MW00532426

JOE NICKELL

SECRETS
OF THE
SIDESHOWS

THE UNIVERSITY PRESS OF KENTUCKY

Publication of this volume was made possible in part by a grant
from the National Endowment for the Humanities.

Scholarly publisher for the Commonwealth, serving Bellarmine University, Berea
College, Centre College of Kentucky, Eastern Kentucky University, The Filson
Historical Society, Georgetown College, Kentucky Historical Society, Kentucky State
University, Morehead State University, Murray State University, Northern Kentucky
University, Transylvania University, University of Kentucky, University of Louisville,
and Western Kentucky University.

Editorial and Sales Offices: The University Press of Kentucky
663 South Limestone Street, Lexington, Kentucky 40508–4008
www.kentuckypress.com

09 08 07 06 05   5 4 3 2 1

Library of Congress Cataloging-in-Publication Data
Nickell, Joe.
  Secrets of the sideshows / Joe Nickell.
     p. cm.
  Includes bibliographical references and index.
  ISBN 0-8131-2358-5 (hardcover : alk. paper)
  1. Sideshows. I. Title.
  GV1835.N53 2005
  791.3'5--dc22   2005007624

This book is printed on acid-free recycled paper meeting the requirements of the
American National Standard for Permanence in Paper for Printed Library Materials.

Manufactured in the United States of America.

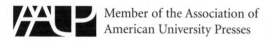

Member of the Association of
American University Presses

In memory of my father,

J. WENDELL NICKELL

(1914–1983),

who taught me magic and took me to my first sideshow

CONTENTS

⦿ ILLUSTRATIONS

ACKNOWLEDGMENTS

In addition to those mentioned in the text, I am grateful to the following for assisting me in various ways: Robert A. Baker, Timothy Binga, D. J. Grothe, Gena Henry, Sandy Lesniak, Linda Lotz, Rob McElroy, Vaughn Rees, and Ed Summer.

Like other authors, I appreciate the understanding and patience of friends and family, especially the love of my life, Diana Harris; my beautiful daughter, Cherette Roycroft; my son-in-law, Randy Roycroft; and my grandsons, Chase and Tyner.

PREFACE

Like Robert Ripley of "Believe It or Not!" fame, I have always been attracted to the odd and the curious. Growing up in a small eastern-Kentucky town, I rarely missed the visiting solo acts—armless wonders or bullwhip artists—who performed at the local ball park. I paid admission to countless magic, hypnotism, and spook shows, not to mention animal and juggling acts, that played at the school auditorium or the local theater. And I must have attended every carnival and circus that came around. Once, in the mid-1950s, my father and I even visited the state fair and its big sideshow. I can still recall being dazzled by the fire-eater, whose feats helped light a boy's interest.

In 1969 I worked as a magic pitchman in the carnival at the Canadian National Exhibition (CNE). It was there that I met El Hoppo the Living Frog Boy and witnessed Atasha the Gorilla Girl, who transformed from beauty to beast before the eyes of frightened spectators (see Nickell 1970). Over the next three years I worked as a magician, learning the secrets of conjuring that lay behind many sideshow performances and illusions. During summers I was resident magician at the Houdini Magical Hall of Fame in Niagara Falls, Ontario. The Falls' Clifton Hill—with its street vendors and attractions such as Ripley's and Tussaud's and Frankenstein's museums—was rather a carnival itself.

When I was not at Houdini's, I spent the remainder of the year performing on the school circuit as Janus the Magician, Mister Twister the Magic Clown, or Mendell the Mentalist. Each fall, I visited the CNE midway. There I saw—

or, more accurately, *studied*—such sideshow exhibits as the bullet-riddled auto of Bonnie and Clyde, a Sasquatch frozen in a block of ice, animal freaks, and such human oddities as the famous Siamese twins Ronnie and Donnie. I also caught the short acts of fellow magicians, at least one of whom recognized me in the crowd and acknowledged my presence with a wink.

During travels in Europe, Asia, and North Africa in 1970 and 1971, I beheld various street acts, including nighttime fire-breathing and Houdini-style escape performances in Paris, a "dancing" bear in Istanbul, a little old wandering conjurer at the Pueblo Español in Barcelona, and a snake charmer and other entertainers at the Medina in Marrakech.

During the summers of 1975 and 1976 I was in Dawson City, Yukon Territory, dealing blackjack in Diamond Tooth Gertie's casino. I also operated a crown-and-anchor game—that is, a wheel of fortune like those on carnival midways. I even created an appropriately carnivalesque spiel: "This train leaves for Lucky Land! Hurry, hurry, last call for winners! Poor man's roulette, just half a buck to bet! It must be down to win!"

In short, I've spent much of my life investigating carnivals, particularly sideshows. Even during my years of graduate work and teaching (1979–1995) and my subsequent work as a full-time paranormal investigator with *Skeptical Inquirer* magazine, I maintained that interest. I often stopped by a roadside carnival or struck off on a weekend to visit a big fair within driving distance. For the past few years, however, recognizing their endangered status, I have more energetically studied these one-time mainstays of circuses and carnivals.

I have met such legendary showmen as Bobby Reynolds and Ward Hall, the last of a vanishing breed, and have been permitted behind-the-scenes access to their shows. My colleague, *Skeptical Inquirer* managing editor Benjamin Radford, who shares my interest, accompanied me on several trips to interview Reynolds, Hall, Hall's partner Chris Christ, and others, as well as to meet such sideshow notables as Poobah the Fire-eating Dwarf.

At one time or another I have petted five-legged cows, inspected trick boxes like the one used for No-Middle Myrtle, witnessed human pincushions (painfully up close), and posed for pictures with snake girls. I have also examined shrunken heads (both real and fake), chatted with sword swallowers and electric girls, obtained the autographs of sideshow notables (including celebrity fat man Harold Huge), and taken close-up photos of Eddie the Blockhead pounding screwdrivers into his nostrils. And that's just for starters.

Sometimes my sideshow studies overlapped my paranormal ones, as I tried my hand (and other body parts) at some of the feats performed by street, fair, and sideshow entertainers. With the guidance of David Willey, physicist and resident "mad scientist" of the *Tonight Show,* I have dipped my hand in molten lead, made a twenty-five-foot fire walk, and laid on a bed of nails while Willey used a sledgehammer to smash a cinder block on my chest.

Secrets of the Sideshows is based on these endeavors, as well as on historical and other research. In the following pages, you will read about the evolution of circuses and carnivals and their accompanying midway features, especially the locations and functions of the so-called freak shows and other types of sideshows. You will learn to "talk carny," as we discuss *roughies* setting up a *ten-in-one* with its distinctive *banner line* and *bally platform.* There you may see an *anatomical wonder* or a *snake charmer,* while the *bally talker* (not a "barker") skillfully *turns the tip.* Inside, you will meet the *lecturer* (still not a "barker"), who will introduce you to such wonders as *Spidora,* encourage you to buy a *pitch card* from an *alligator boy,* and send you to the *blowoff* wondering if the *pickled punks* there are really *gaffed.* You will meet many of the showmen and especially the human oddities and other remarkable performers, even peeking behind the curtains at their often equally remarkable personal lives. You will learn the secrets of illusions such as the headless girl; become an expert on the finer points of fire eating and sword swallowing; and visit menageries, flea circuses, and *single-Os,* such as one featuring a giant rat.

There is much, much more, ladies and gentlemen. Hurry! Step right this way! It's on the inside!

1 ORIGINS OF THE SIDESHOW

THE SIDESHOW, AS ITS NAME IMPLIES, is an adjunct to a main show. But the types of exhibits that came to constitute the sideshow preceded both kinds of shows.

Early Roots

Far back in prehistory, the solitary entertainer vied for the attention and approval of others. Perhaps he had learned some simple feat of acrobatics or juggling. Maybe he was able to perform a clever trick using sleight of hand. Or possibly he had something for show-and-tell, such as a remarkable stone or an exotic trophy. Originally, his would have been an impromptu show, probably performed for a few family members and friends around a communal fire.

From this primitive beginning, performances flourished, eventually involving multiple entertainers appearing before large assemblages. Among the early recorded stories of such entertainers—and the earliest concerning a magician—is one written in the Westcar papyrus of 1550 B.C. It describes the feats of an Egyptian conjurer named Tchatcha-em-ankh—not a contemporary story, but a handed-down tale from the court of Khufu (or Cheops), circa 2680 B.C. As related by the papyrus, in addition to being familiar with all the stars constituting the House of Thoth (a demonstration of his knowledge of astrology), the magician could perform remarkable feats, such as leading a lion about as if with a rope and restoring a head that had been severed. The first of these feats was doubtless an early example of what would eventually become a circus mainstay: lion taming.

As to the restoration of the cut-off head, the papyrus provides a clue by describing the feat of a later conjurer named Dedi, who supposedly could decapitate a goose, a duck, or an ox and then restore the head. No doubt, Dedi did the trick with birds in much the same manner that modern magi do.

1

(Street magician David Blaine performed it on one of his television specials, employing a dove.) Dedi deftly tucked the goose's or duck's head under its wing, at the same time bringing out a dummy head he had hidden in his robe. To restore the bird, he simply reversed the procedure. As for the ox, magical authorities suspect that Dedi only *claimed* that he could do that, relying on his demonstrations with birds to give the claim credence (Gibson 1967, 11–12; Randi 1992, 1–4).

At least as far back as 2400 B.C., ancient Egyptian art depicts jugglers, acrobats, and clowns, along with parades, entertaining the nobility and citizenry. Indeed, Queen Hatshepsut imported giraffes and monkeys—exotic animals that would later appear in circuses worldwide (Granfield 2000, 6). And on the island of Crete—as shown in a blue, white, and gold fresco dated 1600 B.C.—young Minoan daredevils performed acrobatics with charging bulls. The young men and women grasped the animals' horns and then vaulted over the animals' heads with backward somersaults and momentary handstands that were as dangerous as they were entertaining. Some of these bull leapers became the "stars" of society, sporting embroidered outfits, arm bracelets, and elaborate coiffures and makeup—foreshadowing the colorful costuming that would be used by entertainers throughout history (Granfield 2000, 6). Among the entertainments that presaged the modern circus were performances by contortionists (in old China) and wild-animal trainers (in Egypt and elsewhere in the Middle East), as well as such spectator sports as chariot racing (in ancient Greece).

In the Roman era, the writer Juvenal (circa A.D. 60–127) stated that what the public really desired was *panem et circenses*—"bread and circuses." That is, so long as the people were fed and entertained, they would represent a happy citizenry, unlikely to rebel against their leaders. In Juvenal's time, Romans enjoyed nearly 175 days of celebrations and festivals annually (Granfield 2000, 7). During the Roman festivals, spectators gathered in large roofless arenas called *circuses* (figure 1.1). These circuses contained an oval track used for chariot races, various games, and public shows. The first and largest of the circuses was the Circus Maximus, which developed from a modest third-century structure into a stone building seating 150,000 or more spectators. The circus acquired a sinister aspect when Nero used the Circus Caligulas (built in

FIGURE 1.1. In ancient Rome, contests and other entertainments were held in open arenas called circuses. (From a nineteenth-century print)

A.D. 37–41) for spectacles involving the torture of Christians (*Encyclopaedia Britannica* 1960, s.v. "Circus").

Admission to the circuses was free, but hawkers of various types harangued the crowds. Pastry and wine vendors, bookmakers, and prostitutes sought the spectators' money, as did others. Located in nearby booths were astrologers, acrobats, jugglers, and the like—such booths clearly anticipating the later side-shows of circuses and carnivals (*Encyclopaedia Britannica* 1960, s.v. "Circus"; Granfield 2000, 7).

The Fairs and Beyond

During the Middle Ages, when people tended to live out their lives in small communities, traveling entertainers created excitement when they arrived with their dancing bears, trained dogs, and troupes of jugglers and other performers. They drew their wagons into a broad circle, using them as stages. Jesters—forerunners of clowns—teased the onlookers with jokes, riddles, and songs.

In medieval times, *juggling* involved more than keeping several objects in the air simultaneously; it also referred to conjuring—that is, performing magic tricks. Many performers were skilled in conjuring-juggling, ventriloquism, sword swallowing, or even fire eating. The traveling jugglers followed a regular itinerary and often joined with ballad singers, acrobats, musicians, storytellers, and others to give more elaborate performances.

Many of the conjuring tricks performed during the Middle Ages are described by Reginald Scot in his book *The Discoverie of Witchcraft*, published in 1584. Credulous peasants watched as a performer thrust a dagger through his arm or performed a decapitation trick in which a boy's severed head conversed with astonished spectators. (These secrets are discussed in chapters 9 and 10.)

At the edge of the village were set up tents and booths, not unlike the ones at Roman circuses, again heralding the modern circus and carnival sideshows. "Come and see the rare unicorn," the crier might yell. "The only one in the world, and yours to see—for a small fee." Of course, the "unicorn" was merely a horse fitted with a false horn. Even those who suspected trickery lined up anyway and paid the admission fee to satisfy their curiosity. Besides, "People

4

felt the push to buy and see, for the traveling entertainers would be gone in a day, maybe two" (Granfield 2000, 9).

As the medieval crowds gathered, there were other, less entertaining fore-shadowings of American medicine shows and traveling carnivals. Pickpockets took advantage of the spectators' rapt attention to lift their purses, and *mounte-banks* (the term originally referred to quack doctors but has come to mean any type of charlatan) touted the miraculous cures their nostrums could suppos-edly bring to anyone willing to buy a small bag or bottle (Granfield 2000, 9).

In France, *jongleurs* (jugglers) and *trouvères* (troubadours) entertained at various venues. A wedding feast at the home of a wealthy burgher was a gar-gantuan affair with arrays of food and wine barrels in profusion. Such affairs called for entertainment. In their *Life in a Medieval City*, Joseph and Frances Gies (1981, 72) take us back to thirteenth-century Troyes for such a wedding feast: "Jongleurs accompany the successive courses with music, and as soon as the spiced wine, wafers, and fruit are served the entertainment begins. It starts off with handsprings, tumbles, and other acrobatics. Imitations of bird calls, sleight-of-hand tricks, and a juggling act are likely to be on the program. Interspersed are singers who accompany themselves on two musical inven-tions of the Middle Ages: the six-stringed, pear-shaped lute, which is plucked, or the five-stringed viol, the first bowed instrument."

While jugglers, troubadours, and jesters were entertaining village folk in France and England, sixteenth-century Italy was being provoked to laughter by *commedia dell'arte* (comedy of art). Troupes of Italian entertainers toured the rest of Europe performing folk stories in mime. Among the *commedia* characters were Pulchinella, who became Punch in the Punch and Judy puppet shows, and Harlequin, whose colorful patchwork costume would be adopted by clowns ever after (Granfield 2000, 9).

A major venue for the jugglers, mountebanks, jesters, and others was the fair, which became established in the Byzantine Empire as well as in Europe. There were many important fairs, such as those in Frankfurt and Venice and especially the one in Troyes, France. In the early Middle Ages the fairs were largely gatherings for trade. Alongside these commercial fairs grew pleasure fairs, which began to dominate by the beginning of the seventeenth century.

5

The most famous of these was the Bartholomew Fair in London. Henry I had granted rights to the commercial fair to a man by the name of Rahere (who founded St. Bartholomew's hospital). Its almost complete transformation to an entertainment fair made it a classic of that type (*Encyclopaedia Britannica* 1960, s.v. "Fair"). Among the most famous British fairground entertainers was Bartholomew Fair conjurer Isaac Fawkes. At the height of the season in the early 1700s, Fawkes would give as many as six shows a day, performing such feats as causing an apple tree to blossom and bear fruit in less than one minute, which was possibly accomplished by using a mechanical tree (Christopher 1962). Another favorite Bartholomew Fair attraction was the celebrated dwarf Wybrand Lolkes (McKennon 1972, 1:15).

A rare aquatint depicting the Bartholomew Fair in 1721 (Jay 2001) provides a valuable glimpse back in time. Its panoramic view shows the milling crowd among the food and beverage vendors. Individual booths with raised platforms have pictorial background banners announcing "Rope Dancing is here" and "Faux's [i.e., Isaac Fawkes's] Dexterity of hand." Another large booth presents a drama, the cast of which includes a Harlequin. A booth at the side sells novelties. There are other "amusements" (as the print's caption terms them), notably a contraption with three suspended seats that is an obvious, if primitive, forerunner of the modern Ferris wheel. Here in this scene are encapsulated all the elements that would later constitute a carnival midway.

Beginnings of the Modern Circus

Out of these permanent and traveling fairs, which had begun to decline by the eighteenth century, emerged the man who would bring the various elements together to create a modern show form. Philip Astley (1742–1814) did not run away from home to join the circus; instead, he ran away to join the army. He became an expert equestrian and eventually earned the title the Father of the Modern Circus (Granfield 2000, 10).

By the age of twenty-five, Astley had purchased a London field known as Halfpenny Hatch, where he had a riding ring. Every afternoon, astride his horse at the southern end of Lambeth Bridge, he passed out handbills advertising his performance and used his sword to point toward the arena. He astonished spectators with his skill as a trick rider, jumping off and on his

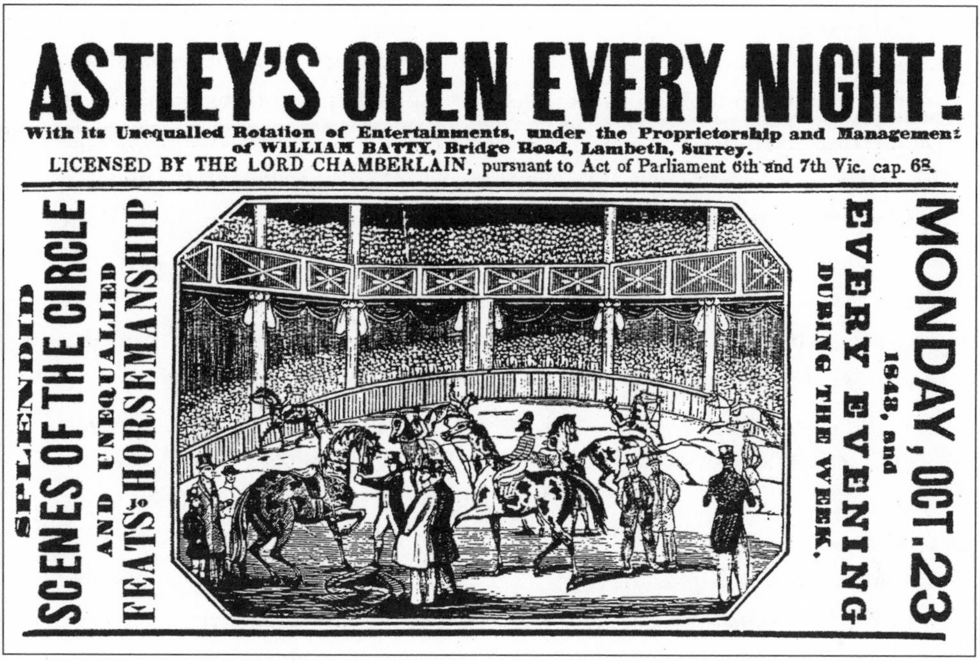

FIGURE 1.2. "Scenes of the Circle" are shown in an 1843 wood engraving advertising the celebrated amphitheater originated by Philip Astley, "Father of the Modern Circus."

galloping horse's back and even standing on his head as it cantered around the ring (Loxton 1997, 10).

Soon the enterprising Astley managed to construct a two-story frame building over the entranceway and erect roofed viewing stands. He trained a troupe of riders and added other entertainers to his show, including musicians, acrobats, and tightrope walkers. He also added clowning and other elements to make what Howard Loxton, in his *Golden Age of the Circus* (1997, 12), terms "a show that begins to be recognizable as what we call a circus."

In 1769 Astley exhibited a "learned" horse and even performed magic tricks on horseback. Soon he had taken his troupe to France. By 1779 he had erected a building called Astley's Amphitheatre Riding House. It was later called the Royal Amphitheatre and a number of other names as it was repeatedly rebuilt after a succession of fires (Loxton 1997, 12–14). (See figure 1.2.)

Ironically, it was not Astley but his chief rival, Charles Hughes, together with his partners, who first used the name *circus*. Hughes opened his Royal Circus in 1782, and his contributions were significant, although Astley is generally considered to have been the better showman. In time, Astley managed to establish no fewer than eighteen circuses across Britain and the European continent (Granfield 2000, 10). Concludes Loxton (1997, 14): "With Astley and Hughes almost all the elements of modern circus, including the name, had been brought together, from rope dancers, clowns, equestrians and trained animals to the grand spectacle that became such a feature of American circus in its heyday."

In France, Astley leased the operation of his circus to a former menagerie cage boy named Antonio Franconi (1737–1836). Franconi had appeared at Astley's Amphitheatre with a bird act, later performed as an equestrian, and in 1786 began his own circus. He and his two sons built their Cirque Olympique and developed it into France's greatest circus of the era. The Franconis made many innovations, including setting the circus ring's diameter at forty-two feet, which remains the standard measurement worldwide. Their descendants came to represent one of Europe's most celebrated circus family dynasties (Granfield 2000, 12; Loxton 1997, 15–16).

Across the Atlantic, eighteenth-century America saw various performances, such as "rope-dancing" (tightrope jigs), exhibitions of exotic animals, and the like. Then in Philadelphia in 1785 an American named Thomas Pool began to perform equestrian routines and to engage a clown to entertain between acts. Thus was formed "the first American circus" (Granfield 2000, 14). (Pool was also active that year in Boston and Baltimore, the following year in New York, and still later in Georgia [Loxton 1997, 19].)

However, an English equestrian named John Bill Ricketts, who brought his own circus from Scotland, is generally credited with creating "the first real circus in the United States" in 1792. A former pupil of Charles Hughes, Ricketts erected an appropriately circular building in Philadelphia to house his circus. The following year he entertained an audience that included George Washington (Loxton 1997, 19).

A newspaper advertisement of that period for "Ricketts' Circus" describes what spectators would see, including Ricketts riding with his knees on the saddle and then leaping over a twelve-foot ribbon and juggling four oranges while riding at full speed. There were also "comic Feats" (clowning) by a Mr. McDonald and "many Surprizing [sic] Feats on the tight Rope" by a "Seignior *Spiracuta*" (Granfield 2000, 15).

The arrival of the nineteenth century saw Ricketts expand his enterprise by erecting two circus buildings in New York City. One of his entertainers was a fellow rider, Thomas Swan, who introduced a locally born equestrienne named Miss Johnson, along with a monkey that did a rope-dancing act. Previously, exotic animals had merely been exhibited; this was "the first evidence of an animal act in America other than horses" (Loxton 1997, 20). Soon Ricketts had many competitors.

Attempts at permanent circuses were not successful, however, and the showmen eventually took to the road. At first, traveling circuses used makeshift timber structures, but they soon adopted tents. The first such circus set up its tent in a New York park in 1823. That practice began to be copied by the touring circuses, which could now afford to make briefer stays in smaller towns. By the 1830s there were more than thirty circuses "on the road" in the eastern United States. Actually, because the roads were so poor, circuses traveled by water whenever possible. One, the Floating Palace, even performed *on* the water. It was constructed on a huge barge capable of accommodating 3,400 spectators and was propelled by a stern-wheeler. It plied both the Ohio and the Mississippi rivers beginning in 1851—exhibiting a menagerie, "curiosities," and performances on stage—but it was burned during the Civil War (Loxton 1997, 21–22).

Meanwhile, by the 1830s, what were called "outside shows" began to align themselves with traveling menageries and circuses. They flourished not as a midway but as separate attractions set up on nearby lots. At first, main shows distanced themselves, even proclaiming in their ads that "no sideshows of pigmy children, overgrown men, abortions, and monstrosities" were permitted to travel with them. In 1850, however, a relationship was established between the sideshows and main shows. One of the former was characterized at its site off the main lot as "vastly amusing" and consisting of "half a dozen supplementary tents" containing a "French Giant," a "Skeleton Man," and other exhibits, complete with pictorial banners (Polacsek 1996).

Barnum the Showman

The name *P. T. Barnum* (figure 1.3) would not enter circus history until 1871, but his influence on circuses—and their sideshows—had already begun. Phineas Taylor Barnum (1810–1891) was operating a grocery business in New York when he learned about a remarkable slave, Joice Heth, who was reputedly 161 years old and had once served as the nursemaid of George Washington. Barnum went to see the slave, who was being exhibited in Philadelphia. Her owner offered to sell her for $3,000, but Barnum struck a bargain for a third of that, sold his store interest, borrowed some more cash, and on August 6, 1835, acquired the blind, partially paralyzed, toothless old woman. Thus was launched Barnum's career as a showman, and he was soon grossing $1,500 a week from Heth's exhibition. When New York crowds began to decline, Barnum took her on a tour through New England.

In his autobiography, Barnum (1927, 49) wrote of Heth that "she was very sociable, and would talk almost incessantly so long as visitors would converse with her. She sang a variety of ancient hymns," he noted, "and was very garrulous when speaking of her protégé 'dear little George,' as she termed the great father of our country." Supposed proof of her authenticity and great age came from a bill of sale from Washington's father, Augustine Washington, dated February 5, 1727. Of course, the whole thing was a hoax, and when ticket sales declined, Barnum hit on a scheme. He knew that a little doubt would fuel controversy and thus boost sales, so he published an anonymous letter in the local paper claiming that Heth was a "curiously constructed automaton, made up of whalebone, India-rubber, and numberless springs," and that her exhibitor was "a ventriloquist."

After Heth suddenly died, Barnum permitted an autopsy, and the examining surgeon declared that she was probably no more than eighty years old. The *New York Sun* announced the next day (February 25, 1836) "the exposure of one of the most precious humbugs that ever was imposed upon a credulous community." Barnum piled hoax upon hoax with the claim, via his assistant, that Joice Heth was still very much alive and well in Connecticut. Supposedly as a prank, the autopsy had been performed on the corpse of a recently deceased old "Negress" from Harlem (Kunhardt et al. 1995, 20–23; Harris 1973, 20–26).

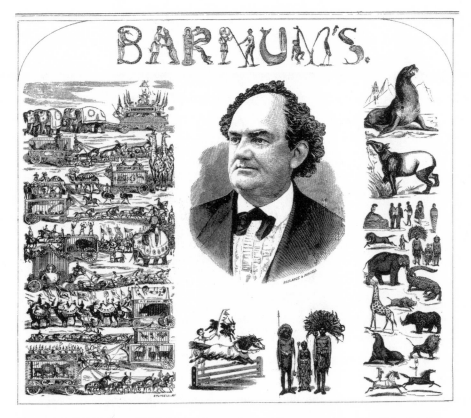

FIGURE 1.3. P. T. Barnum (1810–1891) became the world's greatest showman. This ad is from the *New York Daily Graphic,* October 17, 1873. (Author's collection)

Barnum next engaged a juggler, gave him the exotic name of Signor Vivalla, concocted a fake "rivalry" with another juggler, and soon converted lackluster ticket sales into serious profits. He signed his star and himself with a traveling circus and went on tour. Later Barnum struck off on his own, eventually acquiring—in addition to Vivalla—a group of entertainers. By 1841, however, he was back in New York and had resolved "that I would never again be an itinerant showman" (Barnum 1927, 55–89).

In late 1841 Barnum persuaded a backer to buy a floundering five-story museum and allow him to run it. Renamed Barnum's American Museum (figure 1.4), it began to consume Barnum's life. The entertainment enterprise had featured—in addition to stuffed animals and fossils—contortionists, a banjoist, a lady magician, a lecturer on animal magnetism, a tattooed man, and similar acts (Harris 1973, 40). Barnum began to add even more remarkable exhibits. One was the so-called Fejee Mermaid, which Barnum billed as "the greatest curiosity in the world," although he surely recognized that it was bogus from the beginning. His museum naturalist proclaimed as much, but Barnum was impressed at how closely it could be inspected without obvious signs of artifice. It was, in fact, a monkey's body grafted onto a fish (figure 1.5).

The inevitable accusations of trickery brought Barnum increased notoriety. He featured the Fejee Mermaid in his museum and then sent it on tour, exhibited alongside many genuine curiosities. Eventually there was a public outrage over the fake in South Carolina, and Barnum admitted that it was "a questionable, dead mermaid," telling his partner in the venture, Moses Kimball, "the bubble has burst" (Harris 1973, 22, 62–67; Kunhardt et al. 1995, 40–43).

Barnum's affair with the little mermaid taught him important lessons about human nature. Although the saying "There's a sucker born every minute" is *attributed* to him, there is no proof that he ever said it, and indeed, it seems a bit too harsh for Barnum's nature. Instead, he observed that many people enjoyed being fooled, and he often quoted the poem *Hudibras:* "Doubtless the pleasure is as great / Of being cheated as to cheat" (Kunhardt et al. 1995, 43; Keyes 1992, 6–7).

In a subsequent endeavor, Barnum schemed to have his bearded lady accused of being a man, and a publicized medical examination helped boost both Barnum's credibility and his cash receipts. When one visitor asked whether an exhibit was real or a humbug, the showman replied, "That's just the question: persons who pay their money at the door have a right to form their own opinions after they have got up stairs" (Harris 1973, 67, 77).

Barnum exhibited increasingly diverse oddities—such as albinos, giants, dwarfs, and the Highland Fat Boys—along with ballets, dramas, magic shows, and "scientific demonstrations." When he learned of a five-year-old midget in Bridgeport, Connecticut, named Charles Sherwood Stratton, Barnum arranged for his indenture, dubbed him "General Tom Thumb," and took him on successful tours on both sides of the Atlantic. In England Tom won the

(Above) FIGURE 1.4. Barnum's five-story American Museum—with its exhibits of curios and human oddities and performers—anticipated the modern sideshow. (Contemporary illustration) (Right) FIGURE 1.5. Barnum's Fejee Mermaid, proclaimed "the greatest curiosity in the world," was actually a fake. (Contemporary illustration)

heart of Queen Victoria, who led him by the hand around Buckingham Palace (Barnum 1927, 133–50). Tom Thumb would make Barnum rich and famous beyond his own dreams.

His 1850–1851 tour, featuring the melodious soprano Jenny Lind, the "Swedish Nightingale," was another Barnum triumph (even though, after the ninety-fifth concert, her lawyers and managers persuaded her to pay a $25,000 penalty and continue on her own) (Kunhardt et al. 1995, 48, 92–102).

Meanwhile, Barnum continued to operate his American Museum until, at midday on July 13, 1865, a fire in the museum's engine room spread and consumed the building:

> Desperate efforts were made to save animals, costumes, and some of the more valuable relics, but almost nothing was salvaged except the day's receipts, placed hurriedly in an iron safe by the treasurer, Samuel Hurd. As the animals, including snakes and a tiger, tried to flee the inferno, spectators panicked and some were injured in the crush. The whale tank was broken in an effort to douse the flames in the floors below, and the whales themselves were burned alive. When the statue of Jefferson Davis in petticoats, so recently installed by Barnum, was thrown through the window, spectators caught it and hanged it on a lamppost in Fulton Street. A few rare coins, the fat woman, the learned seal, and some wax figures and small animals were saved, but a collection valued by Barnum at more than four hundred thousand dollars (and insured for only forty thousand dollars) was totally destroyed. (Harris 1973, 169)

Barnum rebuilt on another site (he sold the first property to the *New York Herald* for an inflated sum) and called it the New American Museum. It featured many of the standbys, including General Grant Jr., the midget; Noah Orr, the Ohio giant; and Adelaide Powers and Adah Briggs, the fat ladies. Comments one source, "For the most part, only the names had changed" (Kunhardt et al. 1995, 196.) Alas, the New American Museum was short-lived, succumbing to another fire in March 1868. Barnum considered it the end of his career as a showman.

Then came the "discovery" of the Cardiff giant in August 1869. Believed to be an ancient petrified male colossus, a mysterious statue, or a clever fake, the huge curio drew controversy as soon as it was unearthed on a farm at Cardiff, New York. Displayed in a tent, with ticket sales booming, it came to the attention of P. T. Barnum. He naturally sought to buy it, but when he was rebuffed, he fashioned a copy and displayed it in New York as if it were the genuine stone figure. Actually, this was a hoax of a hoax, since the true story soon emerged: The conception was that of George Hull, who obtained a block of gypsum in Iowa, shipped it to Chicago for carving and artificial "aging," and then transported it by train to a depot near Binghamton, New York. From there it was hauled to the farm site and buried. One year later, it was uncovered by men hired, supposedly, to dig a well (Stein 1993, 13–14; Kunhardt et al. 1995, 214).

The Greatest Show

In the autumn of 1870 Barnum struck a deal with Dan Castello, owner of the Dan Castello Show, and its manager (and part owner) William Cameron Coup. Barnum was to be senior partner, financing the venture and reaping two-thirds of the profits. Thus was born "P. T. Barnum's Grand Traveling Museum, Menagerie, Caravan, Hippodrome & Circus." This was the biggest circus ever in America, although the showman viewed it as a resurrection of his museum, taken on tour (Kunhardt et al. 1995, 222).

Barnum, now sixty years old, did not travel with the show. However, he contributed more than his name, lending his genius for publicity to the enterprise. He sent the massive 100-wagon caravan on the road in 1871, and by the next year, the multiple-tent show was being billed as "Barnum's Magic City." The tents were arranged so as to funnel customers inside—past such forerunners of the sideshows as his museum and menagerie tents—and on to the big top (hippodrome) itself. By this time, Barnum was already heading his advertisements with the phrase destined for history, "The Greatest Show on Earth!" According to one authority, "The golden age of circus had begun!" (Loxton 1997, 25; Kunhardt et al. 1995, 222–24, 229).

Although small circuses had experimented with rail transport in the 1850s, Barnum's great show also began to travel by train. At first, Pennsylvania

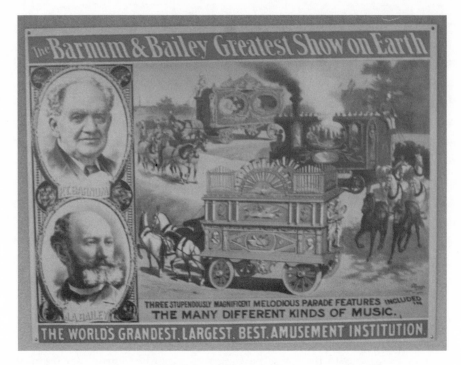

FIGURE 1.6. P. T. Barnum teamed up with competitor J. A. Bailey to give new life to the Greatest Show on Earth. (Circus exhibit, Ontario Science Center)

Railroad cars were used, but they soon gave way to flatcars. These were purchased by the circus and utilized a ramp (invented by Coup) that allowed whole circus wagons to be on-loaded.

As Barnum's show continued to expand, so did its name. In 1873 it became "P. T. Barnum's Great Travelling World's Fair Consisting of Museum, Menagerie, Caravan, Hippodrome, Gallery of Statuary and Fine Arts, Polytechnic Institute, Zoological Garden, and 100,000 Curiosities. Combined with Dan Castello's, Sig Sebastian's and Mr. Atelie's Grand Triple Equestrian and Hippodrome Exposition"—the "Triple . . . Exposition" meaning a three-ring arrangement (Loxton 1997, 28; Granfield 2000, 23).

By 1875 both Castello and Coup had retired, and for the next five years Barnum's circus was operated by a syndicate. (It consisted of four circus speculators who became known as the "Flatfoots" because they "put their foot down flat" in claiming exclusivity for certain areas. To maintain control, they formed partnerships or bought up circuses.) In 1880 Barnum became a partner with his chief competitor, James A. Bailey (figure 1.6), and their celebratory parade in New York the next year featured almost 400 performers, 350 horses, 20 elephants, and 14 camels, plus 4 brass bands.

The following year Barnum & Bailey trumpeted their new treasure, the giant elephant Jumbo. Captured in Africa and acquired by the London Zoological Society, the beast had become temperamental, and the society finally decided to accept Barnum's offer of $10,000. Jumbo's ill temper disappeared with circus life, and the eleven-and-a half-foot-tall, six-and-a-half-ton giant was beloved by millions. Then in 1885 he was accidentally killed by an unscheduled express locomotive in Ontario. Barnum grieved briefly; he then decided to make two exhibits from Jumbo's remains: one the skeleton, the other the stuffed hide. When he learned that the skin could be stretched, Barnum gave orders for the mounted specimen to "show as large as possible" (Kunhardt et al. 1995, 278–81, 298).

About this time, Bailey assumed full control, and half the profits, of the circus. In 1889 Barnum accompanied Bailey on another trip to England, where he again met the queen. He died two years later, on April 7, 1891. The *Boston Herald* summed up his life: P. T. Barnum was "the foremost showman of all time" (Loxton 1997, 29; Kunhardt et al. 1995, 344).

James A. Bailey remained abroad for a five-year tour, while another Barnum & Bailey company continued to tour in the United States. On his return, Bailey found that he had a serious competitor, the Ringling Brothers.

The brothers (sons of German immigrant August Rungeling, who Americanized his name) were fascinated by the circus shows they had seen touring by boat on the Mississippi. In the 1870s the oldest had become a tightrope performer with a traveling circus, and in 1882 he persuaded four of his brothers to join him in forming the Ringling Brothers Classic & Comic Concert Company. They added a trick pig and used paint to transform old farm wagons into circus wagons.

By 1890 the Ringlings were touring small midwestern towns with a dozen rail cars. Mid-decade saw them encroaching into Barnum territory: New England. In 1905 they bought half of Bailey's interest in another enterprise, the Forepaugh Circus. When Bailey died two years later, the brothers purchased the entire Barnum & Bailey show for $410,000. The shows were operated separately until 1919, when the Ringling Brothers and Barnum & Bailey circuses were combined into the world's largest circus.

Carnivals and More

Rivaling the circuses were other traveling shows that proliferated after the Civil War. Among these were independent productions that not only lacked the circus's central arena but also were designed for ease of travel. Joe McKennon, in his *Pictorial History of the American Carnival* (1972, 1:22), states: "The attractions carried by these showmen were not elaborate or pretentious. A trained domestic animal, a living freak of nature, a den of snakes, an act of magic or sleight of hand, or any other single attraction that could be presented in a small enclosure for an admission of five cents. In this enclosure, usually a piece of canvas side walling, the act was presented on the bare ground." Such shows are exactly the same type as the one that traveled along the East Coast in 1719 and featured the "Lyon of Barberry" (McKennon 1972, 1:20), as well as similar shows stretching even farther back in time. They are forerunners of later sideshows, called pit shows (discussed in chapter 3).

Another type of noncircus outdoor entertainment of this period was the so-called medicine show. The snake-oil peddlers (recalling the mountebanks of medieval fairs) used a number of tricks and stunts. The larger traveling shows, employing advance men to herald their arrival, entered town with circuslike fanfare, typically with a band leading the procession of wagons. Skits and other diversions were used to attract audiences, who eventually were treated to the "lecture" (which, when medicine shows expanded into radio, became the commercial). Assistants who moved through the crowds were often garbed as Quakers to lend an air of moral respectability. Native Americans were frequently recruited to promote the notion of "natural" medicines, which were given names such as Wright's Indian Vegetable Pills, Seminole Cough Balsam, and various Kickapoo cures (Holbrook 1959, 196–215; Munsey 1970).

The fascinating story of one such Indian is told in *Tracking Doctor Lonecloud* by Ruth Holmes Whitehead (2002). Born Germain Bartlett Alexis, a Nova Scotian of the Mi'kmaq Indian tribe, he was given the name "Dr. Lonecloud" by "Texas Charlie" Bigelow and Colonel John Healey, proprietors of the Kickapoo Indian Medicine Company. Lonecloud joined up with Healey and Bigelow sometime around 1880. He was paid $7 a week and was given clothing to wear (Indian garb of "buckskin and feathers"). He said in his memoir: "In the show, I lectured, sold medicine, and acted on the stage. All those daring shots. Bursting an apple or potato by shooting it while it was swinging, cutting a card in two edgeways across the hall. . . . I'd shoot and snuff the ashes out of a cigar while it was being smoked." Lonecloud also helped to concoct the Kickapoo medicines and label the bottles.

He worked for other shows as well and sometimes struck out on his own, touring the Maritime Provinces and presenting medicine shows. In one, his future wife played Pocahontas and he played Captain John Smith. Another time, he says, "I got up a show again. I had medicine and three or four Indians, and we put on a show of old Indian ceremonies like Corn Dance and Medicine Dance." Among his nostrums was a hair strengthener. To prove its efficacy, Lonecloud would let another Indian grasp his hair and swing around on it—or so it seemed. Actually, he had concealed beneath the hair a leather strap, secured to his body so as to hold the man's weight. Once when Lonecloud ran out of the tonic, he simply substituted tea in the bottles (Whitehead 2002, 33–34).

In addition to the medicine shows were larger productions. In 1883 William F. "Buffalo Bill" Cody began his Wild West, Rocky Mountain, and Prairie Exhibition. "Though a touring show," explains Loxton (1997, 29), "it was not a circus but presented real-life cowboys and 'Red Indians,' recreating their battles and stage-coach holdups along with demonstrations of trick riding and shooting in an outdoor arena where as many as 300 horsemen rode en masse." (Dr. Lonecloud says that he was with Buffalo Bill's Wild West Show for a winter at Madison Square Garden and at Coney Island afterward [Whitehead 2002, 64].) The Cody show was widely imitated, and many circuses copied the trend with their own "Wild West" features.

But the circus's main rival among outdoor amusements was the independent carnival, with which it is sometimes confused. Actually, a *carnival* is a traveling outdoor amusement enterprise—usually including rides, concessions, games, and sideshows—arrayed around a broad walkway. When the carnival is an adjunct to a circus, fair, or exposition, it is termed a *midway* because, as its name implies, it is located between the entrance and the big top (or pavilion), where the main entertainers perform. Essentially, then, a carnival is *only* a midway, which can be taken on the road or rail by itself (*Encyclopaedia Britannica* 1960, s.v. "Carnival"; Taylor 1997, 94).

The modern carnival midway was an outgrowth of the World's Columbian Exposition held in Chicago in 1893. (This world's fair had been conceived to celebrate Columbus's "discovery" of America in 1492, and it was dedicated on October 21, 1892.) When it opened on May 1, George Ferris's mammoth amusement wheel was unfinished, as were many other projects, and food and drinks were as poorly provided as they were outrageously priced. Crowds were small, but business picked up after Ferris's wheel began to operate and the bad press was countered. This exposition would change fairgrounds entertainment forever.

Dubbed the "White City" (figure 1.7)—because of its temporary buildings with gleaming plaster facades—the fairgrounds had a mile-long entertainment promenade called the Midway Plaisance (or pleasant midway). This was a string of mostly international "villages," such as the Irish Village, the German Village, and so forth, along with Ferris's wheel, a model of the Eiffel Tower, an electric scenic theater, an Egyptian theater featuring dancing girls, a re-creation of a Cairo street, and many other exotic and impressive features (Shepp and Shepp 1893). According to McKennon (1972, 1:37), "There were only two or three attractions on the midway that could be likened to anything known in outdoor amusement business in America prior to 1893." In addition to the Ferris wheel, there was Hagenbeck's Wild Animal Show, but it was contained in a modern pavilion (Shepp and Shepp 1893, 490–91).

Nevertheless, the spirit engendered by the Midway Plaisance continued. Independent showmen and concessionaires came together for the first time to work out solutions to common problems. Why not, they asked, create a *traveling* midway that would play smaller cities and towns? A theater scenic artist named Otto Schmidt persuaded a backer to fund such a trial enterprise in 1893 and again in 1895. Because both attempts were abortive, however, "Schmidt is not credited with being the first full-fledged carnival operator" (McKennon 1972, 1:47). Though true, that is the equivalent of saying that because the Wright brothers got off the ground only briefly in 1903, credit for sustained flight should really go to Alberto Santos-Dumont. (Who? He was a

FIGURE 1.7. The main entrance to the 1893 Chicago world's fair proclaimed admission to the "White City," as shown on this souvenir postcard. (Author's collection)

Frenchman who flew several hundred feet in 1906 [*Lincoln Library* 1946, s.v. "Airplane"].)

In fact, Otto Schmidt was financially successful in Syracuse, New York, in 1895. His Chicago Midway Plaisance Amusement Company featured shows copied from the original Midway Plaisance, such as Streets of Cairo and an Irish Village, plus Bostock's Trained Animal Arena, Old Plantation Minstrels, three illusion shows, Lee's Congress of Wonders, and more. There were no rides, but Schmidt had a shooting gallery and various concessions. Schmidt also had a one-ring circus, but obviously his enterprise was based on the midway, not the circus, model. Therefore, his little circus was just another traveling collection of shows.

In 1896 Frank Bostock and the Ferrari Brothers—all of them animal showmen from England—put together a midway company. It included a carousel and other rides and successfully played several fairs in New England (McKennon 1972, 1:47–49).

GENERAL VIEW OF MIDWAY, SYRACUSE FAIR
SYRACUSE, N.Y.
32198

FIGURE 1.8. Postcard view of the midway at New York's Syracuse Fair, circa 1910–1920. In the center background are banner lines, and at the right, a Wild West show. (Author's collection)

However, it was not the large agricultural fairs (figure 1.8) that led to carnivals' success but the aptly named street fairs. They had been operating in North America possibly as early as 1871, but they were not organized. Then in 1898 the Order of Elks of Akron, Canton, and Zanesville, Ohio, determined to produce cooperative street fairs in their respective cities. They formed a midway committee chaired by hotel keeper Frank W. Gaskill. The events were so successful that Gaskill also launched a carnival week in Alliance, his former hometown, in late fall. Although it rained all week, Gaskill managed to make a profit anyway. He returned to Canton and began to create what would become the "first successful traveling collective amusement company" (McKennon 1972, 1:53). He reasoned, "If I can make money in a bad town with a bad show in bad weather, what can I do in a good town with good weather and a good show?" Gaskill enlisted a contracting agent to begin establishing a route for 1899 and hired two men to assemble the midway.

Gaskill's resulting Canton Carnival Company managed to keep going each week. Whereas Otto Schmidt had had to expend a week's construction time

FIGURE 1.9. Button advertising a Missouri carnival in 1915, when organized carnivals were developing and expanding. (Author's collection)

at each show site, Gaskill used an advance man to see that necessary materials and labor were provided by the show's local sponsor. The advance man supervised the erection of banner frames, platforms, and stages. Thus, showmen could take down a show on Saturday night, load the canvas and other properties in railroad cars, and, on arrival in the next town, set up in a few hours and begin selling tickets (McKennon 1972, 1:55).

On the heels of Gaskill's carnival came another. George Chartier, an exalted ruler of the Elks who had worked with Gaskill on the previous year's trio of street fairs, followed just two weeks later with his Exposition Circuit Company. These carnivals were soon copied by Frank Bostock (whose animal show had briefly been with Schmidt) and a partner. The Bostock Mighty Midway Company employed in-your-face competition; it played the biggest venues the other two shows had promoted, renting adjacent fields and offering free front-gate admission. (Such cutthroat tactics prompted Gaskill and Chartier to begin securing exclusive or "shut-out" contracts in their booked cities.)

By 1903 there were 22 touring carnivals playing street fairs and other "promoted dates," every one of them traveling by railroad (figure 1.9). By 1969 there would be more than 600, selling over 15 million admission tickets. That same year in Toronto, at the Canadian National Exhibition (where I was working as a magic pitchman), Patty Conklin's midway grossed nearly $1.75 million during its short season (McKennon 1972, 1:47, 53–61).

All these various shows contributed to the *sideshow*, but we must consider what the term really means. If it refers to a show that is off to the side—that is, subsidiary to the main one—then the circus can have sideshows but the traveling carnival cannot. P. T. Barnum, who was apparently among the first to use the term (his is the earliest recorded instance in the *Oxford English Dictionary* [1971]), suggested another meaning. In 1855 he wrote in his autobiography, "In attending to what might be termed my 'side shows,' or temporary enterprises, I have never neglected the American Museum." The "temporary" aspect would allow for carnival sideshows, but what about permanent sideshows, such as those at Coney Island?

I think the solution is to recognize that *sideshow* has come to mean "a show with the *characteristics* of a sideshow." Although none of the dictionaries I consulted ascribes to this definition, I commend it to them. The next chapter describes more particularly what these characteristics are, together with the sideshows' place in their typical home, the midway.

2 ON THE MIDWAY

THE MIDWAY IS LOCATED BETWEEN the entranceway and the big top of a circus. A carnival is basically a midway traveling on its own. At a fair, a midway may be an even larger formation, consisting of both the carnival and what is called the "independent midway," which contains *separate* amusements booked by the fair's own committee (Taylor 1997, 94).

Creating the Midway

The traveling aspect of the carnival presents tremendous problems. The owner of such a "collective amusement organization" (known as a *show*) must not only sell the myriad attractions to the public but also compete with other traveling enterprises and *route* the show (that is, lay out the play dates for a season). The booking of a route for a new season begins long before the present one ends. Spots that have proved lucrative are rebooked, if possible. At various *outdoor meetings* (which are actually held indoors) to plan the outdoor show routes, "the amusement park men, the fair managers, the amusement device manufacturers and the outdoor showmen hold simultaneous conventions as they 'wheel and deal' for sales and bookings" (McKennon 1972, 2:151).

Regardless of their size, all outdoor shows require *advance agents* who see that contracts are signed, routes are laid out, and all final arrangements are made. Shows travel by road with fleets of trucks, semis, motor homes, and other vehicles (McKennon 1972, 2:145, 151–52). Only one remaining American carnival, the Strates Shows (founded by Greek immigrant James E. Strates in the early 1900s), still travels by rail with a fifty-five-car train, but even it is adapting to truck travel (Chandler 2002).

The independent owners of rides and shows pay for their *location* (allotted midway space) as well as fees for trailer space, water, electrical connections, and whatever else those in the *office* (the carnival business trailer) require.

After the engagement has played—unless it has been cut short by a *blowdown* (the leveling of tents and equipment by a storm)—the show is *sloughed* (torn down for travel). This *teardown* (see figures 2.1 and 2.2) may begin the night before closing, with the removal of some nonessential elements. On *slough night,* the carnival remains open until the usual closing time; then, except for a couple of central lighting towers and work lights on the rides and other attractions—the midway is darkened.

Empty trucks are pulled onto the midway and loaded. The first ones filled are those that will be required last when the show sets up again. When everything is packed, the *run* (the move between towns) begins. Specially printed arrows that have been tacked to utility poles and the like by advance men may be used to guide the drivers and keep them from *blowing the route* (getting lost) (McKennon 1972, 2:153–54).

It was not always routine getting from one *date* (engagement) to another. Showman Ward Hall (1981, 18) tells of an incident that happened in 1951 in Ogden, Kansas. It rained on opening night, and "a couple of days of rain later, Soldiers with bulldozers from Fort Riley pulled our trailers off the lot just as the water was lapping at the door. A week later the flood-waters had subsided. We got the show out of the mud but could go nowhere for another two weeks as all the roads out of town were washed out. Oh well, we'd had a busy spring and enjoyed the rest."

The history of American outdoor entertainment is filled with similar hardships and even outright disasters, including fatal truck accidents, like the one that took the life of Seal Brothers Circus owner Bud Anderson in 1950 (Hall 1981, 15–16), and train wrecks, including two multiple-fatality derailments in 1918. (The second of those was "the most disastrous wreck in outdoor show history" [McKennon 1972, 1:91, 93].) Accordingly, dates sometimes have to be canceled, but most are met. Whether they are *first of May* carnies (newcomers) or *troupers* (those who have worked at least one full season), carnival people tend to be resilient. At the end of the *jump* (the move between dates), the midway will be resurrected (McKennon 1972, 2:147, 149, 150).

The course of a modern midway is shaped (when possible) like a racetrack. When a carnival arrives at the *lot* (the show grounds), the *lot manager* (or *lot man* or *layout man*) uses a tape line to mark off the area, indicating

26

FIGURE 2.1. During the teardown, a workman partially dismantles the Ferris wheel at a 2003 carnival operated by Hammerl Amusements, Clarence, New York. (Photo by author)

(Below) FIGURE 2.2. The dismantled Ferris wheel is collapsed onto its platform and hauled away. (Photo by author)

the various units by placing pegs at the intended corners as he and his helpers move around the delineated course (Gresham 1953, 30; Keyser 2001).

Then the midway begins to take form, usually with the help of some *roughies* ("green" or temporary help). The *ride jockeys* (the mechanics who put up and take down rides) assemble their pieces like giant erector sets. The fire-resistant canvas tops are spread out and secured with the ringing of sledges on iron stakes; the center poles are then raised and the side walls hung. Light towers are erected, games and concessions set up, and ticket boxes moved into place. The house trailers of the carnies and showmen who have traveled by road are parked behind the rides and tops (Gresham 1953, 31).

When the midway is ready to open, its *front end* includes the entrance and contains some of the flashier concessions and larger rides. The games range along the sides, and the rides are usually in the center of the ringed area. At the *back end* are the sideshows, along with some of the more popular games and rides. Small concession stands may be located nearly anywhere space allows. The setup is designed to invite patrons inside, draw them along to the more sought-after attractions, and then allow them to flow back to the beginning—minus as much of their money as possible (Rinaldo 1991, 53–55; McKennon 1981, 203).

Concessions

A *concession* is a grant of part of some premises—such as a midway—for some particular purpose; the term is also applied to the enterprise or to the activities that are carried on. Any part of the midway can be licensed to a concession-aire, if the carnival does not already own and operate a similar enterprise itself. Games, rides and amusements, and sideshows are treated later in this chapter; here we look at food, beverage, and other concessions (figure 2.3).

Considering that every crowd requires food and drink, vendors of these essentials were present at entertainments and amusements from ancient times. For example, merchants at the Roman circus sold various pastries and beverages, notably wine (Granfield 2000, 7). At London's Bartholomew Fair in 1721, numerous vendors sold their wares. As pictured in an old aquatint (Jay 2001), some set their barrels or baskets directly on the cobblestones, while others rested them on stools or benches. Baskets held fruit (including

FIGURE 2.3. Concession worker prepares for the opening
of his stand at the Erie County Fair in New York, 2004.
(Photo by author)

what appear to be apples, pears, and plums), pastries, or pies, and there were
spigoted kegs dispensing wine or other beverages. The print also shows a small
box-shaped stove that is obviously filled with hot coals, which the vendor (a
woman wearing a broad hat) is blowing with a bellows. The items baking atop
the stove seem oddly modern; indeed, their figure-eight shape indicates that
they are pretzels.

At the World's Columbian Exposition of 1893, concessions for all "tem-
perance" (nonalcoholic) drinks—except lemonade—were awarded exclusively to one Aaron Nusbaum. The lemonade and popcorn privileges went

to Nichols, Gillies, and Martin, and the Waukesha Water Company had another exclusive contract (McKennon 1972, 1:36). Food stands were among the "gaudy" elements of the Midway Plaisance (Nelson 1999, 81), and the hungry, thirsty crowds had a great variety of foods available. For example, one could "dine in as many languages as he chooses" (Shepp and Shepp 1893, 334). One novelty, served at the Ostrich Farm on the Midway Plaisance, was the ostrich egg omelet—or so it was supposed to be. Since about 3,000 tickets were reportedly sold for the attraction daily, and at least half of the patrons paid the extra 50¢ for an omelet, demand was great. Obviously, the few large birds present could not lay sufficient eggs for 1,500 omelets each day. McKennon (1972, 1:39) states wryly: "The poultry farmer, who supplied the hens' eggs for the concession, made his deliveries just before daylight each morning." Elsewhere at the world's fair one could find "excellent ice cream" dispensed in the Woman's Building restaurant (Shepp and Shepp 1893, 334). The first ice cream cones were dispensed at the St. Louis world's fair of 1904 (McKennon 1972, 1:63).

About 1900, Moxie—originally a type of snake oil touted as "nerve medicine"—added carbonation and transformed itself into the prototype of the American mass-market soft drink. Soon, Moxie stands, along with peanut and popcorn stalls, had become staples of fair midways and carnivals (Nelson 1999, 82).

Cotton candy—known to carnies as *floss candy* or simply *floss*—is made by a special machine that spins melted granulated sugar, colored with food dye, into a fluffy mass (figure 2.4). There is controversy over details of the invention, but cotton candy debuted at the St. Louis world's fair in 1904. It was sold by Nashville candy makers William Morrison and John C. Wharton, who called it "fairy floss." It was dispensed in cardboard boxes for 25¢—half the fair's admission price—yet 68,655 servings were sold ("Cotton Candy"; Mariani 1994, 96).

Concession stands at fairgrounds also include those offering full meals (often run by women's clubs or local church groups). They lure midway passersby with the irresistible smells of grilled pork, fried chicken, and roast beef. "For snacks and desserts," states Derek Nelson in his *American State Fair* (1999, 148), "fairgrounds have always been free-for-alls of savory, sweet, high-

FIGURE 2.4. Concessionaire closes her mobile cotton candy stand at the end of the day in 2003. (Photo by author)

calorie goodies: buttered white popcorn (once a novelty, now a staple), huge crocks of pink lemonade, cold bottles of orange drink, and sticky sheaves of green cotton candy."

About that pink lemonade: According to the memoir of circus lion tamer George Conklin (1921, 228–31), the discovery that pink lemonade would out-sell the common variety was accidentally made by his brother Pete in 1857, when he was traveling with the Jerry Mabie show. At the time, says Conklin:

Pete was a youngster and did not mind taking long chances, and, besides, he had saved a little money, so he bought a couple of mules and an old covered wagon and had enough money left to lay in a stock of peanuts, sugar, tartaric acid, and one lemon. In telling the story Pete always says that "that lemon was the best example of a friend I ever met. It stayed with me to the end." With this outfit he followed the circus, and every time the tents were pitched he would mount his box and begin to sing:

"Here's your ice-cold lemonade
Made in the shade.
Stick your finger in the glass,
It'll freeze fast."

How did the lemonade become *pink?* Well, it seems that Pete ran out of water one hot day, and there was no nearby well or spring. Rushing around the show looking for water, he finally got lucky:

Fannie Jamieson, one of the bareback riders, had just finished wringing out a pair of pink tights. The color had run and left the water a deep pink. Without giving any explanation or stopping to answer her questions, Pete grabbed the tub of pink water and ran. It took only a minute to throw in some of the tartaric acid and the pieces of the "property" lemon, and then he began to call out, "Come quickly, buy some fine strawberry lemonade." That day his sales doubled and from then on no first-class circus was without pink lemonade.

Conklin goes on to report some other secrets of the old lemonade concessionaires:

The recipe for circus lemonade has not changed from that day to this. A tub of water—with no particular squeamishness regarding its source—tartaric acid, some sugar, enough aniline dye to give it a rich pink, and for a finish some thin slices of lemon. The slices of lemon are known as "floaters," and any which are left in the tub at the close of a day's business, together with those which have come back in the glasses, are carefully saved over for the next day's use. In this way the same floaters may appear before the public a considerable number of times. The lemonade glasses, too, by the way, like some other things in this world, "are not what they seem." Tall and large in appearance, they give the impression of a generous drink for "only a nickel!" but if examined they are found to taper very rapidly toward the base, to have extra-thick sides, with the bottom nearer the top than it looks, and the thirsty customer actually gets no more of the enticing pink liquid than could easily be poured into an ordinary drinking glass.

Concessionaires who sell candy on the grounds of traveling circuses, menageries, and carnivals are called *candy butchers,* a term that was apparently in use in the 1860s. According to Conklin's memoirs: "The privilege of selling candy in and around the show often brought as much as five thousand dollars for one season. The holder of the privilege employed several men to go along with the show and do the actual selling." The most common candy items then were "barber poles" (red-and-white-striped stick candy). "Sticks that had become dirty from handling and broken pieces," says Conklin (1921, 150–51) "were cut up into small bits and put into paper 'cornies.'" He adds, "These the 'candy butchers' had a trick of selling to the 'rubes' [the locals] and their girls for twenty-five cents each, and represented them as being something 'extra fine.'"

A legendary candy butcher of the Midwest was Mrs. Caroline Jessop, the "Lady Confectioner." With her husband, she hauled candy-making equipment on the fair circuit in the 1850s. When she died in 1916, her recipes—including those for her celebrated taffy and Jessop's Butterscotch Corn—passed to her children. Today the business is continued by the fifth generation of the family at such venues as the Indiana State Fair (Nelson 1999, 150–51).

In addition to tasty treats, carnival and fair midway concessionaires hawk an assortment of toys and novelties. A vendor at the Bartholomew Fair in the eighteenth century is depicted in a booth with an array of small flutes, tin trumpets, little figures of people and animals, and other items displayed on the counter. Shelves behind her are stocked with additional goods, including a framed mirror (see Jay 2001).

Moving ahead a couple of centuries, the Missouri State Fair midway of 1929 not only featured vendors selling caramel apples and ice cream but also "a man with a sewing machine [who] would put your name on a little felt Robin Hood hat for only a quarter." In the 1930s vendor wares included miniature clown hats, little bamboo canes, and monkey-on-a-stick toys (Nelson 1999, 94, 99).

Many concessionaires run *pitch* concessions, which are operated by a *pitchman,* someone who sells merchandise by a combination of demonstrating and lecturing. A pitchman who operates from an elevated platform is called a *high pitchman,* and one working at ground level is, of course, a *low pitchman.* Some of the latter work out of a small case they called a *kiester.* No doubt, pitchmen frequently have occasion (like most carnies) to refer disparagingly to *lot lice,* those people who spend time, but not money, on show grounds (McKennon 1972, 2:149; Taylor 1997, 94).

In the 1950s pitchmen sold "art studies" (pinups), potato peelers, cheap watches, Brazilian (faux) diamond rings, hair restorer, and ever-sharp knives, as well as special decks of magic cards. (I too pitched these "Svengali" decks at the Canadian National Exposition in 1969, along with a selection of other magic tricks.) Vendor wares naturally change with the times. In recent years, as interest has focused on UFOs and other aspects of extraterrestrial mythology, big-eyed, big-headed humanoids in the form of balloons and stuffed toys have appeared at many concession booths. Concessions reflect the culture that they are part of. Their particular forms may change, but the human impulses they attempt to satisfy remain eternal.

Games

Today's carnival game agents are mostly honest, law-abiding folk. But because a carnival is a business whose object is to make money, there are both honest and dishonest carnies. In earlier times, due to carnivals' transient nature, there was little attention—certainly little *informed* attention—from law enforcement. *Caveat emptor* (let the buyer beware) was the rule.

In the period after the Civil War, an advance man called the *fixer* would visit the local police in each town where a circus or other traveling show was scheduled to appear. By skillful use of blarney, money, or both, the fixer attempted to persuade the authorities to look the other way regarding certain "little games of chance." If the town could not be fixed, gamesmen had to take their own chances and perhaps be a bit more careful. "Like all holders of concessions," states George Conklin (1921, 167), "they were obliged to furnish their own transportation. Most of them traveled with a fast horse and buggy, and, no matter if the town were 'fixed' or not, . . . when the crowd was being worked the horses were kept harnessed and ready, with a driver, so that at a moment's notice their owners could flee the town."

Conklin remembers one concessionaire named Sam Gibbons, "an expert three-card-monte man," who "used to work his game with a pair of 'forty-fives' hanging from his belt." Since a queen is typically the target card, the game is sometimes called "Find the Lady." In carny slang, the operator is a *broad tosser* (McKennon 1972, 1:55). He works the game by laying a board across a barrel or, more portably, using a plank suspended on a strap hung around the neck (Conklin 1921, 166, 168). It is a deceptive game, worked by sleight of hand. The gamesman picks up one card by its edges with one hand, and picks up the other two cards with the other hand, the target card being on the front. The cards are shown, and as they are tossed facedown, the card *behind* the target card is secretly substituted for it by a certain practiced "move." Therefore, as the *mark* (victim) tries to follow the target card while the three cards are moved about, he is tracking the wrong one all along.

Rivaling three-card monte for popularity is the shell game. It too involves sleight of hand. It has been termed "the surest and simplest method ever devised to take away a man's money." Also called "thimble rig," it is usually performed not with large thimbles but with walnut shells—hence its common name. In the game, a pea is hidden under one shell and the mark attempts to track it as all three shells are switched around (Gibson 1946, 40–41). The secret is that the "pea" is rubber, and when the shell worker (operator) covers it, he lets the back edge of the shell come down on the pea. He pushes forward on the shell (while doing the same with another, using his other hand), and the rubber pea pops out at the rear. It is deftly clipped with the little finger and stolen away, to be revealed wherever desired by reversing the process.

Despite these minor deceptions, by the early twentieth century, games were considerably less crooked. As Conklin (1921, 165) states, "the roughest show on the road to-day would not dare countenance the least of the methods by which great sums of money were regularly taken from the public by swindlers connected with circuses in the late [eighteen-] 'sixties and early 'seventies."

In the modern carnival, games are located along either side of the midway. Locations on the right side cost concessionaires more than those on the left side, since patrons tend to turn to the right when they enter the grounds. Game operators on the right side therefore get the first opportunity to separate the rubes from their money. In carny parlance, a game is a *joint*. Those along the outer sides of the walkway are dubbed *line joints* because they are in a row; players use only the front of the concession. The inside area of the midway is where the *four-way joints* are located, so named because they can be played from any side (Rinaldo 1991, 53–55).

There are basically three categories of carnival games: *games of skill* (which depend on the player's own ability), *games of chance* (in which the player has no control over the outcome, thus constituting gambling), and *flat games* (in which the player cannot win and is "flat out" swindled). Carnival games are supposed to be of the first category, but sometimes a purported game of skill is actually not. Such a game is called an *alibi store*, because the operator is ready with an "explanation" for why the player did not win: "You threw too hard," for example (Rinaldo 1991, 3, 8).

A *two-way joint* is one that can be operated either fairly or unfairly. A crooked operator is a *grifter* who may use a secret gimmick, termed a *gaff*, to make it difficult or impossible for players to win. A *gaffed* (rigged) game may involve *shills* (short for *shillabers*), who are the grifter's confederates; their job is to pose as patrons and make the game look easy, thus luring the *suckers* or rubes to take a chance. The carny label *Sunday school show* describes a carnival that forbids crooked games (Keyser 2001; Rinaldo 1991).

Among the types of joints are the *hanky panky* (simple games with cheap prizes, such as a fish pond, dart throw, or the like), the *count store* (or *add-up joint*, in which a player wins by scoring a certain number of points), and the *money store* (which pays winners cash rather than merchandise). Some joints make money on a percentage basis. For example, a dozen patrons may each pay $1 to play, while the odds ensure that only one or two players will win a prize worth, say, $3. The operator thus obtains a big profit.

A joint's *stock* (prizes) may be *plaster* (formerly *chalk*, such as ceramic or plaster-of-paris figures, Kewpie dolls, and the like), *plush* (stuffed toys), or *slum* (very cheap merchandise, like most carnival stock) (see figures 2.5, 2.6, and 2.7). Slum is the type of prize used for games that advertise "everyone a winner." Such prizes are bought cheaply in great quantities, so that the cost is much less than the price of playing.

(Left) FIGURE 2.5. Slum prizes are the midway's cheapest. (Antique items from author's collection) (Right) FIGURE 2.6. Chalk (plaster) prizes were common at twentieth-century carnivals. (Author's collection)

FIGURE 2.7. Plush prizes (stuffed toys) are common in today's "joints," like this one at the 2004 Erie County Fair. (Photo by author)

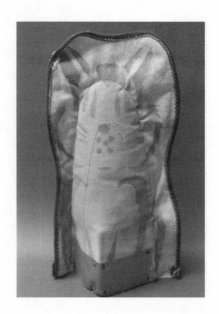

FIGURE 2.8. Old cat-rack figure has canvas instead of the usual fur to make it look easier to hit. (Author's collection)

Like the wares sold by midway concessionaires, the prizes offered by game agents have changed with the times. Take dolls, for instance. Kewpie dolls, six-inch figures based on the good-natured fairies of that name, were popular for several seasons after they first appeared as illustrations for a 1909 children's story. In the early 1930s Charles Lindbergh and Amos and Andy dolls were popular, while those depicting Shirley Temple were the "top choice" in 1935 (Nelson 1999, 91).

The games themselves have also changed, but here are a few common ones that may be seen in today's carnivals and can be operated either fairly or crookedly.

Cat Rack. The object is to knock stuffed cats off their shelves with baseballs. Typically, the cats are hinged, and the operator sets them up by pulling a wire; this raises metal rods behind them, thus pushing the targets upright. The player is given three balls and required to knock over one cat for a small prize, three for an expensive one. Often the player succeeds in toppling two but then fails to knock the next one off the shelf.

The cats look easy to hit, but they are outlined with long, fluffy fur that makes them appear larger than they really are (figure 2.8). Should the player miss on either the first or second throw, the expensive prizes are safe. But two

straight hits may cause the operator to employ a gaff: a secret control that raises the push-up rods behind the cats so they cannot be knocked over (Rinaldo
1991, 24–25; Gibson 1946, 35).

Dime Pitch. The object is to toss dimes onto flat glass dishes; if the dime
stays on the plate, the player wins a big stuffed animal. The game seems easy, but
the stuffed animals hanging over the dishes force the player to toss the dimes on
a straighter angle, thus causing them to glance off (Rinaldo 1991, 30).

Bottle Roll. Two soda bottles are stood side by side, touching, at the bottom
of an inclined platform. The player's goal is to roll a softball down the incline
and knock over both bottles with a single strike. This seems straightforward,
but the ball is lighter than a regulation softball, thus making it essential that it
hit both bottles with equal force. To ensure that it does not, the operator can
set one bottle slightly forward of the other. This causes it to absorb most of
the energy from the ball, with too little left to topple the other bottle (Rinaldo
1991, 28). Hence, the posted rules of one such Bottle Roll in 1988 stated: "Ball
Must Be Rolled / No! Bank Shots / No! Side Shots / No! Rebounds"—$2 per
roll (Brouws and Caron 2001, 104).

Wheel of Fortune. Once a fixture at fairgrounds, the carnival wheel is now
illegal wherever gambling is prohibited. (I have seen them at the Canadian
National Exhibition, however.) To play, one places coins (or chips) on the
laydown, an area of the counter marked with numbers or symbols that cor-
respond to those depicted along the circumference of the wheel. For example,
one type of wheel is called the Crown and Anchor. If the player places a $1 chip
on the anchor symbol on the laydown, and the wheel stops at a section marked
with one crown and two anchors, he is paid double: $2.

The Crown and Anchor (which I once ran in a casino) is a "percentage
wheel." Although carnival wheels have been rigged (Gibson 1946, 58–59),
there is really no need for a "brake pedal" or other controlling gimmick. Over
time, the odds simply favor the operator. (I always joked privately that if I
could have rigged the wheel, it would have been to let players win a bit more
often and thus inspire more playing.)

Even though one may learn much about games and their gaffs, it is well to
recall the words of an expert: "The biggest suckers are those who think they

know all about it. The bunco men like to see them come along" (Gibson 1946, 22).

Rides and Amusements

Carnival rides are the most visible part of the midway. Indeed, the Ferris wheel stands like a beacon to guide people to the location. A forerunner of the wheel, called an "up and down," was one of the earliest fairground rides. The previously mentioned aquatint of the 1721 Bartholomew Fair shows this type of ride, consisting of two parallel crosses with seats suspended between the ends of each of the four arms, the whole thing turning on an axle. Operated by man or horse power, by 1801 these had become octagonal—doubling the number of seats—as illustrated in another print depicting a British fair scene (Jay 2001; McKennon 1972, 1:14).

The true Ferris wheel takes its name from George Ferris (1859–1896). A successful engineer, he had several bridges to his credit when he proposed a giant amusement wheel for the 1893 Chicago world's fair. The fair's management had been seeking some highly visible edifice (like the Eiffel Tower of the 1889 Paris exposition) and had signed contracts for a 560-foot tower with a restaurant. When that project failed to raise sufficient capital, Ferris belatedly got his chance. It was a massive undertaking. When completed, the steel wheel was 264 feet high, and it was driven by two 1,000-horsepower steam engines (figure 2.9). Ferris's wheel had thirty-six cars, each the size of a streetcar—twenty-seven feet long—and each with revolving chairs for 40 people, for a total of 1,440 passengers. In twenty minutes they were treated to two revolutions, with six stops. For this, they paid 50¢, making Ferris's construction a veritable "wheel of fortune" (Shepp and Shepp 1893, 502–3; McKennon 1972, 1:28–35).

Ferris's wheel spawned others, including "a little Ferris wheel, and still a littler one" that graced an amusement area just outside the fair's own Midway Plaisance. The mammoth wheel, a "thirteen hundred ton steel miracle," was the largest single Ferris wheel ever built, although double, triple, and even quadruple wheels were to come. Ferris's behemoth was eventually moved to the St. Louis world's fair in 1904. It lost money and was eventually sold for scrap metal, ending up as part of the USS *Illinois* and a bridge in Indiana (McKennon 1972, 1:34–35, 38–39; Nelson 1999, 97).

FIGURE 2.9. Ferris's giant wheel towered over the 1893 world's fair. (Author's collection)

Subsequent Ferris wheels were popular, but they were heavy and difficult to assemble and break down. In 1900 the Eli Bridge Company in southern Illinois put out a lightweight and more easily handled model. Although known to carnies as a Big Eli Wheel, it and its successors were always popularly termed Ferris wheels (McKennon 1972, 1:51, 69) (see figure 2.10).

Among the traveling midways and carnivals that took to the road and rail after the 1893 world's fair, some, such as Otto Schmidt's, had no rides. That of Bostock and Ferrari, who had come from England, featured several British rides they had brought with them, including a carousel. This led later carnies to refer to carousels as "the first ride" (Nelson 1999, 97). The elaborate Bostock-Ferrari carousel was called the Golden Chariot. It was so successful that it was soon imitated by a lightweight spin-off named the Ocean Wave after its up-and-down motion. However, this version did not fare well because C. W. Parker of Leavenworth, Kansas, and other manufacturers had created

FIGURE 2.10. A large Ferris wheel dominates the midway at the 2004 Erie County Fair. (Photo by author)

the model that was destined to become famous: the jumping-horse merry-go-round (figure 2.11). Parker's carousel (unlike some of the early crude carousels, which had been horse drawn) was powered by a double-cylinder steam engine (McKennon 1972, 1:23, 51, 61, 80).

At some venues, a Ferris wheel and a merry-go-round were the only rides. The next major development in the field was the creation of the Whip by W. E. Mangels in 1915. It soon became a midway mainstay. The Whip featured small, tublike cars fastened to a center post by long metal arms; these, in turn, were attached to a continuous cable. This carried the cars along the straight sides of the course at a steady pace, but at the ends of the course, the cars were "whipped" around at a greatly accelerated speed (Nelson 1999, 105; McKennon 1972, 1:86–87).

The roller coaster was an early ride that was more suitable for permanent amusement parks, such as Coney Island, than for traveling carnivals. Small forerunners of the modern coaster were present in Paris by 1804, and a loop-

FIGURE 2.11. Crude, early carousels led to development of the jumping-horse merry-go-round, still a midway standard. (Photo by author)

ing coaster was demonstrated in France in 1848. However, these were basically sleds on rollers, with limited potential. Then, in 1884, La Marcus Thompson introduced the 450-foot-long Switchback Gravity Pleasure Railway at Coney Island. Four years later a looping coaster, the Flip-Flop, also appeared there, and by the early 1910s, a roller coaster craze swept across the country. Ever more thrilling models appeared at state fairs and other venues (Nelson 1999, 101–3) (see figure 2.12).

In the mid-1930s the Loop-O-Plane enclosed riders in two oblong cars set at the ends of long, vertically sweeping arms. This was among the earliest midway rides to invert passengers, who found the sensation thrilling.

Myriad additional rides appeared. Some were flashes in the pan, while others stuck around and evolved. The 1922 Caterpillar consisted of a train on a circular, undulating track with a canvas cover that slid over it during the ride, a boon to amorous couples. Other rides with undulating courses included the

FIGURE 2.12. A roller coaster thrills midway patrons at a Cleveland fairgrounds in 1933. (Author's collection)

popular Tilt-A-Whirl (which was one of my favorites in the 1950s). No fewer than twenty-one "modern and thrilling riding devices" were advertised by the Nebraska State Fair in 1951. These included the Rollo-plane, Moon Rocket, Ghost Ride, and Wall of Death, as well as those intended for younger children, such as Kiddie Autos. (See figure 2.13.)

Along with the rides, other amusements competed for the midway patron's coin. Such amusements have a long history. For example, the Bartholomew Fair in the 1720s featured large boxes with viewing ports, and a contemporary advertisement described what customers would see:

The Temple of Arts, with two moving pictures, the first being a Consort of Musick performed by several figures playing on various instruments with the greatest Harmoney and truth of time, the other giving a curious prospect of the City and Bay of Gibraltor, with ships of war and transports in their proper motions, as tho' in real action; likewise the Spanish troops marching thro' Old Gibraltor. Also the playing of a Duck in the river, and the Dog diving after it, as natural as

FIGURE 2.13. Many old rides are seen in modernized versions, like this Wave Swinger of the Strates Shows. (Photo by author)

tho' alive. In this curious piece there are about 100 figures, all of which show the motions they represent as perfect as the life; the like of it was never seen in the world.

These peep shows were exhibited by magician Isaac Fawkes. The secret behind them was a Fleet Street clockmaker named Christopher Pinchbeck Sr., who had a genius for constructing clever mechanisms (Christopher 1962, 16–18). Such exhibits are obvious forerunners of the modern penny arcade (in carnivals, an *arcade* is a tent with coin-operated games and other amusements, usually found only in the larger traveling shows and fairground midways).

Such nineteenth-century "dime museum" proprietors as P. T. Barnum (whose admission price was actually 25¢) exhibited a number of amusements that foreshadowed modern ones. These included exhibits of waxworks as well as curious automatons (reminiscent of Pinchbeck's). For example, Barnum featured an "automatic trumpeter," created in 1808 by noted German inventor Johann Maelzel (1772–1838). (Maelzel also devised an ear trumpet for his friend Beethoven, a metronome, and a type of orchestrion called the panharmonion.) In addition, Barnum exhibited remarkable automatons by the great French conjurer Jean Eugene Robert-Houdin (1805–1871; the inspiration for magician Ehrich Weiss to become Harry Houdini). One such figure, called the "dying zouave," bore a wound from which trickled an endless stream of "blood." Barnum also had a Robert-Houdin automaton that could write responses to questions and even draw pictures on request (Kunhardt et al. 1995, 66, 188, 234).

The traveling midways at the turn of the twentieth century had some amusements, distinct from rides and sideshows, that heralded the later arcades and fun houses (figures 2.14 and 2.15). For example, the Bostock-Ferrari Midway Carnival Company advertised in 1901 "Edison's Animated Pictures" and a "$25,000 Crystal Maze, or Palace of Mirrors" (McKennon 1972, 1:58). Such a "Foolish House" was described in 1909: "The floor wallows and shakes. Horrifying bumps confront your feet. What with tempest and earthquakes and night and labyrinthine confusion and stumbling blocks combined, you wish yourself dead. Then relief! A crystal maze, humorous but alarming. A row of concave and convex mirrors, showing you yourself as Humpty Dumpty." It was said to provide five minutes of glee (Hartt 1909).

Describing the early midways, amusement historian Rollin Hartt (1909) mentioned "tintype galleries," "penny vaudevilles," "graphophones" (early phonographs using wax records), "nickel-in-the-slot machines," "strength-testing devices," and "establishments where 'you get your money back if I fail to guess your weight within three pounds.'" Weight guessers—and their brethren who guarantee to "guess your age within two years"—continue to ply the midway. (In carny parlance, they are known as *A&S men*—that is, "age and scale" operators.) According to Derek Nelson (1999, 84), "Folks are always happy to hear someone tell them that they look younger or lighter than they actually are, even if it costs them a nickel to win a penny prize." (See figure 2.16.)

The midway's amusements, especially the rides, have tended to overshadow, and even crowd out, that other important feature, the sideshows.

(Above) FIGURE 2.14. Among today's midway amusements is Ghost Mansion, which combines carnival rides and fun-house features. (Photo by author) (Below) FIGURE 2.15. I examine some descendants of the early automatons at a midway arcade.

FIGURE 2.16. Carnival aficionado Benjamin Radford checks out an age and weight guesser on the midway of the 2001 Allentown, Pennsylvania, Fair. (Photo by author)

Sideshows

The midway shows—the sideshows—can be categorized in various ways. In terms of content, there are *girl shows* (entertainments featuring dancing women), *illusion shows* (those consisting of magical illusions, such as the headless girl), *life shows* (educational exhibits of preserved fetuses illustrating the stages of gestation), *menageries* (animal shows in which the animals do not perform but are merely on exhibit), and others, including *wax shows* (exhibits of wax figures of notables, such as famous outlaws).

In the heyday of the carnival, these shows could take many forms. For example, girl shows could consist of various types of revues, including "Broadway" dances and more exotic theme presentations, such as Hawaiian revues (Stencell 1999). Or they might be the racier *cooch shows,* a carny term taken from the "hootchy-kootchy" dance (Taylor 1998, 93), a burlesque or sideshow derivation of belly dancing that debuted in America at the 1893 Chicago world's fair.

The Midway Plaisance featured over a score of exotic dances, but authoritarian moralists kept them rather tame. Supposedly, Fatima at the Turkish Village was "the wildest of them all." According to carnival historian McKennon (1972, 1:34), "this female impersonator when last heard of in 1933 was the father of five and grandfather of seven." Legend has it that a racy dancer called Little Egypt also performed there, but evidence is lacking. (Possibly someone using that name danced at the unofficial midway that grew just beyond the gates.) Nevertheless, for the next quarter of a century, "an undetermined number of dancing girls calling themselves Little Egypt appeared upon the midways of Street Fairs and carnivals in North America"—invariably billed as "direct from the World's Fair" (McKennon 1972, 1:34).

The first of the traveling girl shows was with Otto Schmidt's pioneering—if failed—carnival of 1895. Schmidt, followed by Gaskill and Bostock-Ferrari, included in his collection of shows a Streets of Cairo exhibit, a traveling version of the popular Midway Plaisance feature of the same name. Cooch shows were only one small part of these entertainments. Working the "streets" were also jugglers and other Middle Eastern types of entertainers, including glassblowers. The Streets of Cairo–type shows were eventually displaced, and "by 1920, the girl shows had evolved into the patterns they have followed ever since" (McKennon 1972, 2:155).

In addition to their content, midway shows are classified by their form and function. For example, a common back-end feature is the *single-O,* a show that consists of only one attraction. With the decline of the large sideshows in the 1980s, these small shows—often designed to utilize a single trailer—were frequently the only sideshows gracing a carnival midway.

This is somewhat ironic, since such individual features were among the earliest attractions of traveling shows. For instance (as mentioned in the previous chapter), in 1719 a showman exhibited a lion along America's Atlantic coast. According to carnival historian Joe McKennon (1972, 1:20), that exhibitor operated in exactly the same manner as did single-attraction showmen near the end of the nineteenth century at street and agricultural fairs.

In contrast to the single-O is a type of show that has become almost synonymous with the term *sideshow*—what the carnies call a *ten-in-one.* This is a midway show that has about ten attractions, often including *freaks* (the carny

FIGURE 2.17. Carnival Diablo is a typical trailer-housed grind show; note the loudspeakers at the upper right. (Photo by author)

term for human oddities), *working acts* (such as fire-eaters), and other special exhibits (figures 2.18 and 2.19).

Whereas the terms *ten-in-one* and *single-O* describe shows by the number of exhibits, others refer to how the show is operated. For example, a *grind show* is one that operates constantly, its ticket sellers and *grinders* (spielers) "grinding away" all day. (Today, the *grind*—a set spiel—is likely to be recorded on an audiotape loop and played over a loudspeaker; see figure 2.17.) Single-Os tend to be grind shows. Another type of sideshow is a *string show,* one with a line of banners along its front (Taylor 1997, 93; McKennon 1972, 2:101, 148, 150). A common type of string show (though usually not a grind show) is the ten-in-one, which is detailed in the next chapter.

(Above) FIGURE 2.18. A large sideshow, like this one at the Hagenbeck & Wallace Circus, typically featured a giant and other oddities and acts. (Author's collection) (Right) FIGURE 2.19. Giant Al Tomaini—billed as eight feet four and a half inches tall—stands beside a man of normal height at the end of a banner line. (Author's collection)

3 THE TEN-IN-ONE

THE QUINTESSENTIAL TYPE OF SIDESHOW, often called a *freak show* (or sometimes a *kid show* to distinguish it from more adult-oriented amusements), is known in circus and carnival parlance as the *ten-in-one*. It was created in 1904 at the Canadian National Exhibition (CNE). Until then, midway attractions were of the single-O type, that is, individual exhibits. These sideshows can be of two types, either *pit shows* or *platform shows*. Pit shows are "typically viewed from above by climbing stairs and filing past a plywood enclosure or small room visible only to the paying patron" (Davies 1996). Platform shows utilize elevated staging (Taylor 1997, 92; Nelson 1999, 155; McKennon 1972, 2:100–101, 149).

In 1904 Walter K. Sibley, an ex-prize fighter and professional bicycle racer turned carny, had some little pit shows—a big snakes exhibit, a pair of fat boys, and a couple of other features, including a baboon that Sibley imaginatively named Zeno the Ape Man. That year the CNE midway was crowded, so Sibley hit on a plan. He consolidated his four pits inside two tents placed side by side, and he showed the exhibits for a single admission price.

Competing showmen complained about Sibley's "four-in-one," which did a thriving business, grossing more than all four shows would have done separately. By the following year Sibley had acquired a special long tent to enclose several exhibits, and that pioneering show debuted at a fair in Waco, Texas. Again his competitors protested, but only briefly, before hastening to get long tents themselves and thus group their attractions (McKennon 1972, 2:101–2).

In the following pages I describe the setup and operation of the ten-in-one, from its main external features—the *banner line* and *bally platform*—to the acts and exhibits inside the *show tent* and culminating in the *blowoff.*

The Banner Line

Being a type of *string show,* the classic ten-in-one has the requisite banner line to visually advertise the wonders of the show (figure 3.1). Stretched in front of the long show tent, this row of banners consists of colorfully painted canvases, typically one for each exhibit or act, which is usually depicted in an exaggerated manner. The banner line is part of the show's front (or outside portion), which also includes such other elements as the ticket booth and signs (figure 3.2); however, there are also non-banner-line fronts (such as the painted panels used for many single-O attractions).

Such banners—for individual amusements—were prominent at eighteenth-century fairs, as shown in the aquatint of London's Bartholomew Fair in 1721 (Jay 2001). One banner illustrates a tightrope walker with his balancing pole and proclaims, "Rope Dancing is here." Another pictures the magician Isaac Fawkes exhibiting his "Dexterity of hand." Among others is one showing three poses of a contortionist, who is dubbed "Famous posture master."

As we know from other rare old prints, traveling British and American showmen used hanging banners to advertise their exhibits. One British itinerant had a canvas depicting a bear, labeled "The Man of the Woods"; another, suitably illustrated, heralded "The Surprising Camel." From a presumably rented building, one banner dangled from a projecting cross-arm, while the other hung flat against the little structure's front. Both banners had their bottom ends stitched around a rod that provided weight and support to keep the cloth unfurled (McKennon 1972, 1:22). These banners were practical. They could be painted by artists who were used to working on canvas. They were also durable and—being lightweight, rollable, and foldable, and thus compact for storage—were ideal for travel.

The British showman's American counterpart displayed an "African Bison" in 1818 in Charleston, South Carolina. The local newspaper, the *Charleston Courier,* made reference to the banner, one of the earliest recorded in America, by stating that the exotic animal's "likeness will be hung at the corner of Meeting and Ellery Street" (Polacsek 1996, 31).

Banners were common to the outside shows—sometimes called sideshows—that followed circuses and menageries in the mid-nineteenth century and set up on nearby lots. One in Ohio in 1858 consisted of about half a dozen

(Above) FIGURE 3.1. A banner line graces the Museum of World Oddities sideshow at the 2004 Erie County Fair. (Photo by author) (Below) FIGURE 3.2. The banner line is part of the sideshow front that includes the ticket booth and other features. (Photo by author)

tents, each with a single attraction and an accompanying banner. According to the *Bucyrus (Ohio) Journal:* "One contained a French Giant, with a Prussian name and an English face, whose portrait outside occupied full 12 feet of canvas. Another hid from public sight the 'Skeleton Man' whose merits and perfections were not only depicted upon canvas, but were noisily heralded to an admiring crowd by a round, brandy-faced Johnny bull [i.e., Englishman]" (Polacsek 1996, 31).

The precise origin of the banner line is uncertain, but it is clear that individual banners began to be juxtaposed in various ways. In 1863 a showman named Joseph Cushing purchased the *privilege* (or concession) to exhibit a sideshow with the L. B. Lent Equescirriculum, an early railroad circus. Cushing conducted his show beneath a *round top* (circular tent) fifty feet in diameter. According to a banner historian, the circular *sidewall* (the canvas wall portion) of Cushing's tent had "every available spot on it covered with full-length paintings" (Polacsek 1996, 31). An 1873 photograph of P. T. Barnum's "Great Show" documents an array of huge pictorial canvases delineating the sideshow area. At one end, a banner bears the cameo portraits of the Bunnell brothers, who were owners of Barnum's sideshow privilege. Although it is difficult to see each banner clearly in the panoramic photo, one obviously depicts a giant (identifiable by the smaller people pictured around him), another a colossal fat lady, and still another a "living skeleton." (I suspect the last two were Hannah Battersby and her husband John, who are discussed in chapter 4) (Kunhardt et al. 1995, 199, 232–33; Bogdan 1990, 210).

Show banners often took "theatrical license" and dramatically or comically exaggerated the exhibits. For example, in 1842 Barnum hung an eight-foot-tall banner outside the New York Concert Hall, where his Fejee Mermaid debuted. The advertisement showed a lovely, bare-breasted, living specimen of the fabled entity, yet visitors discovered inside a hideous, seemingly mummified creature that, Barnum admitted, appeared to have "died in great agony" (Kunhardt et al.1995, 41). As a more modern example, one of the banners of the Hall & Christ Show in the late 1960s (and another in the 1970s) pictured Sealo the Seal Boy with a human head on the body of a seal and accompanied by "other" seals (Hall 1981, 56, 72). (Actually, such "seal children" typically have a deformity in which vestigial feet and hands are attached to the torso,

FIGURE 3.3. Legendary showman Bobby Reynolds strikes a
characteristic pose beneath colorful banners. At left is the
bally platform. (Photo by author)

discussed in chapter 6.) Another clever style of exaggerating was to have,
among the standard-size banners, one that was doubly tall for a giant or exces-
sively wide for a fat lady (Johnson et al. 1996, 160; Barth 2002).

According to *Freak Show* (Bogdan 1990, 101): "Some banners gave the
impression that an attraction was alive when in fact it was in a jar, preserved.
Other banners depicted exhibits in thick jungle fighting wild animals or bat-
tling with their captors. Still others showed the exhibit dressed elegantly and
being received by nobility. Bannerline paintings of midgets depicted exhibits as
being so small that they could stand in the palm of a normal-sized person."

The banner line caught the eye, and the individual placards piqued the curiosity and imagination of the spectator (figure 3.3). The row of canvases might be longer than the tent, or there might be a double-tiered banner line so that the show looked larger than it actually was (rather like the false front used in architecture). If the midway was crowded with attractions, however, the ten-in-one showman might have to "crescent" his line inward to fit the available space. In any case, there was a gap in the middle so that customers could pass from the ticket booth into the tent (Polacsek 1996; Mannix 1996, 73).

Since sideshow exhibits involved many traditional themes—fat lady, midget, Punch and Judy, rubber man, and so forth—paintings representing such typical attractions were advertised ready-made by some artists. For the same reason, the canvases were sometimes offered for sale secondhand.

The early canvases were regarded as examples of fine art, reflecting their origin in the studios of painters. These were often the same artists who did murals, theatrical scenery, and other commercial offerings. Some artists began to specialize, such as the Williamsburg, New York, firm of J. Bruce, Show Painter, who advertised "paintings" of a lady snake charmer, magician, bearded lady, and other standard attractions (Polacsek 1996).

After the advent of the traveling midway at the end of the nineteenth century, show "paintings" gave way to a new genre of sideshow banners. "Banner artwork," states Polacsek (1996, 36), "became more illusionistic—fiction on canvas—rather than depictions of reality." In time, the artwork-like style of the old canvases evolved into the more hard-edged poster, even caricature, style of later banners (Hammer and Bosker 1996). Often a banner sported a *bullet*—a term probably borrowed from sign painters for a large circle of color sporting a word or phrase such as "ALIVE" or "SEE THIS" (Keyser 2001; Johnson et al. 1996).

Among the great twentieth-century banner painters was David "Snap" Wyatt, who had a good compositional sense and a bold, almost cartoonish style. He flourished during the 1950s, 1960s, and 1970s, producing a great quantity of banners from his studio near Tampa, Florida. His nickname came from the vernacular of sign painters, who, lacking work, would take to the road "snapping signs," that is, grabbing whatever sign jobs could be had (Meah 1996). Snap Wyatt told William Lindsay Gresham, author of *Monster Midway* (1953, 157):

"I always try to think of new angles," he told me, lighting a fresh cigar and sweeping a host of paintbrushes and cans away from a corner of a table so I could sit down. He gathered up a handful of brushes, examined them and then threw them into a bin. "These are ready to give away," he explained. "Working on canvas the way I do, it knocks hell out of brushes. Takes a new set for each banner. The canvas I use has got to be tough. If it comes up wind you've got to drop your banner line—if you have time. If you don't use heavy canvas your banners will rip all to hell and gone like boardinghouse sheets. But I'm always trying to figure out a new angle. Like one season I tried out banners all in black and white. You know what I mean—a novelty. Something different. Now I'm back again, using color. But those black and whites were a change from the old stuff. They really stood out, across the midway."

An even greater banner artist was Fred G. Johnson, who had a sixty-five-year career painting canvases for such great circuses as Ringling Brothers and Barnum & Bailey and Clyde Beatty. He began in 1909 as a seventeen-year-old apprentice at the United States Tent and Awning Company, soon progressing to banner artist. During World War I he painted U.S. Army ammunition trucks. He later painted for another tent company and after its bankruptcy in 1929 worked out of his own Chicago garage. Beginning in 1934 he signed on with the O'Henry Tent and Awning Company in Chicago, where he worked for the next forty years. Johnson's banners included "Dickie the Penguin Boy," "Amazon Snake Charmer," "Waltzing Dogs," "Huey the Pretzel Man," "Albino Girl," "World's Smallest Man," and many more. One impressive Johnson banner was a whopping 8 by 19 feet and portrayed "The Royal Family of Strange People: Freaks Past & Present." In 2000, while I was researching voodoo in New Orleans' French quarter, I lucked upon a big Johnson banner in Whisnant Galleries on Chartres Street, self-proclaimed "dealers in unusual collectibles." The banner caught my eye from the sidewalk. At 126 by 116 inches (roughly 10 feet square), it was taking up much of a wall. The gallery graciously permitted me to photograph the painting (see figure 3.4), titled "Major John the Frog Boy" and dated 1940.

FIGURE 3.4. "Major John the Frog Boy," painted by the great banner artist Fred G. Johnson and discovered in a New Orleans gallery. (Photo by author)

Johnson's technique has been recorded (Whisnant 2000):

Much like other painters of the period, he used a traditional orange and yellow framing curtain around a centralized image. Using white crayons, boiled linseed oil, benzene, and Dutch Boy white lead paint, Johnson perfected a technique that permitted him to work on up to five banners simultaneously. He sketched in the outlines with charcoal and then inked the subjects with black paint to maintain the integrity of the outline. Johnson applied a thin coat of white lead paint on top of water, linseed oil, and benzene. With the canvas primed in this manner, he applied the background and figures and then let them dry. The next day he added finishing details. He never varnished the canvas because he feared the canvases might stiffen and crack.

FIGURE 3.5. Banners by the versatile Johnny Meah grace the front of the Hall & Christ World of Wonders sideshow. (Photo by Benjamin Radford)

Fairgrounds art collector Jim Secreto (1996) would add, "The key ingredient in Fred G. Johnson's banner is color—known as FLASH."

One of today's premier banner artists is known affectionately to carnies (and carny aficionados) as "The Great" Johnny Meah. Unusual among modern banner painters, Meah was once a carny himself—a sword swallower, a human blockhead, and a fire-eater—as well as a brush wielder. He has painted many of his visually strong, brilliantly colored canvases (figures 3.5 and 3.6), signed "MEAH Studios," for the Hall & Christ Show, a classic ten-in-one that I had the opportunity to visit on Pennsylvania midways in 2000 and 2001.

The Hall & Christ Show provided an interesting twist on the traditional front. Ward Hall and his longtime partner Chris Christ had an ingenious setup. Their show traveled in two semitrailers—one for living quarters, the other for the rest of the show. Each had banner-style art painted on one side by their friend Johnny Meah; the artwork was covered during travel by hinged panels that opened out to display additional "banners." So, to make a banner line, the

FIGURE 3.6. More banners by Johnny Meah. (Photo by Benjamin Radford)

trucks were parked parallel to the midway, end to end, except for the necessary walkway between. I asked Ward where this idea for double-duty use of the trucks came from. He replied: "It is nothing new. If you look at pictures of the Ringling show—even before the Ringling show, if you look at some pictures of the last years of the Barnum & Bailey Circus, and you'll see that they had a solid front, and it was on wagons. On the Ringling show they had four wagons that folded out and made the front. And then they had a banner that went between the two for the doorway" (Hall 2001).

Whatever its precise form, the banner line has been a mainstay of circus and carnival sideshows, although with the decline of such amusements, the canvases are becoming historical treasures and art collectibles. Johnson's "Major John the Frog Boy," which I happened upon in New Orleans, was priced at $8,500.

Banners, however, are only one part of an effective package that ten-in-one showmen use to draw a crowd. The other includes a spieler and a free sample show held outside on what is called the *bally platform*.

FIGURE 3.7. On the elevated bally platform—part of the front of the World of Wonders side-show—Poobah the Fire-eating Dwarf draws a crowd, known to carnies as a *tip*. (Photo by author)

The Bally Platform

The term *ballyhoo,* meaning flamboyant or sensational publicity, comes to us from the midway—the Midway Plaisance of the 1893 world's fair, in fact. The spielers (as they were then called) used interpreters to summon the Eastern entertainers using a certain Arabic term that has been variously represented (e.g., Mencken 1919). Carnival historian Joe McKennon cites Jean DeKreko, an old carnival showman who was actually at the 1893 fair; DeKreko represented it as *Dehalla Hoon,* which supposedly meant "come here." But for that meaning, the phrase would be *ta'ala huna,* according to Tariq Ismail, an Arabic-speaking friend I consulted. In any case, as McKennon (1972, 1:39) goes on to explain: "If the interpreter was away and the talker wanted his people out front, he used that word himself. He pronounced it a little differently, though. To his Western ear it sounded like 'Ballyhoo.'"

Ever since, outdoor showmen have used the term, often shortened to *bally,* to call their performers out front. *Bally* is also the term for the free entertain-

FIGURE 3.8. The outside talker works the bally at Coney Island's Sideshows by the Seashore. (Photo by author)

ment given outside a sideshow on an elevated stand called a *bally platform* (figure 3.7). The bally is used to draw a crowd—or *tip,* in carny lingo. Showmen speak of *building a tip,* and the goal is to *turn the tip,* that is, convince the spectators to buy tickets for the show.

The spieler who works the bally, in effect a pitchman for a show, is known as a *talker* (figure 3.8). Sometimes this important figure is called the *outside talker* to distinguish him from his counterpart, the *inside talker* or *lecturer* (discussed later). Between ballys, another spieler—usually doubling as the ticket seller—often fills in. This *grinder* is not trying to build and turn a tip but simply trying to move more patrons inside (Keyser 2001; Nelson 1999, 94–95).

McKennon (1972, 1:33) insists that "no talker in outdoor show business has ever been called a barker by fellow showmen." Nevertheless, I have found the term in the memoirs of lion tamer George Conklin (1921, 156), and it may have had currency in circus lingo at one time. In any case, according to Derek Nelson, in his *American State Fair* (1999, 95):

> By the 1950s, barkers had become "talkers," using microphones and loudspeakers, instead of the old megaphones. When the Minnesota fair offered three sideshows (a freak show, "Harlem in Havana," and "Moulin Rouge") on the midway, a corresponding trio of talkers worked the crowd as they made their circuit. Kenneth "Duke" Wilson of Venice, Florida, labeled "king of the talkers" in a contemporary article, was last; the best talker handled the third show because he had the last chance at the crowd's money. As always, psychology was at work. Ticket sellers did their jobs very slowly during the first few sales to make the crowd pile up, which in turn made the people in the back more anxious to get in. Talkers repeated, "Show time! Show time!" over and over, even when the show was 45 minutes away.

One of the great talkers of his day was Nate Eagle. Profiled by the *New Yorker* in 1958, Eagle was called "the last of the great carnival 'talkers.'" He was described as "silky, persuasive, sarcastic, deeply misleading, confidential, ingratiating, hugely adaptable, often insulting, and, at the core, impossible to ruffle by anything attributable to God, man, or nature." A carnival owner, Fred Beckman, once said to Eagle, "You have all the ingredients necessary to rise in your profession—a deceptively honest face, a genius for legitimate fraud, no conscience, a golden tongue, and a feeling that a quarter in somebody else's pocket is a personal rebuke" (Nelson 1999, 95, 121).

Daniel P. Mannix—who once worked for a carnival, then turned his experiences into a quasi-novelized account titled *Step Right Up!*—describes a talker working a bally in the late 1940s:

> The talker was standing on the front edge of the platform talking into the hand mike. "Step right up! Friends, you are now standing in front of the premier attraction of the midway, Krinko's Great Combined Circus Side Shows." His voice came booming back to us from two

loud-speakers hung at both ends of the tent. "Inside here we have the greatest congregation of attractions ever to appear under one top. If you will look from one end of the banner line"—he leaned over the edge of the platform and waved the mike toward the long line of brightly colored canvas paintings in front of the tent—"right down to the other, you will see the acts which we present on the inside."

Mannix continues, describing a common bally feature called a snake charmer (illustrated in chapter 9), among others:

May stepped forward with her snake, and without looking around the talker put his hand on her shoulder. "This is Conchita, whose mother was frightened by a snake, thus giving her innocent child a strange power over reptiles. Over here, we have Bronko Billy, fresh from the plains of the Great West, with genuine cowboy feats to amaze and interest the kiddies." The cowboy, looking very fine in his buckskin suit, spun a loop with his rope, and then sent it shooting up into the air for a flashing second. "Captain Billy, the most tattooed man in the world, and his Bed of Pain!" Captain Billy shucked off his shirt for a moment and turned slowly around. "Madame Roberta, the gypsy queen, who will read your palms and tell your futures by the secret methods of the ancient gypsies combined with modern, scientific techniques!" The elderly lady in the gypsy costume stepped forward and bowed. "And finally, we have Krinko himself! The magician straight from Egypt, presenting mysteries of the Orient for your approval!" Old man Krinko waddled forward, bowing and waving.

After mentioning a five-legged horse, the talker turns the tip, using a common ploy:

"The performers are now leaving the platform and the show is about to start. The admission price is fifty cents to adults and twenty-five cents to kids. But wait!" A few of the people had begun to wander away now that the free show was over, but his shout stopped them. "I'm going to put away those fifty-cent tickets." The ticket seller held up a roll of big, red tickets. "And I'll make kids out of everyone here! Anyone who can get to the ticket box within two minutes by my watch," and he pulled out a large time-piece, "can go in for the twenty-five cents! This is the first show of the evening, folks, so I'll make it an exception. Don't forget this is the premier attraction of the entire midway, so step right up, ladies and gentlemen!"

The entertainers filed off the bally platform as Krinko urgently beat a brass triangle with a metal rod (Mannix 1996, 23–24).

Sometimes, from among the crowd, one or more *sticks* (shills) would hurry forward to get a ticket, thus prompting others to follow. According to *On the Midway* (Keyser 2001): "Without a good shill, an entire tip may stay perfectly still after a bally, all with cash in their hands, and not one of them will go for the ticket boxes, unless some brave soul leads the way. Shills fill the need for such brave souls."

Once, while doing research for this book, fellow carny aficionado Benjamin Radford and I had an opportunity to test the power of shilling. For our benefit, Ward Hall—with the help of Poobah the Fire-eating Dwarf on the bally—had masterfully built a tip. At the appropriate moment, Ben, inspired to get things going, rushed to the ticket booth (which was set up so Ward could do double duty as talker and ticket taker). I was right behind, immediately followed by a line of customers. With a wink of recognition, Ward took the proffered dollar from each of us and, while reaching for the ticket roll, deftly folded the bill and slipped it back with the ticket.

We had first met Ward the previous year and watched the great show-man demonstrate the art of turning the tip. As usual, Poobah (Pete Terhurne, himself a legendary entertainer) ate fire on the bally platform while the show's snake charmer, Ginger, stood by with a great boa wrapped around her (figure 3.9). At the end of the bally, Ward glanced backward from his perch on the ticket stand as if looking into the show tent. "I see the eight-foot woman is standing," he said dramatically, indicating that it was time for the show to begin. Quickly, the crowd began to form a line to buy tickets.

FIGURE 3.9. With (left to right) Poobah the Fire-eating Dwarf and Ginger the Snake Charmer on the bally platform is Ward Hall, the outside talker. The banner of the eight-foot woman is at the far right. (Photo by author)

Later, I commented on the eight-foot woman. She was indeed that tall, just as her towering banner (painted by Johnny Meah) indicated (see figure 3.9). However, once inside, one learned that the lengthy lass was only a mummy—and a gaffed one at that. I laughingly complimented Ward on his effective line about the eight-foot woman having just stood up. "I didn't say that," he protested, his eyes twinkling. "I said, 'The eight-foot woman *is standing.*' She *was* standing, she *is* standing, and she *will be* standing!" (Hall 2000).

In one of the many delightful conversations I've had with Ward's fellow showman and talker, the legendary Bobby Reynolds, I invited his response to the term *barker*. (To the lay public, the word means *talker*, but it is never used by real carny showmen.) Bobby, wittily distinguishing between the amateur and professional terms, quipped: "You know the difference between a barker and a talker? About five hundred dollars a week!" Bobby wanted to be a talker ever since he was a boy. In the early 1950s, he says:

I used to go to Coney Island and I used to shine shoes and pick up bottles, and I used to sleep under the boardwalk. . . . And Coney Island was my playground. . . . That's how, now—I was smitten by the talkers. I always wanted to be a talker. You know I—if it wasn't for the talkers I probably would talk like "dese, dems, an' dose," you know, and say, "when you had dis interview you'd be tawkin' to a guy dat was from Joisey." But unfortunately or fortunately, whichever the case might be, I learned how to be eloquent in my speech.

And so he is. Impromptu, Bobby lets a sample bally spiel roll off his silver tongue. Giving voice to the banner line, he trills:

Frrrreaks, wonders, and curiosities! A panorama of the strange, the weird, the odd, the bizarre, the macabre, and the unusual. Ladies and gentlemen, on the inside, everything that's pictured, painted, and advertised out here you will definitely, positively see on the inside. Frrrreaks, wonders, and curiosities! And put away the fifty-cent tickets. Don't sell any. . . . But if you go right now, for two minutes, by my watch, as long as there's a line going in, I shan't raise the price: It's a quarter. Twenty-five cents. Frrrreaks! Fat Alice from Dallas. . . . (Reynolds 2001)

Now for those "Frrrreaks, wonders, and curiosities!" Ladies and gentlemen, they're on the inside. The line forms right here, and the show is about to begin.

On the Inside

The ten-in-one's traditional home is a long tent. It might seem, therefore, that setting up the show would be simplicity itself. However, Hall (1981, 52) indicates otherwise with an anecdote about an ex–circus juggler named Richard A. Johnson who was joining the Hall & Christ Show: "Dick had never been with a carnival and asked how long it took to set up the show. When I told him it took eight hours, he asked how big the tent was. I told him it was 30 by 90 feet. He replied that it should take less than an hour to erect it. I stated that it did take less than that to get the top up, and when he joined, he learned that the other seven hours were occupied putting together the 'ten thousand' pieces that made [it] into an elaborate show."

Leslie Fiedler, author of *Freaks* (1993, 282), takes us inside the show tent: "beside the Ferris wheel, the kootch show, the hot-dog stand, and the games of chance, the talker spiels and the 'marks' file into the seedy wonderland of the Ten-in-One." Inside, the tent was "usually poorly lit and stuffy with the overpowering smell of old canvas" (Ray 1993, 10).

The attractions might be arranged on one or more platforms. A show I recall from the 1969 Canadian National Exhibition had a single long platform, with a curtain at the back. The platform was divided along its length into roughly ten workstations. With such a setup, one area might consist of a magician's table, another a huge chair for the fat lady, still another a stand of swords, and so on—whatever is needed for that act or exhibit.

An alternative setup consists of a staging area, called the *pit*, where the acts are performed. This may be a roped-off area of the bare ground or grass or, more likely, a large rectangle of planking. The necessary props are set up in this area. For example, for the Hall & Christ sideshow of 2000, there was a bed of nails, an electric chair, and a ladder of swords, among other items. (These are discussed in later chapters.)

Whether the ten-in-one is a platform type or a pit type, the show is conducted by an *inside talker* or *lecturer*. He introduces each of the features, either moving along the platform from one exhibit to the next or working as a sort of ringmaster in the pit. Frequently, the attractions—especially the *freaks* (or human oddities)—do their own lectures, perhaps talking briefly about their deformities and life histories. "Theatrical license" is freely utilized, and the presentations typically make use of one of two major types of exaggerations: the exotic, whereby the exhibit is represented as being from some distant land (Borneo rather than Brooklyn), or the aggrandized, in which the oddity is endowed with some status-boosting characteristic, such as having appeared before royalty, possessing some talent or ability, or coming from a prototypically normal American family (Bogdan 1990, 97).

At the end of some acts or exhibits, spectators might be offered a pitched item, such as a "true-life" booklet; a photograph, known as a *pitch card* (figure

3.10); or some other item, such as an envelope of magic tricks. Frequently, giants sell huge finger rings (figure 3.11), and midgets offer miniature Bibles. Such an extra, inside sale is known as an *aftercatch* (Taylor 1997, 91, 95; Bogdan 1990, 103).

Meanwhile, the outside talker may appear at the entrance and call "Bally!" Immediately, a couple of those who have finished their performances will hasten outside to take their place on the bally platform and help build the next tip (Mannix 1996, 24). Alternatively, there may be two or three performers—such as a fire-eater and a snake charmer—who exclusively work the bally in order to be available as needed. Ten-in-ones operate more or less continuously. New customers who enter, say, during the sword swallower's performance would follow the lecturer during the next several features—magician, fat lady, giant, and so on—and when the sword swallower is on again, that is their signal to exit the show.

There are many variations in how ten-in-ones are framed and operated—whether based on idiosyncrasies, practicality, inspiration, or whatever. Showman Doug Higley once told me in this regard that "Whatever you say is true," because almost every possible approach has been tried sometime by somebody.

The term *ten-in-one* refers to how many exhibits or acts are featured. Although Fiedler (1993, 282) states that "even the number of performers is set at no more nor less than the magic ten," actually, there are frequently more than ten attractions (Bogdan 1990, 45); Gresham (1953, 8) refers to the "ten (more or less)-acts-in-one show." *Ten-in-one* is an insider term, never appearing in the show's billing, and a show would not fail to open for lack of an act or two. According to Ray (1993, 8), "as few as four performers sometimes make up the 'ten' Side Show acts—the Rubber Girl doubling up (so to speak) as the Electric Girl and maybe even as the target for the Knife Thrower!"

I found an example of versatile performers doing such double duty when my research took me to Coney Island's Sideshows by the Seashore, the country's only permanent ten-in-one. The continuous, all-day show is performed in a small theater, with a handful of performers doing multiple acts. For example, the inside lecturer opens with a magic routine, then does a human blockhead act (in which nails and an ice pick are pounded up his nose), fol-

J. G. TARVER, Dallas, Texas
Height 8 Feet 2. Age 24 Years. Weight 325 Lbs.

FIGURE 3.10. Giant J. G. Tarver was one of several who used the appellation the "Texas Giant." (Author's collection)

FIGURE 3.11. Giants often sold oversized finger rings as pitch items. (Author's collection)

lowed by sword swallowing. Madame Twisto not only is the star of the blade box (an illusion in which she is harmlessly dissected by numerous broad blades) but also doubles as Serpentina, the snake charmer. (These and other acts and exhibits are discussed in subsequent chapters.)

Ward Hall, who uses the term *five-in-one* for a show of intermediate size between the single-O and the ten-in-one, once took the idea of performers doing multiple acts to the extreme. When his then-partner Harry Leonard was suffering ill health, he and Ward *framed* (built) a new, efficient little show called Pigmy Village. It had banners for six acts, with Harry lecturing and Ward making bally and selling tickets. The "pigmy" show was little in more ways than one: the whole thing could be loaded in the showmen's house trailer, and "Once inside, we find only one pigmy," stated Sally Rand in a 1963 television special. She added, "But then Mr. Hall didn't promise six pigmies; he only promised six acts." All of them were performed by the multitalented Pete Terhurne (aka Poobah the Fire-eating Dwarf, profiled in chapter 4). After a few seasons, Pete was stricken by exhaustion and high blood pressure, and he collapsed. Luckily, Ward's new partner, Chris Christ, caught him and kept him from falling from the platform. The incident sealed their resolve to return to "the big-sideshow field," where the burden of work would be shared by more performers (Hall 1981, 38–48).

Nor were the ten-in-ones the largest sideshows. Some circuses had very large shows. For example, Ringling Brothers and Barnum & Bailey Circus had a great Congress of Freaks sideshow. During the 1920s and 1930s, their annual "class photograph" at New York's Madison Square Garden, taken by photographer Edward J. Kelty (Barth and Siegel 2002, 102–9), averaged thirty or more people, including—in circus and carnival terminology—both *freaks* and *working acts* (those other than the oddities, who exhibit special skills) (Taylor 1997, 92, 96). The freaks typically included a giant, one or more fat ladies, a "family" of midgets, a human skeleton, a "What Is It?" (Barnum's term for a microcephalic dwarf), and a human torso (an armless and legless person). In addition, there were "made" freaks, such as a tattooed woman. Some years the show also included a giantess or two, a leopard-skin girl, albinos, a bearded lady, and others, including the famous Jo-Jo the Dog-Faced Boy. The working acts usually included a sword swallower, a rubber man (contortionist), a snake charmer, a pair of wild men, and various *anatomical wonders* (performers whose oddities could be seen only by demonstration), including an elastic-skin man and a backward boy (who could turn his head 180 degrees). Such large shows eventually declined. In 1973 Hall and Christ "put together I think probably the last *big, big* sideshow—I'm talking about twenty acts, everything you can imagine, for the Ringling show in Washington, D.C." (Hall 2000).

In short, sideshows come in all sizes, from the single-O to the five-in-one and ten-in-one to shows twice as big or more. The ten-in-one, however, is the classic size, but it can take many forms. It is frequently called a freak show, and, indeed, human oddities are often a major or even the sole theme. At the Indiana State Fair in 1934, a wide banner behind the bally platform screamed "FREAKS" in huge letters, followed by "ALL ALIVE." The show was headlined by "Roberta-Robert / Hermaphrodite" (a *half and half* in carny lingo, often billed as "half-man/half-woman" on banners). Other shows have advertised "Strange Human Freaks," "Famous Freak Show," "Strange and Curious People," "Oddities of the World," "Freaks / Oddities / Curiosities," "World's Strangest People," and just "Freaks" (Nelson 1999, 116, 122; Taylor 1998, 94; McKennon 1972, 1:107, 199; Johnson et al. 1996, 30; Hall 1981, 18, 50, 73).

There have also been large sideshows devoted to *illusions* (the term has the same meaning as when used by stage magicians to describe a large magic feature, such as sawing a woman in half). One such *illusion show* (which can be a single-O or larger show, as long as all the exhibits are magic tricks) was photographed at Palisades Park, New Jersey, in 1926 (Barth 2002, 54). Called Temple of Wonders, it had a front composed of some fifteen framed banners, featuring, for example, "Leona the Girl of Mystery," shown being pierced by swords, and the "Human Butterfly," depicted as a human head on an insect's body (similar to Spidora in chapter 10). Two banners—one advertising a "2 Headed Girl" and another for "Maxine the Half Lady"—might be thought to represent human oddities, but such sideshow features exist in both freak and illusion forms (as discussed in later chapters). Posing for the photo on the bally platform is the "Prof. of Magic" performing a levitation trick.

Especially with illusion shows, a talker might go too far. McKennon (1972, 1:143) tells a story illustrating this truth:

One talker on an Illusion Show promised the crowd in front of his bally that the four-legged girl would strip and run up and down the aisles. He turned quite a few from his "tips" with that spiel. Naturally, the two girls in this illusion couldn't leave the apparatus; but the show was good and the "Marks" got their ten cents worth. He used this "opening" for half a season without any "heat" other than occasional "squawk" from some disgruntled seeker of things erotic. Finally, one night in Wichita, Kansas, he made a pitch to a big "tip" and "turned" almost all of them over the bally. After the performance was over, instead of using the regular exit, the crowd of sex seeking Sun Flower Staters came back out "over the bally." The talker took refuge on top of one of the Ferris wheels. In the resultant "Hey Rube" [a battle with locals] many heads were bruised and possibly a few bones broken. The show's doctor didn't treat the injuries of the townspeople. This was on one of the big railroad shows, and this talker had to find another show for the remainder of that season.

In addition to freaks and illusions, another theme is depicted by a large, nine-by-thirty-foot banner painted circa 1965 by Snap Wyatt. It proclaims, "World's Strangest Girls!" The illustrations on it and accompanying banners show a female fire-eater and sword swallower, a tattooed lady, a frog girl, and others. Apparently, this was a ten-in-one show operated by Dick Best, featuring "all woman freaks or working acts" (Johnson et al. 1996, 110–14, 158).

Still another theme is represented by the all-animal sideshow. One I saw in 1972 at the Canadian National Exhibition was set up like a ten-in-one with a banner line, but it had no bally platform, since it was operated as a *grind show* (a continuous entertainment). Such a show is called a *walk-through,* where the exhibits are viewed at the patron's own pace. This show included a ram with four horns, a cow with five legs, and other oddities. As billed, the "World's Smallest Horse" was a "preserved exhibit" (a fetus pickled in a jar), and the "World's Largest Horse" was in "photographic form." To distinguish the living exhibits from such *curios* (as I describe them in chapter 12), banners still typically feature bullets of color that scream the word "ALIVE" (Nickell 1999).

Another word that began to appear on banner bullets in the 1960s is

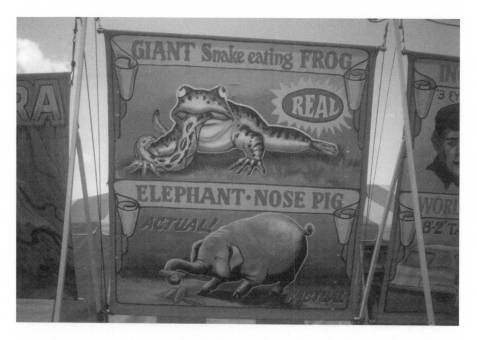

FIGURE 3.12. "Real," proclaims a bullet of color advertising a "Giant Snake eating Frog." This is a clever play on words, since the exhibit is actually a large snake that eats frogs. (Photo by author)

"REAL" (figure 3.12). It is often used with a wink, for although it seems to mean "genuine," it might only mean, for example, that the "extraterrestrial" specimen is made of real rubber. In response to the spectator's query about an exhibit, "Is it real?" Ward Hall answers for carnies everywhere: "Oh, it's *all* real. Some of it's really real, some of it's really fake, but it's all really good" (Taylor 1997, 81). Echoing the sentiment is Bobby Reynolds, whose traveling International Circus Sideshow Museum & Gallery features a banner touting "The Really Real Frog Band! Real Frogs!" Outfitted with miniature clarinets, drums, and other instruments is a band of stuffed amphibians. Has Reynolds gotten any complaints from patrons? "No. They'd look at it, they'd say, 'Do these frogs play?' and I'd say, 'Well, they used to.' 'Are they real frogs?' 'They're real frogs.' 'Why don't they play?' 'They're dead'" (Taylor 1997, 22–23).

Showmen like Reynolds and Hall know that they are in the sideshow business to make a living and that their success is measured by how well they can turn the tip. Reynolds consequently emphasizes the importance of the outside elements, stating, "The banners are almost as important as the talker." What about the inside? He says, "You could have nothing in there. Who gives a damn, you know?" It seems I've caught him at a particularly cynical moment. "They'll come out—. No matter what you have in there they wouldn't like it anyways; so what's the difference, you know? Might as well enjoy it, you know. They're gonna—. On my tombstone, you know what they're going to write? 'Screw you. I got your dollar'" (Reynolds 2001).

When I asked Ward which part of the sideshow was the most important, he had the following to say (Hall 2001):

> One part is no more important than any other part. First of all, the show has to be booked at spots where it can get money. I'm not going to mention the name, but I had been asked this year to take the sideshow on a circus, a certain circus. And though I would love to have been with that circus, I couldn't have made a living, because they have not enough business, and you have to have a lot of people, they've got to be in front of you, in order for you to sell tickets. So first you have to book spots where you know you're going to have people. Then you have to have assurance from the carnival company or the fair or whatever, that you're going to have a good location, because you can get put fifty feet out of the money, you know, at the fair. Then it is necessary, of course, to have a show, because if you're going to bally you got to have something to talk about.

Showmen often take yet another crack at getting their patrons' money, in addition to the cost of a ticket and the extra proceeds from the sale of after-catches (which usually go directly to the performers as a bonus). There is still one more ploy: the blowoff.

The Blowoff

Shows need to divest themselves of patrons from time to time to make way for new ones. P. T. Barnum effected this by means of a clever gag. Signs in his museum proclaimed, "This way to the Egress"—apparently a major exhibit. When people suddenly found themselves back out on the street, they might realize that *egress* means "exit" (Wilson et al. 1996, 63). Barnum's approach was good for a walk-through show. Bobby Reynolds, whose traveling sideshow museum has many homages to Barnum, displays his own egress sign. He is delighted if a patron gets the joke.

Carnival showmen call the crowd leaving a show the *blowoff* (or simply the *blow*). The most dramatic blowoff I have witnessed was at the single-O sideshow featuring Atasha the Gorilla Girl, which actually frightened patrons out of the show. When the illusion was complete and Atasha had been transformed into a wild gorilla, the beast leaped out of its cage and lunged at the crowd (for a more detailed description, see chapter 10). Passersby on the midway would see people running out of the tent, perhaps laughing nervously, and that blowoff would help gather a tip for the next show (Nickell 1970).

The term *blowoff* is also applied to an extra inside attraction that functions like an aftercatch for the entire show. It is sometimes called an *annex* (Gresham 1953, 13); in his autobiography, Hall (1981, 38) describes it as an "annex attraction." Either a patron can pay to go behind the curtain and see the feature, or he can *blow off*, meaning to exit the show. For the extra admission charge, one might see a five-legged horse or an illusion such as the headless woman. The 2000 Hall & Christ ten-in-one featured a human pincushion as a blowoff (Mannix 1996, 24; Bogdan 1990, 103–4; Taylor 1997, 92; Keyser 2001). Some showmen reserve their best acts or exhibits for the blowoff. Reportedly, the revenue from a good blowoff feature can *make the nut* for the show—that is, cover its entire expenses. (Showmen speak of the *daily nut* or the *weekly nut*. If a show is *on the nut*, it has not yet made expenses; when it begins to make a profit, it is deemed *off the nut* [Mannix 1996, 21; McKennon 1972, 2:149; Keyser 2001].)

During the heyday of the sideshows, the extra feature was introduced by the lecturer in much the same way that the talker on the outside bally introduced the show initially. The spiel might specifically indicate what the patrons would see, but often the showman used a *blind opening*, one that could apply to any exhibit. It typically emphasized the mysterious, unusual nature of the exhibit and permitted the showman to change the blowoff at any time without having to alter the spiel.

Sometimes only the men in the audience were offered the extra attraction.

The lecturer might indicate that there was something risqué about the act or exhibit, or that it was only for those with strong stomachs. Sometimes this was true. "More often, however," according to Bogdan (1990, 104), "it was just a trick to get the man to pay more." (This ruse was used with the blade box illusion, discussed in chapter 10.) During what Reynolds calls this "small intermission," there might be some amusement for the children (Taylor 1997).

Bobby Reynolds, who defines a blowoff succinctly—"That's where you get an extra quarter"—gave me this blind opening for a blowoff, which he delivered impromptu:

> Ladies and gentlemen, if you gather down close, everything that's pictured, painted, and advertised on the front you will see on these long elevated stages for your general admission. The attraction I have back here tonight, if I didn't tell you about, you wouldn't even know it was here. Now I've been in this business for a number of years and I've introduced a lot of strange people. People like Frank Lentini, a man with three legs, sixteen toes, and four feet. Betty Lou Williams, a girl that had her baby sister growing out of her stomach. The attraction I have back here this evening is equally as strange as the two I just mentioned. Now there is a small admission to see this. We don't apologize for it. There'll be no show out here on these stages until this attraction is over. And if you would like to go, it's only a quarter, 25¢.

He added: "I didn't tell them what the hell's in there. You can have anything in there, you know. It's all done with Christian Science and rubber bands" (Reynolds 2001).

Reynolds illustrates this point with a humorous anecdote. Showman Dave Rosen had an animal ten-in-one that included armadillos and something called the Jungle Mother. In the blowoff, Rosen had Johanna the Bear Girl, but on this occasion—a busy Fourth of July—she was a no-show. Rosen was frantic at the prospect of lost revenue, so he turned to his lecturer, Reynolds:

> And he says, "Bobby—." I says, "She's not here, what am I going to sell?" He says, "Well." He brings out these two little monkeys.

"They're simian monkeys." I says, "They're simian monkeys." He says, you know, "simian monkeys." I says, "Dave, you want me to sell 'em like they're Siamese monkeys? Is that what you're tryin' to tell me?" He says, "Yeah." So I says, "Okay Dave, put 'em in there." And I go through this—through the antics. I got everybody in there. The place was packed. He says, "Okay Bob." I says, "Okay what?" He says, "Tell 'em about the simian monk—." I says, "No. I did my job. They're in there. *You* tell 'em about the simian monkeys, *not me!*" And he goes in, and I don't know what the hell he told 'em. He probably told 'em they were worth $5 million apiece, and . . . they all come out going, "What the hell's a simian monkey?" You know, but that's part of my life. (Reynolds 2001)

Of course, walk-through shows, which lack an inside lecturer, would not have a blowoff—unless they were run by someone like the irrepressible Bobby Reynolds. In 1999 his traveling sideshow museum—which he dubs his "Freakatorium"—included a small, screened-off area near the egress posted with banner-style signs. "Human 2-Headed Baby" they proclaimed, with pictures of a cute, if double-headed, infant. "Real," they promised, although the astute reader of this book would have noticed that the word "Alive" was missing. This blowoff simply had its own ticket seller and featured a preserved fetal specimen. (The following year, the same exhibit was operated as a single-O grind show, with its own location on the midway.)

Now that you have seen the banner line, listened to the talker, watched the bally, and gone into the top of the ten-in-one; now that you have listened to the inside lecturer, viewed the working acts, and been caught by an aftercatch or two, it is time to blow off this chapter. If you will come this way, Ladies and Gentlemen, you will actually go behind the scenes to learn the secrets of the exhibits and meet the remarkable people who make up the show. This way, please.

HUMAN ODDITIES
Large and Small

WITH AN INCREASED UNDERSTANDING OF GENETIC and other causes of deformities, the word *freaks* has given way to such euphemisms as *anomalies, mistakes of nature, abnormalities, curiosities,* and *phenomènes.* In London in 1898, some members of the Barnum & Bailey sideshow troupe held a meeting to protest being called freaks. Among them were bearded lady Annie Jones and an armless wonder, who recorded the minutes by writing with his foot. They finally settled on *prodigies,* but that label failed to catch on in America, and it has been suggested that "the whole affair may have been dreamed up by the Barnum and Bailey public-relations staff"(Fiedler 1993, 15). Frederick Drimmer (1991) expressed his own preferred euphemism in the title of his book, *Very Special People,* but glossed it in the subtitle: *The Struggles, Love and Triumphs of Human Oddities.*

Nevertheless, *freaks* is the usual circus and carnival term, and a *freak show* is one where freaks are exhibited and where "freakish working acts [are] performed" (Keyser 2001). The esteemed literary and cultural critic Leslie Fiedler (1993, 23–24) notes that the word *freak* is perhaps "as obsolescent as the Freak show itself," but he finds that it still has a certain "resonance." Although there are disabled people who evoke primarily pity rather than awe, he says:

> The true Freak, however, stirs both supernatural terror and natural sympathy, since, unlike the fabulous monsters, he is one of us, the human child of human parents, however altered by forces we do not quite understand into something mythic and mysterious, as no mere cripple ever is. Passing either on the street, we may be simultaneously tempted to avert our eyes and to stare; but in the latter case we feel no threat to those desperately maintained boundaries on which any definition of sanity ultimately depends. Only the true Freak challenges the

conventional boundaries between male and female, sexed and sexless, animal and human, large and small, self and other, and consequently between reality and illusion, experience and fantasy, fact and myth.

In this chapter we look at oddities who primarily challenge our concept of scale: giants, fat people, living skeletons, dwarfs, and midgets. Like other oddities, they help define what those who encounter them think of as "normal." According to William Lindsay Gresham in his *Monster Midway* (1953, 101), "Any variation from the norm can serve as a side-show attraction."

Giants

Throughout literature, giants have provoked feelings of wonder and terror. In the Old Testament, the Philistine champion whose name became a synonym for giant, Goliath, challenged the warriors of Israel's King Saul to individual combat. When none responded, David came forth, armed only with a sling, and toppled Goliath with a pebble (1 Samuel 17:1–58). Although the Authorized (King James) Version gives Goliath's height as "six cubits and a span" (about nine feet nine inches), other texts, such as the Dead Sea Scrolls and the Septuagint, state four cubits and a span (about six feet nine inches).

Many of the giants of fairy tales are ogres, like the one in the popular children's story of Jack the Giant-Killer. So, typically, are those of literary works, such as the Cyclops in Homer's *Odyssey;* Nimrod, leader of a group of "horrible giants" in Milton's *Paradise Lost;* and even the man-made monster in Mary Shelley's horror classic *Frankenstein.* In contrast are the typical giants of advertising, such as the "fakelore" figure Paul Bunyan, who was largely the contrivance of a lumber company ad executive (Dorson 1959), and, of course, the Jolly Green Giant of canned and frozen vegetable fame. More ambiguous is the temperament of the alleged man-beast—known variously as Bigfoot, the Abominable Snowman, and other appellations—who appears less frequently in folklore than in "pranklore" (Nickell 1995).

Imaginary giants aside, true gigantism is a rare condition characterized by overgrowth of the long bones. Its usual cause is overactivity of the anterior pituitary gland (often caused by a benign tumor), occurring before normal

tion is complete. After maturity, a syndrome called acromegaly may occur, resulting in enlargement of the head, hands, and feet. Still later in gigantism, there may be a coarsening of the facial features, with protruding jaws and excessive spacing of the teeth (*Taber's* 2001; *Encyclopaedia Britannica* 1960, s.v. "Gigantism").

Historically, giants were used as soldiers, displayed (since Roman times) in arenas, and stationed (chiefly in England) as show guards at palace gates. One of these palace guards was Walter Parsons, who served in that capacity for King James I. Born in Staffordshire, he was apprenticed at a young age to a smith but grew so tall that he had to stand in a knee-deep hole in the ground to keep him on a par with the other workmen. Apparently standing more than seven feet tall, Parsons found a more appropriate station in life at the tall gates of royal palaces. After James died, he continued as porter to Charles I, reportedly dying about 1628. It was said that "if affronted by a man of ordinary stature, he only took him up by the waistband of his breeches and hung him up upon one of the hooks in the shambles [butchers' stalls], to be ridicul'd by the people and so went on his way" (quoted in Thompson 1968, 144).

The supply of giants could not meet the royals' demand. Indeed, according to Fiedler (1993, 108):

Frederick I of Prussia was particularly unscrupulous in his methods of impressment, shanghaiing anyone seven foot or over he could find and kidnapping women of appropriate size to couple with them and produce a second generation. Hearing, for instance, of an outsize carpenter called Zimmerman, Frederick sent an agent to him to commission the building of a coffin large enough to fit someone just his size. It was, the agent explained, for a recently dead soldier too large for any standard box. When the job was done, he expressed doubt about whether even the huge coffin Zimmerman had produced would be adequate, asking him to stretch out in it himself to make sure. Once his dull-witted victim was safely inside, the recruiter nailed the lid shut and shipped him off by carriage to Potsdam, where he arrived dead of suffocation. But that scarcely mattered, since even the bones of a Giant were enough to please the ruler, apparently as proud of the seven-foot-one skeleton in his closet as of the eight-foot-three living Scotsman who was the tallest of his elite corps.

It is unknown when the first giant was exhibited in the tradition of sideshows, but certainly the practice was common in seventeenth-century London. For instance, a "Monstrous Tartar" from Hungary was exhibited in 1664 at "Ye Globe in the ould Baily." Described as "a creature of extraordinary strength and valour," he had been captured during a battle with Christians after expending all his arrows. A comely twenty-three-year-old giantess from northern Ireland, who stood seven feet tall without shoes, was shown in London in 1696 and at the fair in Montpelier, France, in 1701 (Thompson 1968, 149–50).

Anatomists coveted the skeletons of giants, none more so than that of Charlie Byrne (1761–1783), known as the Irish Giant. Aware that his skeleton was sought and that physicians and their agents surrounded his house like vultures, the dying Byrne made his friends promise that they would weight his body and bury it in the Irish Sea. Nevertheless, the celebrated English anatomist John Hunter obtained it for a reported 500 pounds, boiled it to obtain the bones, and exhibited the skeleton in the Hunterian Museum. Today it is in the Royal College of Surgeons in London, where it stands just under seven feet nine inches tall.

In an exaggerated fashion that would become standard for giants, Byrne had been exhibited as "the *Tallest man in the world*," with his height represented as "*eight foot two inches* and in full proportion accordingly" (Drimmer 1991, 222–26). It was common in sideshow presentations—following the exaggerations of the banners—for the talker and lecturer to add a foot or more to a giant's height. (For a chart of famous giants' claimed versus actual heights, see McWhirter 1981, 14.) Standing on the platform, often in high-heeled boots, the giant seemed to be as tall as the claimed height. Other tricks included cutting giants' shirts large to make them appear wider, and making the cuffs too short so that it would seem impossible to obtain a shirt with sleeves that were long enough. Sometimes women wore headdresses with plumes; a man might wear a "40 gallon" cowboy hat to go with his boots, or he might be a "goliath" with a tall helmet (Minor 1996) (figures 4.1 and 4.2).

FIGURE 4.1. A giantess names Mariedl from the Tirol region of Austria posed with her sister for this postcard photo. Note the large headdress. (Author's collection)

MARIEDL, die Riesin aus Tirol, mit ihrer Schwester.

For publicity photographs, giants were typically shot from an especially low angle so that they seemed to tower above the viewer. Another ploy was to stand them beside midgets (see figure 4.2). Barnum had giantess Anna Swan pose with his Lilliputian King sitting in her outstretched hand (Kunhardt et al. 1995, 174). Giants could also be posed beside ordinary but relatively short people or next to specially made, undersized furniture (Minor 1996). It was common for giants to be under contract not to allow themselves to be measured (McWhirter 1981, 14).

Barnum exhibited a number of giants at his American Museum, including the Arabian Giant (Colonel Routh Goshen) and the Belgian Giant (aka the French Giant, Monsieur E. Bihin) (Kunhardt et al. 1995, 175). In his autobiography, Barnum (1927, 131–32) related a story about the two men, showing that they had ordinary human foibles. According to the great showman, the giants generally got along with each other, despite some jealousy. One day, however, they had a quarrel and traded racial epithets. They ran to Barnum's

FIGURE 4.2. A carnival giant enhanced his height by wearing a tall hat and posing beside a midget. (Author's collection)

collection of arms, one grabbing a war club and the other a crusader's sword. The disturbance brought Barnum from his office. He pretended to think that their fighting was a grand idea, as long as it was duly advertised and promoted. "No performance of yours would be a greater attraction," he told the two, "and if you [want to] kill each other, our engagement can end with your duel." In *Barnum's Own Story* he recalled, "This proposition, made in apparent earnest, so delighted the giants that they at once burst into a laugh, shook hands, and quarreled no more."

These behind-the-scenes incidents in the lives of giants and other oddities tell us much more about them—and about us—than do their sideshow appearances. Take the case of Anna Swan, one of Barnum's favorites. Anna came to him from Nova Scotia when she was seventeen. Her father, a Scottish immigrant, was just five feet four inches tall, and her mother stood only five feet tall. Anna, the third of their thirteen children, weighed a whopping eighteen pounds at her birth in 1846, and at age six she was as tall as her mother. By age fifteen she had reached seven feet and was still growing, eventually adding another five and a half inches. A friendly and intelligent woman, she lectured on giants to the museum's patrons.

Like Barnum's other performers, Anna lived in the museum and was there when fire swept through it in 1865. A reporter published a detailed account of her rescue. Supposedly, her huge, 400-pound body would not fit through any door, and a loft derrick was used to remove her through a hole made in an outer wall by enlarging a window. Barnum, who had had nothing to do with creating the exaggerated account, termed the report "facetious."

Later Anna toured the West and, in 1869, Europe, appearing before Queen Victoria (Drimmer 1991, 231–35). Among Anna's companions on the European tour was another giant, Captain Martin Van Buren Bates. Born in Whitesburg, Kentucky, in 1845, Martin Bates was known locally as the Giant of Letcher County. Although all ten of his brothers and sisters were, like his parents, of average height, Bates was six feet tall by age fifteen and eventually reached a height of seven feet two and a half inches. He was attending college in Virginia when the Civil War began, and he joined the Confederacy by enlisting in the Fifth Kentucky Infantry. He became a first lieutenant and later a captain. After the war, he began to capitalize on his stature and toured in

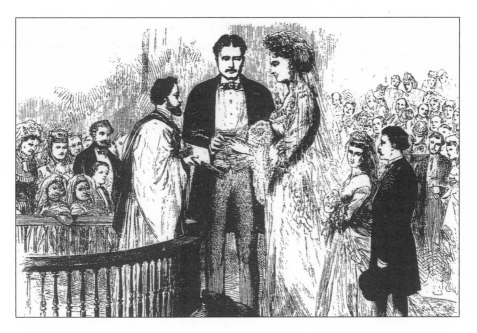

FIGURE 4.3. P. T. Barnum's giants—Anna Swan and Captain Martin Van Buren Bates—made a distinctive wedding couple.

exhibitions across the United States and Canada. In New Jersey he met Anna, who was three inches taller than he.

While they were on tour, the Nova Scotia Giantess and the Kentucky Giant decided to marry (figure 4.3). The wedding took place in London on June 17, 1871, with Anna wearing a white satin gown decorated with orange blossoms. This had been a gift from Queen Victoria, who also gave her a cluster diamond ring and presented Captain Bates with an engraved watch. Less than a year later, Anna gave birth to a baby girl weighing eighteen pounds and measuring twenty-seven inches. Tragically, the giant infant died at birth (Kleber 1992, 59–60; Bogdan 1990, 206–7; Drimmer 1991, 235–37).

Eventually, the couple retired to a farm at Seville, Ohio, where they built a house "the like of which," according to Drimmer (1991, 237), "had not been seen since the days of Jack the Giant Killer." The eighteen-room mansion had a main wing with twelve- to fourteen-foot ceilings and doors eight and a half feet tall. The local Baptist church built a large pew especially for the couple.

In 1878 Anna became pregnant again. On January 15 of the next year she began to have labor pains, but it was thirty-six hours before they became serious. Reports Drimmer (1991, 239):

> Late in the afternoon of January 18, the bag of waters burst. Six gallons of fluid poured out. Then the baby's head appeared. But it moved no further. Anna's abdominal muscles had stopped their action.
>
> Dr. Beach took out his forceps. The head was enormous, with a circumference of nineteen inches. Although most of it emerged, the baby was caught by its great shoulders.

Then,

> Realizing he needed help, Dr. Beach wired another physician, Dr. Robinson of Wooster. He arrived the next morning. After a vain attempt at using the forceps again, the two doctors slipped a bandage over the infant's neck. One of them pulled the baby to the side, and the other finally managed to draw out an arm. More careful manipulation and the shoulders came free. At last the baby had been delivered.

Dr. Beach reported the infant boy's weight as twenty-three and three-quarters pounds and his height as thirty inches—taller than the midgets Anna had performed with. Sadly, however, he did not survive a full day. His gravestone reads, simply, "Babe."

The giants made no further attempts at parenthood. But for years, Seville residents would recall how, as children, they had been held in Anna's great lap or had been quieted by the otherwise gruff Captain Bates, who would hold his huge watch to their ear.

In 1888, just a day short of her forty-second birthday, Anna died suddenly. Her funeral was delayed while the captain obtained a large enough casket. When his own death came in 1919, the funeral director made a necessary decision: the six pallbearers Bates himself had named were relegated "honorary pallbearers," and eight strong men were chosen to carry the coffin. It protruded from the hearse, whose doors were held together with rope around the box's end (Drimmer 1991, 238–41).

Other noted giants included the "other" Irish Giant, Patrick Cotter (1760–1806), who used the name O'Brien. He stood nearly seven feet eleven inches, although he claimed to be taller. A journalist reported: "Mr. O'Brien enjoyed his early pipe and the lamps of the town afforded himself an easy method of lighting it. When at the door of Mr. Dent in Bridge Street, he withdrew the cap of the lamp, whiffed his tobacco into a flame and stalked away as if no uncommon event had taken place" (quoted in Drimmer 1991, 227).

There was also Chang Yu Sing, the Chinese Giant, described in an 1891 Barnum ad as "Tallest Man in the World" and "The Unquestioned Goliath of the Century." He was "Nearly 9 Feet High in His Stocking Feet," the ad stated, although he was probably a foot shorter. He had a penchant for expensive clothing and wore robes of embroidered silk and other finery (Bogdan 1990, 99; Parker 1994, 165; Gardner 1962, 137).

The tallest person who ever lived, whose height was unquestionably verified, was American Robert Wadlow (1918–1940). He stood eight feet eleven and a half inches when he was measured not long before his untimely death at age twenty-two (*Guinness* 1998, 96). Like many giants, Wadlow—who weighed 439 pounds—had leg trouble and walked with a cane. A new brace scraped his ankle, causing an infection that led to his death (Drimmer 1991, 251–52).

Wadlow's parents had tried to give him as normal a life as possible. He traveled for a shoe company using his great height—and size thirty-seven shoes—to attract crowds. He rationalized that he was in advertising, not being exhibited as a freak. He did agree to appear with Ringling Brothers at Madison Square Garden and the Boston Garden, but only in the center ring, never in the sideshow. He refused a Ringling request to wear a top hat and tails, and he challenged overblown reports—such as one claiming that his food intake was four times that of an average person—as "deliberate falsehoods" (Bogdan 1990, 272–74; Packard et al. 2001, 36). Therefore, concludes Drimmer (1991, 274), "Although very tall, he was not a giant."

An anecdote further illustrating this distinction concerns Jack Earle. His extreme height brought him to the attention of Ringling Brothers sideshow manager Clyde Ingalls in the mid-1920s. "How would you like to be a giant?" the showman is said to have asked, indicating the important difference between merely being noticeable and being a sideshow star (Bogdan 1990, 2–3, 25). Earle had visited the circus in El Paso, Texas, to view the giant Jim Tarver, who was some three or four inches shorter than Earle. Soon Earle became the Texas Giant and replaced Tarver as the reigning "Tallest Man in the World," being decked out in western attire with high-heeled boots, tall cowboy hat, and a red outfit trimmed with gold braid (Fiedler 1993, 104; Drimmer 1991, 245).

Before his sideshow debut, Earle—born Jacob Ehrlich in 1906—had had a movie career. Hollywood producers changed his name and featured him in nearly fifty comedies. Then, a fall from collapsed scaffolding during filming resulted in a broken nose and blurred vision, followed by blindness. He was found to have a benign tumor on the pituitary gland, and it was pressing against the optic nerve. Months of X-ray treatment shrank the tumor, restoring his sight but also ending his growth at a height of seven feet seven and a half inches. Earle never resumed his Hollywood career.

Earle was an introspective man who wrote melancholy poetry. (Near the end of his life he published a volume of poems titled *The Long Shadows* [Earle 1952].) A shy man, he had found his movie career—and now circus life—challenging. Nevertheless, he had good friends in the Ringling Brothers show, especially among the midgets. He seemed to exemplify Gresham's (1953, 100) generalization: "While midgets are traditionally pugnacious, giants are usually gentle with a tendency to melancholy. In side shows a giant and a midget will often become inseparable friends, complementing each other in character traits." That certainly seems to be true in the case of Jack Earle. As Drimmer (1991, 244) relates: "A familiar sight in the circus was the giant walking between the tents, his big voice booming in reply to a high-pitched remark from little Harry Doll or some other midget who was perched on his shoulder. In Jack's first season with the circus, Harry, in particular, was very helpful to him. When Jack felt ill at ease the midget pointed out to him that there were more 'freaks' in the audience than there were on the sideshow platform."

Earle finally left the sideshow at the close of the 1940 season, and he embarked on a third career as a salesman for a wine company. Naturally, he was billed as the World's Tallest Traveling Salesman. He lived to the age of forty-six, dying in 1952.

Another later Texas Giant was Dave Ballard, who was with the Hall & Christ Show until he suffered a terminal illness in the fall of 1968. Once, a woman approached Ward Hall at a fair in Berea, Ohio, and asked if he would employ her nineteen-year-old son. Recalls Hall (1981, 55): "We could use another ticket seller so I agreed. She said, 'I don't think you understand; he is a rather tall boy.' My ears perked up as I asked, 'How tall is he?' To which she replied, 'He is seven foot eight and would like to travel with your show.' And so he did." As Hall continues: "Since I had Dave Ballard, the Texas Giant featured, we dressed Bob Collins in a Roman outfit with a high helmet, and sat him on the outside stage [the bally platform] with a sign reading, 'My name is Bob. I'm 7' 8" but if you think I am tall see the Texas Giant inside.' It created a lot of interest and really stimulated business."

Still another famous giant was Johann K. Petursson, who was born in Iceland and later toured Europe's vaudeville theaters with two midgets until World War II. He was performing in Copenhagen when the Nazis came, and he spent the rest of the war as a shipyard worker. In 1948 Petursson was brought to America by the Ringling Brothers Barnum & Bailey Circus, where he was transformed from the Icelandic Giant, a gentleman wearing formal dress and a top hat, into the Viking Giant, a bearded figure with cape and plumed helmet. He reportedly stood eight feet nine and a half inches tall and weighed over 400 pounds; however, a knowledgeable source gives his height as just over seven feet eight inches and his weight as nearly 360 pounds. In any event, his home, trailer, and vehicles, as well as his furniture and clothing, were fashioned to accommodate his great size (Hall 1991, 6–7; "Tallest Man" 2003; Taylor and Kotcher 2002, 13–15).

Among other sideshow giants was African American Tyrone Reeder. He was slightly shorter than Petursson, with whom he appeared in 1973 at a Ringling Brothers Barnum & Bailey Circus sideshow in Washington, D.C. (Petursson came out of retirement for the exhibition.) Ward Hall and Chris Christ produced the sideshow and decided to give Reeder "a more exotic aura," so they had a special costume made and billed him as Abdul the Egyptian Giant. Wishing to be helpful, Reeder jumped up when the lecturer introduced him, and the purported Egyptian drawled, "'Hi Ya' All, Hi Ya' All'" (Hall 1991, 7). Except for the lecturer, says Hall, everyone was amused.

Fat People

While giants are measured by their height, other sideshow attractions are characterized by girth and weight. Obesity, or corpulence, is the excessive accumulation of fat beneath the skin and in and around certain internal organs. It results from an imbalance between the amount of food eaten and the energy expended. It may be due to a number of complex factors, including genetics, hormonal imbalance, neurological influences, overfeeding (especially on fats and carbohydrates), overimbibing of fluids (particularly beer and sweet wine), and a sedentary lifestyle. Health is threatened because exercise becomes difficult and the functions of the thoracic and abdominal organs are affected (*Taber's* 2001; *Encyclopaedia Britannica* 1960, s.v. "Corpulence").

Fat people have been variously regarded in different places and eras. In biblical times, fatness could be a sign of prosperity tending to ungodliness (Deuteronomy 31:20) or a symbol of pride (Psalms 119:69–70). In general, the ancients were contemptuous of fat people, although the Chinese had a different view, believing that in the Celestial Kingdom physical bulk indicated proportional intellectual endowment. Some humanists in the Middle Ages regarded obesity as an outward, visible manifestation of the inward, invisible indolence and apathy that were characteristic of some decadent clerics. Some Western rulers—including William the Conqueror, Charles the Fat, and Pope Leo X—were corpulent, along with at least one saint, Thomas Aquinas, who, despite weighing some 300 pounds, was alleged to levitate (Fiedler 1993, 126–27).

Not until the eighteenth century did fat people begin "to come into their own as show Freaks for the popular audience," according to Fiedler (1993, 127–28). The most famous such person of that time was Englishman Daniel Lambert (d. 1809), who was described by a contemporary as "a stupendous mass of flesh, for his thighs are so covered by his belly that nothing but his knees are to be seen, while the flesh of his legs, which resemble pillows, projects in such a matter as to nearly bury his feet." Lambert weighed 739 pounds and measured nine feet four inches around (Fiedler 1993, 128).

FIGURE 4.4. A fat lady poses for a *cartes de visite* photo in the second half of the nineteenth century. (Author's collection)

Guinness lists no fewer than ten men who weighed over 800 pounds, the heaviest of whom may have been Jon Brower Minnoch (b. 1941). His weight was estimated by an endocrinologist as "probably more than 1,400 pounds" before he began dieting and diminished to 450 pounds. The largest "precisely measured weight for a human," according to *Guinness,* is 1,069 pounds accorded to Robert Earl Hughes (1926–1958). When he died of uremia, he was buried in a coffin the size of a piano crate, which was lowered into the huge grave by a crane (McWhirter 1981, 20–22).

Fat ladies (figures 4.4 and 4.5) have included some over 800 pounds. That was the maximum weight that hospital scales could register when Mrs. Percy Pearl Washington (1926–1972) was weighed, although she was thought to be about 880 pounds. An earlier weight record of 850 pounds had been achieved by another woman. However, Ida Maitland's (1898–1932) alleged 911-pound weight is unsubstantiated.

Along with fat ladies and fat men, there were fat children, such as Barnum's Highland Mammoth Boys, three brothers exhibited in the 1840s. Currier and Ives produced a lithograph with an exaggerated depiction of Barnum's

93

Impresario Olof Wiese, Berlin N. 4, Kesselstr. 17.

Jlona, die ungarische Kolossaldame
ca. 485 Pfund schwer.

FIGURE 4.5. A German fat lady, Jlona, reportedly tipped the scales at 485 pounds. (Author's collection)

seven-year-old Vantile Mack, who supposedly weighed 257 pounds and had a sixty-one-inch chest (Kunhardt et al. 1995, 38–39, 73–74). Among fat adult siblings were the Carlson sisters, known as the Wrestling Fat Girls, who were photographed at Coney Island about 1925 (Barth and Siegel 2002, 14, 43). The world's fattest brothers were Billy and Benny McCrary (alias Billy and Benny McGuire), who were born in 1946 and came to weigh 743 and 723 pounds, respectively. They dwarfed the minibikes they rode. In 1979 Billy fell from his bike and died soon afterward of heart failure (McWhirter 1981, 20, 22).

Johnny Meah (1996) provides this serious assessment of the sideshow genre of fat people:

Although I readily acknowledge Fat People as a popular attraction, I've never regarded them in the same way I regard Midgets and Giants. A Midget, Dwarf or Giant has a course charted for them at birth by their pituitary gland. Most professional Fat People (mind you, I say most), are self-made freaks who have literally eaten their way into the spotlight. I've worked with at least twenty sideshow Fat People and with the possible exception of one, never knew any of them to suffer from any type of glandular disorder. This is not to say they weren't overweight to start with, but, in most cases, a problem correctable by proper diet and exercise. These people aspired to super corpulence to enable them to exhibit themselves. One man freely admitted to drinking copious quantities of sugar water in an effort to become "The Fattest Man in The World." Another man, tiring of the "Fat-For-A-Fee" business, returned to his original occupation as a musician and dropped to a relatively normal weight of two hundred and fifty pounds.

Meah (1996) suspects that whoever first yoked together the words *jolly* and *fat* had probably "never spent much time around Fat People; however these two words have enjoyed the longest marriage ever recorded." Daniel Lambert was known as the Jolly Gaoler of Leicester. Others have been billed as Happy Jack, Jolly Irene, or Happy Jenny (see figure 4.6). No doubt, many have fit the stereotype, although Carrie Akers, who performed in the 1880s as a dwarf fat lady (allegedly thirty-five inches tall and about 300 pounds), acquired the sobriquet Quarrelsome Carrie (Fiedler 1993, 128–30; Bogdan 1990, 165).

Certainly, fat folk are often billed in humorous fashion, with names like Jolly Dolly, Alice from Dallas, Baby Ruth, Tom Ton, Tiny Brown, and so on. Comic elements may be used in the banners, bally, and lecture. Fat ladies often dress in dainty, little-girl outfits. One banner depicts "Sweet Marie" devouring a feast with a fork in one hand, a spoon in the other. A banner bullet claims "643 lbs." Another banner, headed "Oh My! But She Is Fat," portrays a huge woman in a skimpy bikini. Still another, for "Ruth the Acrobat," shows a corpulent woman in an unlikely contortionistic position (Fiedler 1993, 130–31; Bogdan 1990, 114; Barth 2002, 42–43; Nelson 1999, 119–20; Johnson et al. 1996, 83–91). (See figure 4.7.)

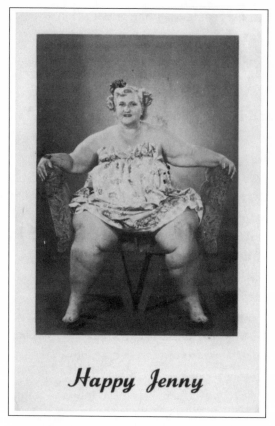

Happy Jenny

(Left) FIGURE 4.6. Fat lady Happy Jenny sits on a special chair for her pitch card photograph. (Author's collection) (Right) FIGURE 4.7. The pitch card of Miss Peggy boasts a weight of 558 pounds. She poses in front of her huge banner, which has her resembling a pig. (Author's collection)

Ward Hall (2001) talks from the bally: "They're here, they're alive, and they're performing on stage. Here's where you see the biggest, fattest, funniest man in the world: Harold Huge. He's alive. He weighs 712 pounds. Alive! The biggest, fattest man on earth." And Bobby Reynolds (2001) spiels: "Frrrreaks! Fat Alice from Dallas. She's so big and so fat it takes four men to hug her and a boxcar to lug her. And when she starts to dance, she quivers like a bowl of grandmother's jelly on a cold frosty morn. Hell, it must be jelly 'cause jam don't shake like that. That's right, 532 pounds of female pulchritude. Mmmm boy! She's a big one."

As part of the billing, fat people's size was often exaggerated by up to 200 pounds (Meah 1996). For their photographs, their garments were sometimes "stuffed with rags to add to their size." Written on the back of one 1880s photo of "The Ohio Fat Boy" (R. J. James) were instructions for a retake, using looser

clothing to make him appear larger (Bogdan 1990, 13). In addition, "A fat lady used to be paid in proportion to her weight; if she added pounds to her girth, the management added dollars to her salary" (Drimmer 1991, 272–73).

Jolly Dixie was with the Nat Reiss Shows in 1927 when she was photographed standing beneath her double-width banner. It proclaimed her weight as 603 pounds, but she looked little more than half that (Barth 2002, 42). Another fat lady, Jolly Dolly (Joann Winters of upstate New York), was also a lightweight; worse, she seemed to be losing pounds when she joined the Ringling Brothers sideshow in 1973. "Finally," says Hall (1991, 29), "when a customer walked up to her and asked her where the fat girl was, it was decided to transfer her to the ticket department."

The story of Baby Ruth illustrates the difficulty of "normal" life for a fat lady. She had been born to a Ringling Brothers sideshow fat lady and had obviously inherited her mother's glandular imbalance, weighting sixteen pounds at birth and fifty on her first birthday. She attempted to lead an ordinary life as a secretary but, drawing too many gawkers, soon surrendered to the sideshow and for a time appeared with her mother. She married circus balloon man Joe Pontico and enjoyed star status with Ringling, where she was advertised with a claimed weight of 815 pounds.

One day, she decided to visit her girlhood home, Muncie, Indiana, and see her sister. A specially built ramp permitted her to board a railroad baggage car for transport and, at the other end, to disembark. She used the ramp again to reach the back of a piano mover's truck for the ride across town. At her sister's house she managed to cross the rickety porch, which had been hastily reinforced for her visit. All seemed well until, suddenly, Baby Ruth plunged through the floor of the living room and landed, relatively unhurt, in the basement. A derrick had to be used to lift her by cable through a large hole sawed in the roof. According to a brief biography by Ned Sonntag (1996, 142), "Baby Ruth left her childhood home in Muncie with no further celebration, and," he adds pointedly, "fled back to the blessed safety of the circus."

Life for a sideshow fat person can have its funny moments. According to Hall (1981, 46) regarding the 1965 season: "The fat man I had that winter used to sleep a lot while on exhibit, so I had a sign made with a large pin attached to it which read, 'If the fat man is asleep, stick him with this pin. He will wake

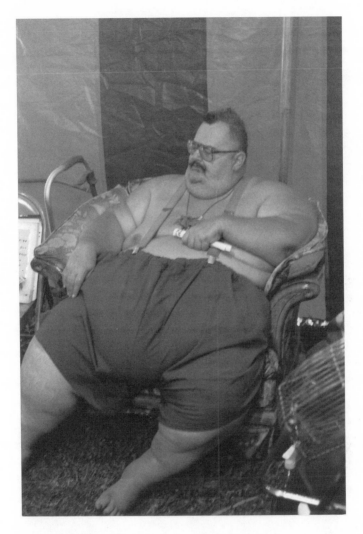

FIGURE 4.8. Fat man Bruce Snowden. (Photo by author)

up and entertain you.' It worked once and then sign and pin mysteriously disappeared."

When I met the Hall & Christ Show's "Harold Huge," Bruce Snowden (figures 4.8 and 4.9), he seemed understandably bored. Sitting by the exit with his pitch cards, he was reading a book. Asked about his act, Snowden sloshed his great belly "like a waterbed," and replied:

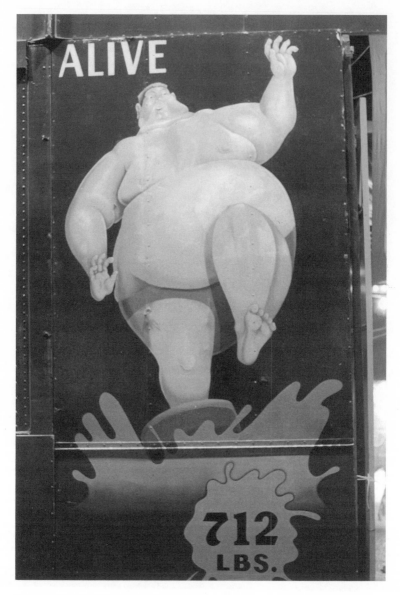

FIGURE 4.9. Snowden's banner at the Hall & Christ Show, York, Pennsylvania, 2000. (Photo by author)

I have a routine about how I eat 50,000 calories worth of food at a time. I probably only eat about twice as much again as you do. You might be able to eat one TV dinner with dessert. Instead, I'll eat two TV dinners. But I don't eat 25 chickens and a barrel of beer, thirty pancakes, two dozen eggs, sixteen pounds of bacon. That could kill a sperm whale, never mind a human being. Two things: Yes, I do like to eat too much and I'm not very active. I also have a tendency, of course, to "be heavy." I probably am the heaviest man who ever lived in my family, but not by more than a century. My father used to bounce up and down from 250 to 350 and back again. And when he was on the way down, life in that family was hell. He was one of those people that, if he was miserable, he wanted everybody else to be miserable. If there's a bitchy type of human being, it's somebody on a diet. You're driving down the street and you cut somebody off, you just drive in front of them, they might snarl at you. But every now and then, it's a lot worse. They're the ones on the diets. (Taylor and Kotcher 2002, 84)

Daniel Mannix (1996, 36) asked one fat lady, who worked the blowoff, if she were happy. She replied: "Oh, sure. On a carny lot, everybody is different from ordinary people, so I'm all right. And I guess you get a kick out of doing anything you can do real well. I'm a real good freak and I know every night there's hundreds of people willing to pay money to see me." She continued: "I bring in more people than any ordinary act and I know it. The other carnies appreciate it. Instead of just being a freak, I'm somebody important. That's a good feeling." No doubt she spoke for many.

Living Skeletons

In 1870 Barnum's famous fat lady Hannah Perkins, who reportedly weighed in at 688 (or 700) pounds, married fellow circus sideshow attraction John Battersby, a "living skeleton" who supposedly weighed a mere 40 (or 45) pounds. They appeared in sideshows together for many years. Another such union was the later marriage of Ringling Brothers' living skeleton, 58-pound Pete Robinson, to 467-pound (allegedly) fat lady Bunny Smith, with the ceremony taking place at Madison Square Garden (Kunhardt et al. 1995, 154; Bogdan 1990, 210).

Such romantic storybook pairings recall the seventeenth-century nursery rhyme by Mother Goose:

Jack Sprat
Could eat no fat,
His wife could eat no lean;
And so betwixt them both,
They lick'd the platter clean.

Indeed, in a Ringling publicity photo, Bunny Smith is shown feeding her thin husband, capitalizing on their respective stereotypes. Marriages like these were promoted by showmen as one more gimmick to create interest in their attractions (Bogdan 1990, 210). However, according to Fiedler (1993, 134), "Most reported marriages of Fats and Thins turn out, in fact, to have been fraudulent inventions of public relations men."

Also called "human skeletons," the more aptly named "living skeletons" were usually men who appeared to be emaciated. Distinguished from anorexia nervosa (a psychological aberration that affects mostly teenage girls and young women), their condition was physiological: many suffered from a condition called acute muscular atrophy, which resulted in withered, limp arms and legs but normal heads. This condition seems to have afflicted Frenchman Claude Seurat (1797–1826), who was so thin that spectators "were alarmed, amused and amazed actually to *see* his heartbeats!" Although feeble and having a weak voice, he was otherwise perfectly healthy (Parker 1994, 181–83). (See figure 4.10.)

Harry V. Lewis, called "Shadow Harry," was a truly sick man. Born in Iowa in 1895, he began to notice a weakness in his shoulders and hips and eventually wasted away to seventy-five pounds, although he stood a normal five feet seven and a half inches. Lewis was diagnosed with "the juvenile form of generalized muscular dystrophy" and, to keep from losing strength in his muscles, was instructed to spend as much time on his feet as possible. Obediently, according to Drimmer (1991, 287), "He spent about eleven or twelve hours of that time on the sideshow platform, standing, it seemed, in one spot." He even read and ate while standing.

According to the *Guinness Book of World Records* (McWhirter 1981, 20),

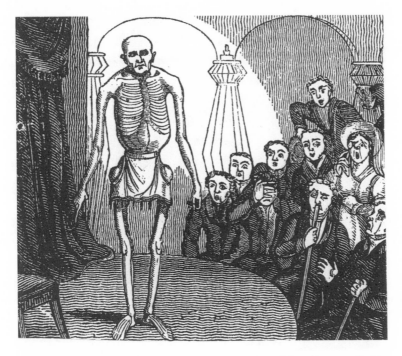

FIGURE 4.10. Living skeleton Claude Seurat amazed English audiences with his emaciated appearance.

"The thinnest recorded adults of normal height are those suffering from Simmonds' disease (hypophyseal cachexia), which can produce weight losses of up to 65% in the case of females." Emma Shaller (1868–1890), who was five feet two inches tall, weighed just forty-eight pounds.

Isaac W. Sprague was a living skeleton at Barnum's American Museum in the 1860s. While temporarily out of work following the burning of the museum, Sprague took the opportunity to court and marry a Massachusetts woman, Tamar Moore, and subsequently raised three boys. All were, he stated, "well developed, large and strong" and showed "no signs of the malady . . . which distinguished me." Sprague's photo pitch card bills him as "Age 38 years. Height 5 feet 5½ inches. Weight 46 pounds." Standing beside his normal-appearing family, Sprague is dressed in the usual fashion for the type, with short sleeves and tight-fitting pants to show off his remarkably spindly limbs (Kunhardt et al. 1995, 275). According to a contemporary circus fan (quoted in Drimmer 1991, 286): "He used to lecture on himself and said he had never had a sick day in his life. He would stand up during this lecture to show he was strong and would close his talk putting up his fists in fighting position and offer one thousand dollars to any man of his size and weight that he could not whip. This always caused a laugh."

Among other Barnum living skeletons was fifty-four-pound Alexander Montarg, who entertained by playing the violin. He measured just four inches through the chest, and his arms were reportedly only slightly more than an inch in diameter (Kunhardt et al. 1995, 161).

One of the most famous thin men was J. W. Coffey, who began his career in Chicago dime museums in 1884. Billed as the "Ohio Skeleton," he later had a makeover. Dressing as a swank gentleman in formal (but, of course, very close-fitting) attire—complete with monocle, waxed mustache, and cane—Coffey cleverly reinvented himself as the "Skeleton Dude." Playing the role of a dapper bachelor, he flirted with the ladies in the audience and punned self-deprecatingly, "Most women don't like their Coffey thin." In his circa 1890 publicity photograph—taken by Charles Eisenmann, celebrated photographer of freaks and other notables—Coffey posed with his "valet" in a posh setting. Coffey's presentation was copied by others; at least one, Edward C. Hagner (1892–1962), alias "Eddie Masher," even lifted the sobriquet "Skeleton Dude." He allegedly weighed just forty-eight pounds while standing five feet seven inches tall (McWhirter 1981, 20).

Hall (1991, 26) provides this portrait of another such attraction:

Slim Curtis, known as "The Human Skeleton," wasn't much more than skin and bones. He wore black tights to show his skinny legs, plus top hat, white tie and tails. A friendly humorous gent, he carried a cane. His voice didn't fit his appearance. He had a powerful deep voice. Slim was the show's M.C. He was the kind of drinker who sipped all day. As the day wore on, his drink would increase in size, while his voice would become steadily weaker. The late-night shows would find him unable to mutter even a whisper. Unable to announce the acts, he would bang his cane on the stage and wave at the act—staggering from stage to stage.

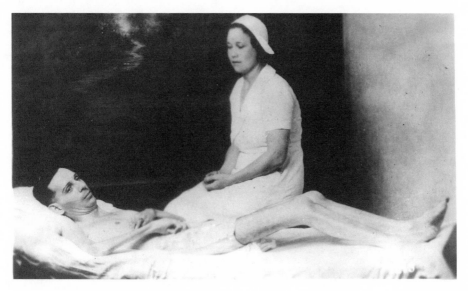

FIGURE 4.11. John Shouse, billed as the "Stone Man." (Author's collection)

Sometimes a living skeleton was billed as the "Cigarette Fiend" (Nelson 1999, 119) or other imaginative name. A banner depicted one such bag of bones playing tennis with a normal-size person; it read, "Age 38 years / Weight 68 Lbs." (Johnson et al. 1996, 38).

Perhaps the tallest thin person was Baltimore's Slim the Shadow. His claimed size, according to a Ripley's compendium (Mooney et al. 2002, 74), was seven feet tall with a weight of only ninety pounds, which he reportedly maintained for sixteen years. He posed for an advertising photo in tights and a top hat (no doubt to increase his tall appearance).

Somewhat related to the living skeletons were so-called ossified people—those who had a condition such as cerebral palsy that gave them atrophied muscles and stiff joints. Among these were George White, the "Ossified Man" (Bodgan 1990, 54, 229); Dolly Reagan, the "Ossified Girl" (Taylor and Kotcher 2002, 11); and John Shouse, the "Stone Man" (figure 4.11).

Dwarfs

In contrast to giants, dwarfs (of which there are different types) define normal size at the opposite end of the spectrum. Just as nine feet is the upper limit for giants, twenty-three inches may be regarded as the lower limit for mature dwarfs (compared with eighteen to twenty inches—the average length of newborn infants) (McWhirter 1981, 15–17). Dwarfism "may result from a variety of genetic defects, endocrine deficiencies, nutritional lacks or a combination of these factors" (*Encyclopaedia Britannica* 1960, s.v. "Dwarfism").

Early writers did not differentiate among the various types of conspicuously small persons. The first dwarf who is known to us by name was Khnumhotou, who lived about 2500 B.C. and was keeper of the pharaoh's wardrobe. "He was probably of noble blood," states Drimmer (1991, 191), "and his tomb was an imposing one."

There have been races of diminutive people, notably certain tribespeople of equatorial Africa called *Pygmies*. Herodotus and Homer wrote of a race of small people living in a distant land to the south—indeed, where Pygmies were "discovered" relatively recently. The shortest such tribespeople are the Mbuti, who live in a remote region of the Congo (formerly Zaire). Their average height is four feet six inches for men, and an inch less for women (McWhirter 1981, 19; Thompson 1968, 185).

It is now common to distinguish two other main types of little people: *midgets* (discussed in the next section of this chapter), who have normal proportions, and *dwarfs*, whose features are disproportionate. William Lindsay Gresham, in his *Monster Midway* (1953, 99), gives this frank characterization:

Dwarfs are entirely different from midgets, and although medical literature tends to lump both together under the common term "dwarf," midgets resent this classification. An achondroplastic dwarf is the result of some malfunction of the thyroid gland. His head is the size of a normal man's but has a bulging forehead. The nose is usually saddle-shaped and broad. The arms and legs are short and bowed, the fingers and toes of equal length, making hands and feet unusually broad. The spine tends to curve in, causing the abdomen to be prominent. Their voices are of normal timbre, although frequently very deep. In show business, because of their grotesque appearance, dwarfs do clown routines. They are usually intelligent people, warmhearted and generous, if they make a successful inner adjustment to the so-called normal world.

Their psychological problem differs from that of the midget. No one ever mistakes a dwarf for a child, and it seems easier for a man to resign himself to being thought ugly than for him to be considered "cute."

Attila the Hun (406?–453) might have been a dwarf. Historian Edward Gibbon described him as having "a large head, a swarthy complexion, small, deep-seated eyes, a flat nose, a few hairs in the place of a beard, broad shoulders, and a short square body, of nervous strength, though of a disproportioned form" (quoted in Drimmer 1991, 192). Unfortunately, we do not know just how short he was. Fiedler (1993, 60) offers a note of skepticism, pointing out that Attila reportedly had a court midget, a Moor named Zercon, whom he had won in a battle with a Roman general. Fiedler finds it "difficult, though somehow titillating, to imagine a Dwarf ruler with a pet Dwarf."

The early Scandinavians and Germans wove legends of mystery and magic about dwarfs, who were known in the folklore as goblins, elves, and gnomish figures called Kobolds. These supernatural dwarfs supposedly lived in caves and often kept great treasures.

Real dwarfs of sixteenth- and seventeenth-century Europe became increasingly popular as house servants and entertainers. A dwarf who was particularly clever—especially if also a hunchback—might become a court jester (Drimmer 1991, 190, 192; *Encyclopaedia Britannica* 1960, s.v. "Oberon").

A diminutive strongman was Owen Farrell, the "Irish Dwarf," who was described as "little more than half the stature of a man with the strength of two." Born of poor parents, he became footman to a Dublin colonel in 1716. He stood only three feet nine inches but was exceptionally bulky and strong; he could reportedly carry four men at a time, two seated on each arm. Believing that he could successfully exhibit himself, he traveled, eventually reaching London. However, being "uncouth" and dressed in ragged clothing, he was often found begging in the streets. Artists did paint and engrave his image (see Fiedler 1993, 60), and before his death (about 1742) he subsisted on "a weekly pittance" supplied by a surgeon in return for his promised skeleton (now at the Museum of the University of Glasgow) (Thompson 1968, 212).

Today, many of the sideshow dwarfs and midgets—like other attractions and showmen—winter in a place known to carnies as *Gibtown*—actually

Gibsonton, Florida, population 5,000, located south of Tampa on Tampa Bay. The Gibsonton post office installed a special low counter to be used by the little people each winter (McKennon 1972, 2:148).

Similarly scaled down was the home of at least one dwarf couple who resided in Gibtown—that of dwarf tattoo artist, magician, and ventriloquist Billy Taylor and his wife Bobbie, who was exhibited as the "Bull Dog Girl." Explains Hall (1991, 15), "Her descriptive title was the result of a misshaped face and rather bent arms." Billy and Bobbie's house was custom built: cupboards and other furnishings, including tables and chairs, were constructed on a scale appropriate for the couple's small size. Bobbie outlived Billy in retirement. Once, while attending a dinner at the Showmen's Club in Gibtown, she was approached by an old acquaintance. "Bobbie the Bull Dog Girl!" he exclaimed. "I haven't seen you in years." She replied, "You still haven't seen her. I retired that act twenty years ago."

One of the most celebrated dwarfs of the modern midway is Pete Terhurne, introduced in the preceding chapter as the six-act star of Hall & Leonard's (later Hall & Christ's) Pigmy Village sideshow. What Hall (1981, 26) calls "the bright spot of 1954" occurred in Breckenridge, Minnesota. One of the show's bally girls asked Hall if he had seen the curly-headed dwarf who lived in town, and she offered to recruit him. Hall gave her the go-ahead, and in an hour she had returned with "Little Pete" in tow. In his book *My Very Unusual Friends*, Hall (1991, 18) provides some background on Norbert "Pete" Terhurne: "Pete's parents were overly protective of him, to his detriment. On his first day of school, some other boys made fun of his dwarfism. He came home in tears. His mother never allowed him to return to school, resulting in his being illiterate. After a few days, the other school children would have become accustomed to his difference. He would have been accepted and educated, since the basic intelligence exists, and he learns fast."

Terhurne was extremely shy, but he spent a week with Hall & Leonard, appearing on the bally and taking tickets. Harry Leonard dubbed him "Poobah" after the character (Pooh-Bah) in Gilbert and Sullivan's comic opera *The Mikado*. Terhurne later arranged to stay with his sister in Fargo, North Dakota, so that he could work with the show when it appeared there. When they traveled back through Terhurne's hometown on the way to the South Dakota State Fair in Huron, he had Ward Hall ask his mother if he could accompany the show there as well. She agreed, but she made Hall promise to put her son on a bus home when the fair closed. Soon, however, it was obvious that Terhurne was unhappy; assuming that he was homesick, Hall reassured the young man that he would be home shortly. But the problem was just the opposite: Terhurne wanted to stay with the sideshow. Since Terhurne was twenty-four—old enough to make his own decisions—Hall agreed, and they sent his mother a telegram to that effect. At the next opening in Spencer, Iowa, however, they were paid a call by a Clay County deputy sheriff, who asked to speak privately with Terhurne. Terhurne's mother just wanted to make sure that he was all right and that he was where he wanted to be. The matter was quickly settled. Terhurne did go home for the winter, but thereafter (except for the occasional visit to Minnesota), his home was in Gibtown.

Hall observes that Terhurne "had been treated as a child until he joined the show." It was "the first time he was treated like a man." An incident underscores the difference. One Sunday off, Hall, Leonard, and Terhurne went to the movies. The ticket seller—apparently not paying attention, and so betraying Gresham's avowal (quoted earlier) that "No one ever mistakes a dwarf for a child"—asked, "Two adults and one for the little boy?" Terhurne grasped the ticket-box ledge, pulled himself up on his tiptoes, and said indignantly, "I'm no little boy. I'm a man!" And so he was (Hall 1991, 17–19).

Terhurne has been "Pete the Clown" at Ringling Brothers and Barnum & Bailey and other circuses; for theater and nightclub shows, in which he performed in comedy routines, he was billed as "Little Lord Leon"; and he has appeared on numerous television shows and had parts in several movies. For sideshows, however, he has always been "Poobah." He also learned a variety of working-act skills, including the *iron tongue act,* in which the performer places a hook in his pierced tongue and lifts weights with it (Hall 1991, 17). For his one-man Pigmy Village show, Terhurne was dressed in a leopard-skin costume, but, admits Hall, he "wasn't very ferocious looking." In addition to the iron tongue act, he has eaten fire, juggled, danced barefoot on a bed of broken glass, handled a giant snake, and let Leonard throw knives around him. (These working acts are analyzed in chapter 9.)

I first met Terhurne at the Hall & Christ sideshow in York, Pennsylvania.

(Above) FIGURE 4.12. Norbert "Little Pete" Terhurne, aka "Poobah the Fire-eating Dwarf," poses with me. (Right) FIGURE 4.13. Terhurne eats fire on the bally platform of the Hall & Christ World of Wonders sideshow. (Photo by author)

Mr. Chas. Decker,
21 Years Old--Height 31 Inches--Weight 45 Lbs.

FIGURE 4.14. Nineteenth-century midget Charles Decker. (Author's collection)

He was eating fire on the bally (see figures 4.12 and 4.13). As I can attest, even without his torch, his smile can light up the midway.

Midgets

In contrast to dwarfs, whose features are disproportionate, midgets (or ateliotic dwarfs) have normal proportions. They look like ordinary people, only in miniature (figures 4.14 and 4.15). There are several main types of midget, each of which is due to a growth hormone (pituitary) deficiency:

- Primordial midgets are born tiny but seem to grow at a normal pace, reaching puberty at about age fifteen. They remain well under four feet tall.
- "True" midgets are born normal size, often weighing up to nine pounds, but between the ages of two and seven years they stop growing. Puberty arrives late for them, usually when they are in their twenties.
- Infantile midgets remain children physically but develop an adult mentality.

THE FAMOUS LILLIPUTIAN COMPANY

UNDER THE MANAGEMENT OF
CASPAR H. WEIS

FIGURE 4.15. In the early twentieth century, the Famous Lilliputian Company was a group of performing midgets. (Author's collection)

- Progerian midgets suffer from a rare disorder called progeria. They are primordial midgets who are born tiny, reach puberty in only a few years, then advance through traits of middle age to premature senility and death (Gresham 1953, 98–99; McWhirter 1981, 17–18; *Taber's* 2001).

In earlier times, when people were generally shorter, midgets tended to be shorter as well. The shortest mature person whose height has been established was Pauline Musters (1876–1895), a Dutch midget exhibited as "Princess Pauline." She was billed as only 19 inches tall, but a medical examination actually yielded 23.2 inches (McWhirter 1981, 17). She was, sadly, plagued by alcoholism and died in New York at age nineteen from meningitis and pneumonia (Parker 1994, 155).

The shortest male midget was Calvin Phillips (1791–1812) of Bridgewater, Massachusetts. At age nineteen he was recorded as standing twenty-six and a half inches tall and weighing just twelve pounds. He died two years later of progeria (McWhirter 1981, 18).

In the seventeenth century, inspired by the old superstition that fairies sometimes exchanged a human baby for a fairy one, showmen exhibited midgets as "changelings" or "fairy children." In 1680, for example, a "Changling Child" was to be seen in London "next door to the 'Black Raven.'" Nine years old, the boy was allegedly only two and a half feet tall, never spoke, was toothless, but had a voracious appetite. Another, the "Little Farey Woman"—a midget from Italy—was just "two feet two inches high and in no ways deformed." She was exhibited at the Harts-Horn Inn in Pye Corner circa 1670 (Thompson 1968, 206).

A midget couple, the Black Prince and his Fairy Queen, were exhibited along with a miniature horse. Their seventeenth-century bill advertised the prince as "a little *Black Man* being but 3 Foot High and 31 Years of Age, straight and proportionable in every way," who "has been shown before most Kings and Princes in *Christendom*." A man who saw them said that the wife "could dance extraordinarily well" and that the little horse "shewed many diverting and surprising tricks at the word of command" (Thompson 1968, 199–200).

The most notorious sideshow midget was Estelle Ridley, who exhibited herself in a circus until the early 1870s, when she hit on a better scheme for profiting from her diminutive size. According to Mike Parker's *Fantastic Freaks* (1994, 157–58), "Using cunning make-up and child's clothes, she was able to transform herself from a hard-living, foul-speaking 40-year-old woman into a pretty, innocent-looking 'little girl' called Fanchon Moncare." She regularly took ocean-liner cruises with a female accomplice, who told fellow passengers that the girl was the orphan of wealthy parents. On their return to New York, "Fanchon" would happily skip through American customs clutching her cherished china doll. No one imagined that, once she was beyond the dock, the "child" would unscrew the doll's head and pour out a fortune in stolen European gems. The jewels were destined for Chinatown's Wing To, an elderly crime figure who would fence them. Alas, Ridley was betrayed by another woman, her rival for the affections of a local gambler, and was sentenced to life in prison; she later hanged herself in her cell.

History's most famous midget was Charles Sherwood Stratton (1838–1883). He was discovered by P. T. Barnum when the showman spent a night in Bridgeport, Connecticut, in 1842. Barnum hired the boy, not quite five years old, accompanied by his mother, for exhibition at the American Museum. Barnum exaggerated the boy's age as eleven to make his small size seem even more remarkable, and he had bills printed advertising "General Tom Thumb," taking the name from nursery tales and adding the comically imposing rank. Witty, lively, and talkative, "Tom" soon became a celebrity, and Barnum reengaged him, increasing his salary. When Barnum decided to take him to England, Charlie's father agreed to accompany his wife and son and to sell tickets for the performances. The "General" charmed everyone. "I feel as big as anybody," he would say, strutting in the little uniform Barnum had had tailored for him. To show off his smallness, the showman would ask for a little boy to come on stage for comparison. "I would rather have a little miss," Tom would say. He would subsequently dismiss the comparative giantess with a kiss on the cheek (Drimmer 1991, 155–59).

In London, little Tom charmed Queen Victoria, who took him by the hand and led him about the Buckingham Palace gallery. When it was time to leave, Barnum followed custom by backing away from the queen. Tom tried to imitate him but could not keep up with the longer-legged showman, so he would periodically turn and run a few steps, then again face the queen and continue backing out. The running midget excited the queen's poodle, who charged after him, barking and forcing Tom to hold the dog off with his little cane. Along with her companions, the queen laughed merrily (Barnum 1927).

Tours of the English provinces, France, Spain, and Belgium were followed by a return to England and then tours of Scotland and Ireland. Tom arrived at his appearances in a miniature coach that Barnum had had made especially for him, drawn by four tiny ponies and with two boys serving as coachman and footman. After three years, in 1847, Tom returned to the American Museum, then went on a tour of the United States and Cuba. He was now, says Drimmer (1991, 168) "a rich little man," and famous in show business. He vacationed with his parents in Bridgeport, and Tom's father, a carpenter, built a special little apartment for him with small-scale furnishings. After his father died in 1855, Tom toured by himself or with his mother or other relatives.

When Barnum suffered financial reverses over a failed investment, Tom Thumb wrote him a letter, characteristic of both his wit and his deep friendship:

My dear Mr. Barnum, I understand your friends, and that means "all creation," intend to get up some benefits for your family. Now, my dear sir, just be good enough to remember that I belong to that mighty crowd, and I must have a finger (or at least a "thumb") in that pie. . . .

I have just started on my western tour, and have my carriage, ponies and assistants all here, but I am ready to go on to New York, bag and baggage, and remain at Mrs. Barnum's service as long as I, in my small way, can be useful.

Although Barnum (1927, 272–73) declined the offer, he reconsidered a year later—in 1857—and invited his tiny friend to again tour Europe with him. Capacity houses during the three-year tour put the showman back on his feet.

As a man in his twenties, Tom stood two feet eleven inches tall, weighed fifty-two pounds, and sported a mustache. In 1863 he became smitten with a new attraction at Barnum's museum, a pretty midget named Mercy Lavinia Warren Bump (Kunhardt et al. 1995, 164–65). Born in 1841, Lavinia Warren (Barnum persuaded her to drop her last name) was thirty-two inches tall and weighed only twenty-nine pounds when Tom met her. He hurried to the office, quite excited, and said: "Mr. Barnum, that is the most charming little lady I ever saw, and I believe she was created on purpose to be my wife! Now," he continued, "you have always been a friend of mine, and I want you to say a good word for me to her. I have got plenty of money, and I want to marry and settle down in life, and I really feel as if I must marry that young lady." Barnum (1927, 338) got a rise out of Tom by saying that Lavinia was "engaged already," but then confessed that it was to him, for exhibit purposes. Barnum agreed to help but insisted, "You must do your own courting." And he warned Tom of a jealous rival for Lavinia's affection, another midget named "Commodore Nutt" (George Washington Morrison Nutt).

Matters between the rivals—the General and the temperamental Commodore—eventually boiled over, and one day the two had a scuffle. The lithe, wiry Nutt threw the older, heavier Tom on his back. Nevertheless, Tom persevered, making frequent visits to see Lavinia, and he finally asked Barnum to invite them to his home in Bridgeport. Tom arrived with his mother, who apparently had no inkling of what her son was up to. After dinner, Mrs. Stratton left, Barnum's family retired early, and the little couple was left alone. Upon learning that Lavinia wanted him to accompany her on her upcoming tour, Tom became emboldened and finally proposed marriage. She agreed, subject to her mother's consent. Soon, as Barnum (1927, 347) recalled, "Tom Thumb came rushing into my room, and closing the door, he caught hold of my hand in a high state of excitement and whispered: 'We are engaged, Mr. Barnum! We are engaged! We are engaged!' and he jumped up and down in the greatest glee."

Lavinia's mother withheld her consent until she was persuaded that the marriage was not a publicity stunt, and then the event was announced. It *was* good for publicity—and business. Barnum observed that for weeks Lavinia sold her *cartes de visite* (visiting-card-size photos)—the usual pitch cards of the period—at the rate of over $300 worth daily. Museum receipts each day were often more than $3,000 (Barnum 1927, 350)—and that was when a dollar was a significant sum.

The wedding, on February 10, 1863 (figures 4.16 and 4.17), was such a social affair that wealthy persons offered tidy sums for admission. However, Barnum proudly said of the event—which he thought suitably lavish for a prince and princess—"not a ticket was sold." Legally, the wedded couple was Charles and Lavinia Stratton, but to the world, they were "Mr. and Mrs. Tom Thumb." On their honeymoon they were received by President Lincoln at the White House (Barnum 1927, 352). Lincoln was struck by Lavinia's striking resemblance to Mrs. Lincoln—albeit in miniature. Standing beside Tom, the tallest president in history remarked to his son Tad, "God likes to do funny things; here you have the long and the short of it" (Drimmer 1991, 178).

In due course, the little couple became the parents of a normal-sized baby—or did they? The birth is reported as fact by some reference sources, such as the *Dictionary of American Biography;* actually, however, Tom and Lavinia merely posed with a baby, provided by Barnum, for a publicity photo taken by Mathew Brady (figure 4.18). The picture was widely sold. When they toured Europe, they "exhibited English babies in England; French babies in France; and German babies in Germany." Eventually, they announced that the child had died of a brain inflammation. Lavinia admitted the pretense in

THE MARRIAGE.

General Tom Thumb and his Bride in their Wedding Costume.

TOM THUMB FAMILY

(Above, left) FIGURE 4.16. The wedding of P. T. Barnum's midgets Charles Stratton ("General Tom Thumb") and Lavinia Warren in 1863 was a great social event. The honeymooning couple was even received by President Lincoln at the White House. (Author's collection) (Above, right) FIGURE 4.17. The bride and groom: General and Mrs. Tom Thumb. (Author's collection) (Right) FIGURE 4.18. The "Tom Thumb Family" was a scam. Barnum had the childless midget couple pose with various borrowed babies. (Author's collection)

an interview in the May 4, 1901, *Billboard*. Whether the couple was infertile or chose not to risk the dangers of childbirth for a woman of her size is not known (Lavinia's midget sister would suffer a painful delivery in 1878, resulting in the death of both mother and infant daughter) (Bogdan 1990, 157).

The couple toured as part of the "General Tom Thumb Company," which included Commodore Nutt and Lavinia's sister Minnie. The entourage sang and danced and performed skits and impersonations. By 1883 the General—who had reached the height of forty inches—looked portly, tired, and old, although he was only forty-five. On July 15, Charles Stratton died of a stroke. He was buried in a four-foot coffin in the Mountain Grove Cemetery in Bridgeport. Not far away, Barnum was buried in 1891, and Lavinia (who later married another midget, Count Primo Magri) followed in 1919, buried beside the General. Her headstone reads simply, "Wife." Until her death, she wore a locket bearing a picture of the man she called Charles and whom the world knew as General Tom Thumb (Bogdan 1990, 157–59; Drimmer 1991, 180–82).

Barnum's promotion of Tom and Lavinia had been, if not entirely original, brilliantly carried out. Few midgets enjoyed the success of General and Mrs. Tom Thumb, who led remarkable lives full of financial rewards and admiration. Yet when she wrote her memoirs (never published), Lavinia would lament, "If nature endowed me with any superior personal attraction it was comparatively small compensation for the inconvenience, trouble, and annoyance imposed upon me by my diminutive stature" (quoted by Drimmer 1991, 182). She might have been speaking for little people everywhere.

In sideshows before and after, however, midgets found a ready niche. Indeed, a perusal of old circus and sideshow photographs by Edward J. Kelty (Barth and Siegel 2002) shows that—while dwarfs were invariably cast as clowns in the big top—midgets, usually juxtaposed with giants, dominated the sideshows. Photographing them with giants was only one way to enhance their smallness; more subtly, a midget might be posed beside an ordinary but tall person or stood in an oversized chair (Minor 1996). Of course, the size of a midget is always exaggerated downward, and many have claimed to be the "World's Smallest" (see figure 4.19).

Times change, and with them, so do the meanings of words. At its most dis-

FIGURE 4.19. "Little Gloria," whom I met in 2001, is only one of many little people billed as the "world's smallest." (Photo by author)

passionate, *freak* meant simply "freak of nature" (Fiedler 1993, 19). Today it is called "an ugly word" (Drimmer 1991, xii), even judged to be "taboo" (Stone and Johnson 1996, 11). But there are uglier words. From ancient history, abnormal creatures—both animal and human—were termed *monstrosities*. The births of these so-called monsters were often explained in superstitious, supernatural, terms. They might be thought to presage calamity and disaster, or they might be considered evidence of divine wrath. Some believed that they were the result of mating with animals (Thompson 1968, 17). These beings, like some of those examined in the next chapter, were often put to death (Fiedler 1993, 21).

HUMAN ODDITIES
Between a half and two

IN ADDITION TO THOSE WHO DEFY normal parameters by their size, there are those who do so as versions of a single, complete individual.

Siamese Twins

Siamese twins—today called conjoined twins—are monozygotic ("one egg") twins who are not completely separated. The fertilized egg divides incompletely at an early stage, and the two parts continue to develop into two anatomically linked individuals. They may be paired in various ways, such as a single head with double neck, trunk, and limbs; a doubled head, shoulders, and arms, but with a single trunk and pair of legs; or a rare type with a "Janus head," that is, two faces on one head and body (*Encyclopaedia Britannica* 1960, s.v. "Monster").

Authentic records of conjoined twins in ancient times are sparse, but Cicero (106–43 B.C.) mentioned the birth of a girl with two heads. During the reign of Theodosius (346?–395) a child was reportedly born with two heads, two chests, and two pairs of arms, yet a single leg. According to the account (quoted in Thompson 1968, 31), the conjoined twins had different personalities: "One head might be crying while the other laughed, or one eating while the other was sleeping. They quarreled sometimes and occasionally came to blows. They are said to have lived two years, when one died four days before the other."

In A.D. 945 two Armenian boys, joined at the abdomens, were exhibited in Constantinople. "They excited great interest and curiosity," states Thompson (1968, 30–31), "but they were removed by order of the authorities, as it was considered at the time that such abnormal creatures presaged evil."

The earliest known English conjoined twins who actually survived were

FIGURE 5.1. The Biddenden Maids were the earliest known English conjoined twins. (From an old print)

Mary and Eliza Chulkhurst. They were called "Ye Maydes of Biddenden" (the Biddenden Maids) after the village in which they were born about 1100. Joined at the shoulders and hips, they were otherwise separate and lived until 1134, when first one died and then, necessarily, the other died within hours. They are still remembered on Easter Monday, when the locals distribute Biddenden Maids' cakes imprinted with their image from boxwood dies cut in 1814 (Thompson 1968, 32–36; Parker 1994, 79–80). (See figure 5.1.)

The sixteenth century brought a number of works on "monstrosities" and "prodigies" and often included wood engravings of double-headed "monsters" and other conjoinings. One pair of such twins who lived in Switzerland had reached age thirty in 1538: "Each of the heads possessed a beard, and their two bodies were fused together at the umbilicus into a single lower extremity. They resembled one another in features and face, and were so joined that they could see each other. They had a single wife with whom they are said to have lived in harmony" (Thompson 1968, 37–48).

London has been characterized as something of a Mecca for "every variety of monstrosity" in the seventeenth century. Conjoined twins were among those exhibited. For example, during the reign of William and Mary (1689–1694), a twenty-one-year-old, single-headed person with two distinct bodies was brought to London and exhibited by Sir Thomas Grantham at the Blew-Boar's Head in Fleet Street and later at the King's Head in the Strand. Eventually, he "proved a great attraction" at the famous Bartholomew Fair (Thompson 1968, 63–66).

The most famous conjoined pair was Chang and Eng, the original "Siamese twins" (figure 5.2). Born in Meklong province, Siam, on May 11, 1811, they were linked by a three-and-a-half–inch armlike tube of flesh. They were of Chinese ancestry, their father and maternal grandfather having been Chinese. The family consisted of fourteen children, including other pairs of twins. Reportedly, the superstitious king of Siam wanted them put to death but was eventually persuaded that they were not only harmless but could function well enough to support themselves. And so they did.

At the age of eighteen, after a two-month visit to Boston, where they were examined by Harvard professor J. C. Warren, they sailed to England for exhibition. They first appeared at the Egyptian Hall in Piccadilly, London. After touring Europe they eventually returned to America, where they were exhibited as an individual attraction in dime museums and other venues (Thompson 1968, 79–80; Parker 1994, 76–78). An early handbill depicted them in oriental dress with pigtails and heralded them as "Siamese twins" called "The United Brothers, Chang-Eng." The bill stated "Admission 50 cents" with date, time, and place to be filled in. The twins sold a pamphlet about their lives and also had "a few copies of a very superior likeness, executed in lithograph and suitable for framing—price 25 cents" (Kunhardt et al. 1995, 144).

They became world famous, but after seven years of exhibition in the United States, Chang and Eng retired in 1838. They became American citizens, adopted the surname of Bunker, and purchased a North Carolina plantation

THE SIAMESE TWINS—CHANG AND ENG.

FIGURE 5.2. Chang and Eng Bunker (1811–1874) were the original "Siamese twins"—born in Siam, exhibited in London, and later under contract to P. T. Barnum. (Wood engraving from *Life of Barnum*)

and, eventually, thirty-three slaves. The Bunkers married sisters, whom they decorously set up in separate houses and took turns visiting a few days at a time. They eventually fathered twenty-two children.

P. T. Barnum was aware of the retired pair, and in the late 1840s he installed a wax figure of them in his American Museum. In 1860 he got his chance to exhibit the living twins when they decided to come out of retirement to raise money to send their many children to college. They did not like Barnum, who in turn found them troublesome. Their wives bickered, and Chang, a heavy drinker, feuded with his teetotaler brother. According to a newspaper account (quoted in Kunhardt et al. 1995, 147): "They had a sleeping room in Barnum's museum, as did the other curiosities; and one night a rumpus was heard in it. On breaking open the door, the twins were found fighting. Eng was on the floor, underneath Chang, who was choking him."

Their six-week engagement at the museum was very profitable, but the Bunkers rejected Barnum's offer for a countrywide tour. Instead, they had decided to plan their own western tour, then sail from California for their first visit to Siam in three decades. However, secession and civil war forced them to scrap their plans and rush home for the duration. The war devastated their wealth, and afterward they permitted Barnum to send them on a tour of Europe to rebuild it.

Promotion of the Bunkers required little in the way of deception. Unlike oddities whose size could be exaggerated, they were unique as they were. There was one little secret about their height, however: although Eng was five feet two inches, Chang was an inch shorter (due to a slightly curved spine) and so wore thick-soled boots to compensate. The twins were most comfortable in specially made chairs that were wide enough for them to sit in together. One from Chang's home was shown on the *Antiques Roadshow* television program (December 30, 2001) by his granddaughter; an identical one had been at Eng's house. As well, at each respective home, they—and one wife—shared "what was perhaps understatedly described as a 'very large bed'" (Parker 1994, 78).

In 1870 Chang suffered a stroke and thereafter had to be partially carried by Eng. Four years later, on January 17, 1874, Chang died in his sleep at age sixty-two. Eng resigned himself to his fate and asked that his brother's body be shifted closer to him; he lived for about two more hours (Kunhardt et al. 1995, 147; Thompson 1968, 83–84).

Although "Siamese twins" could be gaffed (see chapter 8), real conjoined twins, suitable for exhibition, were not common—especially after advances in surgical separation techniques. Among those conjoined pairs who were exhibited as human oddities were the Millie-Christine sisters (figure 5.3). Also billed as the "United African Twins," the girls, who had been born into

FIGURE 5.3. Millie-Christine, the "United African Twins," were born slaves. (From an 1896 color lithograph; author's collection)

slavery, were joined back to back at the buttocks. They were exhibited by being shuttled "back and forth across state lines" and were finally taken to England. Later they were exhibited by Barnum, who styled the pair as the "Two-Headed Nightingale," with Millie singing alto, Christine soprano. They also danced and even skipped rope. To prove that they were genuinely conjoined, their point of connection was shown to spectators "without any infringement of modesty." A pamphlet sold as a pitch item at their exhibitions contained "Medical Descriptions," revealing that they had "a common anus . . . and actually discharge their feces and urine at the same time" (Kunhardt et al. 1995, 209; Fiedler 1993, 209).

Another pair of back-to-back conjoined girls was the beautiful, charming Hilton sisters, Daisy and Violet, who were born in Brighton, England, in 1908. Their mother, barmaid Kate Skinner, turned the girls over to bar owner Mary Hilton, who became their guardian. From the age of three, the Hilton girls were exhibited at fairs, circuses, and carnivals as the "United Twins." They toured Europe and Australia. Later, in the United States, after Mary Hilton died, the twins' lives were taken over by her daughter and son-in-law. They taught the twins to play saxophone and transferred them from the sideshow to vaudeville. "We are our own Jazz Band," they joked to a reporter in 1924, when they were fifteen (Drimmer 1991, 53–57).

The Hilton sisters' 1926 pitch booklet, titled "Life Story and Facts of the San Antonio Siamese Twins," took liberties, beginning with the details of their origin. Instead of being born out of wedlock with an unknown father and a mother who did not want them, the booklet claimed that they were "the daughters of an English Army Officer. Their mother died a year after their birth. Their father was killed in Belgium in 1914" (quoted in Bogdan 1990, 169–70). These fictions were elaborated in their "autobiography" (Hilton and Hilton 1942), which claimed that "Captain Hilton" had "married Mother in Texas." One early pitch-card photo was captioned "Daisy and Violet / Texas Siamese Twins," although an earlier one was captioned "Violet and Daisy / English Siamese Twins" (Taylor and Kotcher 2002, 52, 61).

In 1932 they won a $100,000 judgment against their "guardians" and gained their independence. They acted in movies, including Tod Browning's cult classic *Freaks* (1932). (Browning, a circus contortionist turned filmmaker, hired real sideshow oddities and built a realistic carnival set for his film. The plot featured freaks taking revenge on an aerialist and her strongman lover for their evil deeds.) The Hilton twins also starred in a quasi-autobiographical film, *Chained for Life,* which bombed in the early 1940s (Wilson et al. 1996, 150–58, 201–9). The girls each suffered a failed marriage, and Daisy became a blonde (Hilton and Hilton 1942). Although they once earned $5,000 a week, by 1969, when they died of influenza at age sixty, they were employed by a Charlotte, North Carolina, supermarket. Fiedler (1993, 209) reports, somewhat imaginatively, that they were working "as a double checkout girl—one bagging, no doubt, as the other rang up the bill on the cash register."

Perhaps the last of the famous sideshow Siamese twins are Ronnie and Donnie Galyon (figure 5.4). Born October 28, 1951, the boys were rejected by their mother but cared for by their father, Wesley. They spent their first twenty months undergoing X-ray and other examinations. The twins were joined facing each other, being connected from the lower end of the breastbone to the

FIGURE 5.4. Ronnie and Donnie Galyon, conjoined twins born in 1951, were once promoted by this pitch pamphlet. (Author's collection)

abdomen, and they shared a single rectum and set of male organs; separation was considered impossible. Wesley Galyon put his sons on exhibit, rationalizing, "What else can Siamese twins do?" An early poster declared, "$10,000 Reward if the Boys Are Not Alive" (Hall 1991, 40; *Sideshow* 2000).

I saw the Galyons about 1970 or 1971 at the Canadian National Exhibition in Toronto. Their single-O sideshow consisted of an air-conditioned trailer that had a picture window so that customers could view the teenagers while filing past. I recall them eating while watching television, then getting up to put their plates away, necessarily walking sideways.

Ronnie and Donnie were the only conjoined twins exhibiting in 1991 when Ward Hall wrote his book *My Very Unusual Friends.* At that time, they were appearing in Central and South America, where they were often called

"Doonie and Roonie" but were treated with more respect than in the United States and Canada. They traveled on a single passport. The Galyons are now retired, having earned enough money to buy their own home.

One-and-a-Halfs

Sometimes the incomplete division of the fertilized egg that produces conjoined twins is even more flawed. Instead of dividing into a pair of nearly equal and symmetrical individuals, the result is one normal body and a stunted or vestigial one growing out of it (figure 5.5). As Drimmer (1991, 29) explains: "The little twin might be almost complete. It might be a whole small body from the neck down. Or a whole small body from the waist down. It might be the upper part of a body, with a large, deformed head. The twin might be just one or two legs. It might be just a head—fused to the head of its completely normal twin. Sometimes a portion of the partial twin might be enclosed within the body of the larger twin. Doctors call the larger twin an 'autosite,' the smaller one a 'parasite.'"

Among the best known of these "one-and-a-halfs," as they are sometimes called (Fiedler 1993, 219; DeBurke 1996), was a Hindu man known as Laloo (figure 5.6). Born in India in about 1874—the second of four otherwise normal children—Laloo had a small, headless, parasitic body attached to his lower breastbone. He was described in the July 1886 *Indian Medical Gazette*. He toured England in 1891 and later traveled to the United States, where he became part of Barnum's show. He married in Philadelphia in 1894, and his wife subsequently traveled with him (Thompson 1968, 219; Drimmer 1991, 32).

In Laloo's sideshow and dime museum appearances, his managers advertised that the vestigial twin was Laloo's sister; to promote the idea, they dressed the small body in feminine clothing. Of course, like Siamese twins, such parasites are always the same sex as their autosite; if they had developed properly, they would have been "identical" twins, because they came from the same fertilized egg. ("Fraternal" twins are produced from different eggs and may be as different as any two siblings.) In fact, although Laloo's stunted twin lacked testicles, it did have a rudimentary penis. Laloo reportedly boasted privately that it urinated and even had erections. (Fiedler 1993, 219; Drimmer 1991,

128

FIGURE 5.5. Perumal, a Hindu one-and-a-half, named his parasitic twin Sami. (Contemporary publicity photo)

32–33). However, Thompson (1968, 93) states that the ancillary body "was incapable of active motion and no pulse could be felt."

Another famous one-and-a-half was Betty Lou Williams, the "Double-Bodied Girl." Apart from her miniature twin—consisting of the lower half of a stunted body with a misplaced arm and two legs—she was an attractive black woman. She posed, smiling, in a two-piece bathing suit, one hand placed on her hip, the other supporting the vestigial twin extending from her abdomen

WEEK BEGINNING MONDAY, DEC. 7th.

DOORS OPEN DAILY FROM 10 A. M. TO 10 P. M.

THE REIGNING SENSATION!
ENGAGED FOR THIS WEEK ONLY.

LALOO

The Greatest Curiosity in Existence!

LALOO IS A

HANDSOME
HEALTHY
HAPPY
HINDOO
HE HAS

4 ARMS
LEGS
HANDS
FEET

20 Toes--20 Fingers--2 Bodies
AND ONLY ONE HEAD.
HE'S ALIVE!

Highest Salaried Marvel Ever Exhibited.
The Medical World Amazed and Startled.

ASK YOUR FAMILY PHYSICIAN ABOUT

LALOO
Then go to the MUSEE-THEATRE, see him,
touch him, clasp each one of his four arms and
legs, prove to your own satisfaction that he is
ALIVE

Not an Offensive Curiosity but a Good Looking, Intelligent Boy and his Sister.

Prof. Wilton's Cat Circus, 20 Educated Felines.   Punch and Judy Show.
Walker & Reedy's London Marionettes.   Return of the Hungarian Band.

New Eden Musee, Art Gallery, Menagerie, Prairie Dog Village, Etc.

10c. GENERAL ADMISSION 10c.
Secure your seats early.   Reserved Seats, 5, 10 and 15 cts. extra.   Box Seats, 25 cts.

FIGURE 5.6. Laloo's parasitic twin was genuine but was falsely presented as female. (Author's collection)

(Drimmer 1991, 33). When not on exhibit to the public, she cleverly wore maternity clothes, permitting her to move unnoticed through the "normal" world (Hall 1991, 23, 54).

In the case of autosite-parasite twins who were joined at the lower body and could not be exhibited in full without exposing the genitalia, showmen covered up all but the extra twin's limbs and billed the attraction accordingly. Thus Myrtle Corbin, who had two small extra legs hanging between her own, was billed as the "Four-legged Woman from Texas." She began to be exhibited at age thirteen, and her first pitch book (a pamphlet titled "Biography of Myrtle Corbin," published in 1881) described her as being "gentle of disposition as the summer sunshine and as happy as the day is long." The birth of her first child was reported in at least three medical journals, and she later posed with her husband and little girl for a pitch-card photograph (Wilson et al. 1996, 52–53; Bogdan 1990, 230; Drimmer 1991, 37). Corbin exhibited with the Ringling Brothers and other circus and carnival sideshows for many years. Her later promotional literature described her as having two vaginas, alleging that she had borne three children from one vagina and two from the other (Drimmer 1991, 37).

Another oddity of this type was Sicilian-born Francesco A. "Frank" Lentini (1889–1966), who was billed in circus sideshows as the "Three-Legged Wonder." His extra leg was shorter than the others and was joined to his skeleton by an underdeveloped pelvis. He also had an extra, rudimentary set of genitals or, as the showmen who promoted him proclaimed, "two complete sets of male organs." Lentini (n.d.) was philosophical about his condition:

> One time I was taken to an institution where I saw a number of blind children and children who were badly crippled and otherwise mistreated by fate, and then and there, I realized that my lot wasn't so bad after all. Even though a child, I could appreciate the fact that I was possessed of all my faculties and senses. I could hear, talk, understand and appreciate and enjoy the beauties of life. I could read and they couldn't. I could talk to my friends, but some of them couldn't because they were dumb. I could hear and enjoy beautiful music, while some of them couldn't because they were deaf. I have my men-

tal faculties and began to look forward to my education, and some of them couldn't because they were idiots. The visit to that institution, unpleasant though it was because of the misery that I saw, was the best thing that could have happened to me. From that time to this I have never complained. I think life is beautiful and I enjoy living it.

As a child, Lentini and his family immigrated to America, and he traveled for years with Buffalo Bill's Wild West Show, the Walter Main Circus, Ringling Brothers and Barnum & Bailey Circus, and other shows (Parker 1994, 67; Drimmer 1991, 35). During the 1930s, while he was with Craft Big Shows, he was featured on a banner that showed him kicking a football. It read, "Only 3 Legged Football Player in the World!—Alive" (Johnson et al. 1996, 39, 154). Although "Football Player" was an exaggeration, his pictured feat was not: According to Jeanie Tomaini (the "World's Only Living Half Girl," described later in this chapter), "he could kick a football the whole length of the show with that leg" (quoted in Taylor and Kotcher 2002, 1).

Asked how he purchased the extra shoe he needed, Lentini (n.d.) said, "I buy two pairs and give the extra left shoe to a one-legged friend of mine who had the misfortune to lose his right leg." An early pitch card, showing him nude from the rear, claimed that he was "The only man in the world with 3 legs, 4 feet, 16 toes, 2 bodies from the waist down." (The extra partial foot and toe grew from the side of the extra leg.) Lentini married and fathered four normal children.

In 1963 Lentini left the Wanous Family Show, ambitiously creating his own ten-in-one sideshow that he operated at the Nebraska State Fair. Ward Hall (1991, 21), who had a small competing show (the Hall & Leonard Pigmy Village), sought to coexist with Lentini on the midway: "Knowing he was vain in regards to his drawing power as an attraction, after telling him of my conflicting acts, I said 'Of course we know the people don't come to your show because of a fire eater or snake charmer. They all want to see you, for there is only one Lentini!' He certainly agreed with that statement and as we worked in competition, we remained friends. After completing his contractual obligations, he closed his show and returned to the Wanous Show, where he remained until fatal illness struck him down while traveling between towns."

Armless and Legless Wonders

People without arms or legs—or lacking both—have frequently shown a remarkable ability to triumph over their handicap. For example, a legless youth born about 1699 near Vienna was seen and admired by many European royals. A man who saw him at age fourteen reported: "He stands and walks and climbs and leaps from the ground upon a table and sits on a corner of it. . . . He jumps, dances and shows artfull tricks than any other person can do with thighs and legs." Moreover, he was able to speak "five different languages" (Thompson 1968, 58).

Probably the most celebrated legless wonder was Eli Bowen (b. 1844), whose career began at age thirteen and lasted more than half a century (figure 5.7). His pitch cards evolved from showing the image of a young bachelor to that of a family man with a wife and four children. An 1880 pitch book mixed pride with wit to pronounce: "Above these and all others of this class of curiosity, Mr. Bowen, the subject of this narrative, rises and towers conspicuously in this—that he has no lower limbs at all—in fact not a leg to stand on, and yet is able to move off very swiftly and gracefully to the astonishment of all who witness his dexterous movements—in fact I do not believe any country of any age has ever produced anything like unto him." Though legless, Bowen did have feet. He used his extensively developed arms to perform impressive acrobatics for his audiences. Aided by wooden blocks gripped in his hands, he could raise his hips sufficiently to permit him to swing his torso between his arms. He also tumbled, did stunts on a pole, and performed other feats (Bogdan 1990, 212–15).

Several legless wonders were advertised as "half" people (see figure 5.8). One notable example was Johnny Eck, "The Only Living Half Boy, Nature's Greatest Mistake." Like Bowen, he performed acrobatics and even trapeze feats and was featured in Browning's film *Freaks*.

Another was Jeanie Tomaini, the "World's Only Living Half Girl." Born Bernice Swift, she was exhibited at a local fair at age three and began touring with a carnival called Dodson's World Fair Show when she was eleven. She later appeared with other circus and carnival sideshows. She performed cartwheels, did handstands, and climbed a ladder upside down. Jeanie married giant Al Tomaini (see figure 2.19), whose advertised height was eight feet four

FIGURE 5.7. Eli Bowen, the celebrated legless wonder, is shown in a posed publicity photograph at age thirty-six. (Author's collection)

and a half inches. He had a stage beside hers when she eventually returned to Dodson's show. They honeymooned at Niagara Falls, then resumed show life, performing at fairs, dime museums, boardwalks, and nightclubs and even running their own sideshows, including a ten-in-one. They retired in 1949 to run the Giant's Tourist Camp at Gibsonton, Florida (figure 5.9). After twenty-six years of marriage, Al died at age fifty; Jeanie lived for another thirty years, dying August 10, 1999 (Bogdan 1990, 210–12, 215–16; Taylor and Kotcher 2002, 26–44).

In contrast to the legless wonders were armless ones. For example, John Valerius, born in 1667 in Germany, lacked arms yet, according to a contemporary, showed "such tricks with his feet that nobody can do with both arms, hands and feet." He cut his own quill pens with a penknife and wrote in five languages. He could thread a needle and sew "very prettily." He was a marksman with firearms and performed acrobatics, including jumping and vaulting. He went to London in 1698 and exhibited for several years (Thompson 1968, 58–59).

Mlle. GABRIEL
The living half woman

FIGURE 5.8. Mademoiselle Gabriel—the "living half woman," as she is styled on her pitch card—appeared for a time at the Dreamland Circus sideshow at Coney Island. (Author's collection)

The first armless wonder to be publicly exhibited in the United States was probably Sanders K. G. Nellis. He debuted at age thirteen in 1830 and progressed from private showrooms to the Peale Museum in New York, later becoming a regular attraction at Barnum's American Museum. Billed as the "Wonder of the World," he could shoot a bow and arrow, play several musical instruments, and cut silhouettes with scissors.

Carl Unthan (1848–1929) was another celebrated armless wonder who became known as the "Armless Fiddler." He performed in circuses, fairs, and vaudeville venues, and he also lectured amputees in hospitals of his native Germany during World War I. In addition to playing the violin, he demonstrated such everyday activities as slipping on his coat, lighting a cigar, and—popping the cork—filling glasses with wine. He taught himself to type

FIGURE 5.9. Half-woman Jeanie Tomaini and her husband, giant Al Tomaini, ran the Giant's Tourist Camp at Gibsonton, Florida—shown here on the restaurant's menu. (Author's collection)

using—instead of two fingers—two pencils, eraser-ends down, grasped with his feet (Drimmer 1991, 73–86; Bogdan 1990, 222–23).

Among the female armless wonders was Mrs. Ann E. Leak Thompson. Her 1871 pitch book sought public support for herself and her elderly parents, hoping to "draw forth the sympathy and consideration of every heart that witnesses her operations, or to whom this little volume may come." She superstitiously attributed her armlessness to an impression her mother had had concerning her drinking, quarreling father during her pregnancy: "Her mother learned of his being in a scrap down in the town, and when she saw him coming home, he had his overcoat thrown over his shoulders without his arms in the sleeves." Mrs. Thompson did crocheting and embroidered scriptural phrases, such as "Holiness to the Lord" (Zechariah 14:20) and, with irony, "A Lamp unto My Feet" (Psalms 119:105). An 1884 photograph by Charles Eisenmann, showing her with her husband and little boy, displays samples of her handiwork (Bogdan 1990, 218–19).

Another female armless wonder was Mademoiselle Tunison of Long Island. Instead of her feet, she used her mouth to produce linen doilies and crayon drawings in the early twentieth century. Her advertisement (figure 5.10) does not say that she exhibited herself (instead giving her "Permanent Address" for mail orders) but notes, "Palmistry a Specialty."

The best-known armless wonder of the sideshows was Charles Tripp of Woodstock, Canada. In 1872 Tripp, then seventeen, is said to have traveled to New York looking for Barnum, who hired him at once. Tripp exhibited for more than half a century, appearing in many circus sideshows. For his last seventeen years he toured with carnivals so that he could be with his wife, whom he married late in life. Mrs. Tripp sold tickets for rides, and Tripp exhibited his penmanship, artwork, carpentry, and paper cuttings. He poured and drank tea for many of his pitch cards, which, over his long career, went from *cartes de visite* to cabinet photographs to photo postcards (Bogdan 1990, 219–22). A snapshot shows the clever Tripp, the "Armless Wonder," and his witty friend Eli Bowen, the "Legless Wonder" (discussed earlier), riding a bicycle built for two. They also engaged in humorous exchanges: Tripp liked to caution, "Bowen, watch your step!" And Bowen would exclaim, "Keep your hands off me!" (Drimmer 1991, 87–90).

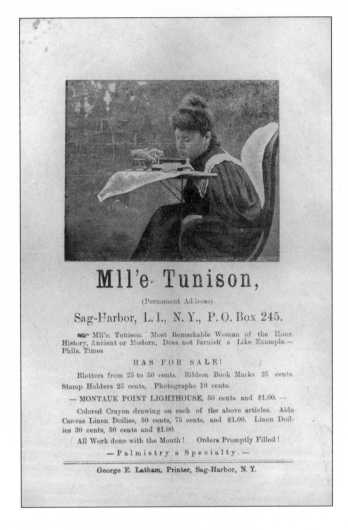

Figure 5.10. Armless wonder Mademoiselle Tunison produced artworks using her mouth. She also read palms. (Author's collection)

More amazing than either the armless or legless wonders were those who were both. The most famous of these was Matthew Buchinger (b. 1674), who had only flipperlike feet attached directly to his torso and upper-arm stumps. Known as the "Little Man of Nuremberg," he was an accomplished calligrapher, musician (on dulcimer, trumpet, and bagpipes), and magician (dexter-

FIGURE 5.11. Prince Randian, the "Caterpillar Man," was an armless, legless wonder who rolled and lit a cigarette with his lips as part of his act. (Author's collection)

ously performing the cups-and-balls feat). He dressed in the fashion of the day with coat, vest, and powdered wig. Buchinger married at least twice and fathered fourteen children. An often-quoted story about him comes from a contemporary:

> He got a great deal of mony but his last wife was a very perverse woman who would spend all his mony very prodigally and luxuriously in eating, drinking, and clothes and would not permit him to eat nor drink as she did and did Beat him Cruelly, which he had born patiently but one day, she having beat him before company, that so provoked him, that he flew at her with such force that he threw her down and getting upon her belly and Brest and did so beat her with his stumps that he almost killed her, threatening to beat her in the same manner

139

if she ever did so any more—and she became after a very dutiful and loving wife. (Fiedler 1993, 52–53; Jay 1987, 44–57)

A more recent armless and legless wonder was billed as the Caterpillar Man or the Snake Man. He dressed in a sacklike woolen garment and wriggled on the platform like a serpent (figure 5.11). He was also billed in royal fashion as Prince Randian, the Human Living Torso, presented with his wife, Princess Sarah, and their four children. He demonstrated how he shaved himself and rolled and lit a cigarette using only his lips (Bogdan 1990, 114–15). Randian was brought from British Guiana to the United States by P. T. Barnum in 1889. He first appeared in Hubert's Museum, then traveled with Barnum's Greatest Show on Earth. He performed for forty-five years (Drimmer 1991, 102–3).

6 OTHER HUMAN ODDITIES

 AMONG THE MANY TYPES OF human oddities are those who do not readily fit into traditional categories.

"Animal" People

A diverse group of human oddities consists of those whose deformities can be likened to some animal—hence "alligator" boys and girls, "frog" people, and others, such as the Lobster Boy and Sealo.

"Alligator" people (unless they are gaffed—see chapter 8) suffer from *ichthyosis*, or "fishskin disease," which is characterized by profoundly dry, scaly skin (figure 6.1). There are several different types of ichthyosis, many of which are hereditary. One type does not manifest until sometime between one and four years of age; another type is sex-linked, being present only in males (transmitted by females through a recessive gene), and is apparent in early infancy. Ichthyosis is incurable, but symptoms may be relieved by skin-softening ointments (Gould and Pyle 1896; *Taber's* 2001).

Among the early oddities with this condition was a "fish-boy" or "merman" born in 1684 in Italy and exhibited in London at the age of ten. Named Bernardin, he was "quite covered with the scales of fishes." Another, shown in London in 1820, was described as "a new species of Man," covered with scales except for his face, palms, and soles.

In 1879 two youths from my own home county in eastern Kentucky made news with their ichthyosis. One newspaper represented James and Henry Elam, aged eight and twelve respectively, as "The Alligator Children of Morgan County," while another characterized them as "Mistakes of Nature, The Boyfishes," noting their affinity for water (Nickell 1991a). Actually, the water provided relief from their condition. Those suffering from extreme ichthyosis cannot perspire, so in hot weather they may seek relief by immersing them-

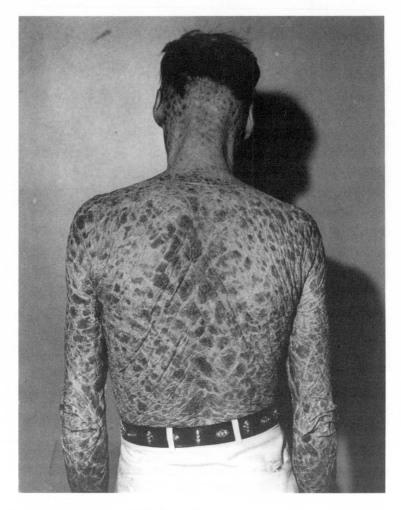

FIGURE 6.1. "Alligator" people suffer from the disease ichthyosis, characterized by profoundly scaly skin. (Author's collection)

selves in cool water (Meah 1996). According to a newspaper account: "They may have to keep their bodies greased when not in the water. When the body becomes dry the skin cracks open." The boys' heads were covered with scales, which also prevented the growth of hair. Lapsing into superstition about their reptilian appearance, the account continues: "The boys handle snakes with impunity and delight, frequently quarreling over a single reptile, but satisfied when each has one, and snakes have no antipathy to them, but follow them like a dog does his master" (quoted in Nickell 1991a). According to a later news-paper article, "The alligator children of Morgan County are to be exhibited in Central Kentucky for the benefit of their parents," who were probably poor. Attempts to learn more about the boys—including a query to Circus World Museum in Baraboo, Wisconsin—were futile.

There were many other alligator children, and banner artists have had great fun with such attractions. For example, under the heading "Alligator Boy," one such artwork features in typical fashion a hybrid creature with the upper half human and the lower half reptilian; it is shown attracting the inter-est of real alligators. Less frequent were banner depictions closer to the exhib-it's real appearance, such as "Alligator Girl" by legendary banner painter Snap Wyatt. Her scantily clad body merely exhibits a boldly checked appearance (Johnson et al. 1996, 62, 121, 122). Banner artist Johnny Meah (1996, 120) says of the more realistic depictions: "I've pictorialized numerous alligator skinned people. In rendering them one must constantly bear in mind that the banner will be viewed from many feet away, therefore very bold lines and exaggerated light and dark contrast must be used in depicting the unusual skin. As is the case with most banner art, you constantly repress the urge to use softer more subtle effects as they are lost when viewed from a distance."

The banner described earlier, featuring the hybrid human-alligator crea-ture, may have been used to advertise Emmitt Bejano. Born in Punta Gorda, Florida, he was adopted by "the dean of the sideshow men of the nineteen twenties and thirties, Johnny Bejano" (Hall 1991, 45). Emmitt was exhibited in Texas and sold such promotional items as alligator and snakeskin pocket-books. He later worked for showman Karl Lauther, who had a dime museum show and later a ten-in-one midway sideshow. Bejano was advertised as the "Alligator Boy" and "Alligator Man." In 1938 Emmitt eloped with Lauther's adopted daughter, who performed as Percilla the Monkey Girl (discussed later in this chapter). They exhibited with the Ringling Brothers circus sideshow and "some of the most prominent carnival sideshows of this century" (Taylor and Kotcher 2002, 186–203).

A 1950s alligator boy, William Parnell, starred with Claude Bentley's Freak Circus, a sideshow traveling with the James E. Strates Shows. Born in 1925 in North Carolina, Parnell "suffered with an obscure skin disease that left him covered with greenish white patches, a condition that most people agreed looked distinctly reptilian." Reportedly, the local school administrators found him so repellent that they would not admit him, so at the age of nine he ran away with a carnival. "I don't mind when they look at me; that's what I get paid for," he was quoted as saying in a 1952 magazine. "But then they ask me, is it a fake? Really, I wish it was a fake" (Nelson 1999, 121–22).

Among the famous ladies of the genre was Mona Osanbaugh, the "Alligator Skin Girl," who once posed with one-and-a-half Betty Lou Williams (mentioned in chapter 5). Similarly billed were Christine Doto, shown in a 1968 photo wearing only a top and miniskirt to show off her skin condition (and trim body), and Mildred Durks, wife of Bill Durks, who was known variously as the "Man with Three Eyes" and the "Two-Faced Man" (discussed later) (Hall 1991, 53–56; Taylor and Kotcher 2002, 133, 135–36).

A variant of the alligator person is the performer whose skin is roughly textured or loose and baggy (Taylor and Kotcher 2002, 243). Such was Charlotte "Suzy" Vogel from Germany, where she was a medical curiosity at the University of Freiburg in the early 1920s. The artwork on an early poster depicts her on a platform with a small elephant behind her. The poster is headed "Suzy / Nature's Enigma" and "A Puzzle to the entire scientific world" (Meah 1996, 120). She was also known as "Suzy the Elephant Skin Girl." She was recruited by Ward Hall as an attraction for Peter Hennen's sideshow in 1960, and she remained with Hennen for several years. Says Hall (1991, 21): "On one occasion, he had signs advertising her as an 'Outer Space Monster.' She was hurt by this and she protested, 'I am not a monster.' The signs were removed." After Hennen ended his sideshow, Charlotte Vogel retired to her native Germany. Hall recalls her as having "a very sweet disposition." Like many others with her condition, she showed the truth of the old adage (penned by John Davies in 1606), "Beauty's but skin deep."

A different skin disorder is the explanation for certain "leopard" people (figure 6.2). *Vitiligo,* a condition characterized by a lack of skin pigment in patchy areas, affects people of all races but is more noticeable in those with dark complexions (*Taber's* 2001). P. T. Barnum exhibited a "leopard child" at his American Museum; she was an African American girl with large white splotches on her face, chest, arms, and legs (Kunhardt et al. 1995, 188).

FIGURE 6.2. A "leopard" child, with splotchy skin, is shown in an 1896 color lithograph. (Author's collection)

Frenchwoman Irma Loustau, a Caucasian "Leopard-Spotted Woman" (probably of the latter nineteenth century) with prominent dark patches, was billed as "Femme Panthére" (Panther Woman) at age twenty-four (Taylor and Kotcher 2002, 176). During the mid to late 1920s, the Ringling Brothers and Barnum & Bailey Congress of Freaks show exhibited various leopard girls, mostly African American, as shown in the circus photographs of Edward J. Kelty (Barth and Siegel 2002, 104–6).

Another type of fancified human-animal hybrid is the amphibianesque oddity exemplified by Samuel D. Parks (1874–1923), "Hopp the Frog Boy." His cognomen may have been inspired by Edgar Allan Poe's story "Hop-Frog." (The king of a fabled land kept a jester, a clumsy-gaited dwarf whom he cruelly mocked and abused. However, on the pretext of contriving a masquerade, Hop-Frog manages to lure the king and his councilors into adopting the guise of apes, with the use of tar and flax. Then he hangs them, chained, from a great chandelier and burns them to "a fetid, blackened, hideous and indistinguishable mass.")

Parks was featured on his banner as a human-headed frog. He first appeared before medical students at the 1893 Chicago world's fair and later joined the Barnum & Bailey Circus for a European tour. Hopp the Frog Boy subsequently "exhibited all over the United States and Europe in the leading circuses and largest carnival companies," according to a tribute in *Billboard*. It was written by his second wife, who described herself as "a Connecticut midget." She stated: "Hopp was the only attraction of his kind in the World. His face, hands, and feet were human but the rest of his body was deformed similar to that of a frog. When he got down on all fours he looked exactly like a huge bullfrog" (quoted in Drimmer 1991, 306).

As mentioned earlier in the discussion of banners (see chapter 3), another such sideshow oddity was Major John the Frog Boy, who was depicted by banner painter Fred G. Johnson in 1940 (see figure 3.4). He was portrayed in the usual hybrid fashion, as was Otis Jordan, an African American who had (according to one of his many admirers) the body of a four-year-old but a normal head with "a noble, scholarly face" (Meah 1998, 56; Johnson et al. 1996, 16). Jordan performed as "Otis the Frog Boy," beginning in 1963. Part of his routine was to roll, light, and smoke a cigarette using only his lips. When his act was shut down in 1984 after a woman complained about the exhibition of disabled people, Jordan moved to Coney Island, where he continued with the more politically correct billing the "Human Cigarette Factory" (Bogdan 1990, 1, 279–81; Taylor 1998, 55–61).

Among others of the genre was Flip the Frog Boy, who was with the Hagenbeck-Wallace Circus Sideshow in the 1930s. His upper body was normal, but he had diminished legs and tiny feet that required him "to hop like a frog" (Mannix 1999, 12). Another was Carl Norwood, an African American dwarf with tiny legs who was featured as "Carl the Frog Boy" and the "World's Smallest Man" in a single-O launched by Hall & Christ in 1973 (Hall 1981, 71, 100; 1991, 51).

Any one of a number of deformities might qualify one as a frog boy (figure 6.3). In 1969, when I worked at the Canadian National Exhibition, I visited the

FIGURE 6.3. A hunchback midget, like this man
from around 1890, might be styled as a "frog boy."
(Author's collection)

ten-in-one that included El Hoppo the Living Frog Boy. Although the banner
depicted him in the usual fashion—a youth with a frog's hindquarters—in actuality, "Hoppy" was a gray-bearded man in a wheelchair; he had spindly limbs
and a distended stomach. To make him look more like his banner image, he
was stripped to the waist and dressed in green tights (Nickell 1999). Sometime
later, in downtown Toronto, I saw a man who looked remarkably like "Hoppy"
selling the *Telegram* newspapers from his wheelchair. Was he really the frog
boy? Some three decades later, while researching this book, I queried showman
Doug Higley. He wrote to say that since "El Hoppo" was "not a well known freak
performer, I would guess that he was just some poor unfortunate . . . picked off
the street and created on the spot for that one date" (Higley 2000).

Most frog people are males, but there was at least one "frog girl show." It ran afoul of a Florida statute prohibiting the exhibition of anyone with a deformity or disfigurement for profit, but the law was successfully challenged by Ward Hall, "Little Pete" Terhurne, and Sealo (Taylor and Kotcher 2002, 9–11).

"Sealo the Seal Boy" was Stanley Berent, whose condition is called *phocomelia;* it is a congenital malformation in which the limbs are poorly developed or entirely absent, so that the hands and feet are attached to the trunk (*Taber's* 2001). When exhibited, individuals with this condition are typically described as "seal" or "penguin" people. A friend of Sealo's (Melvin Burkhart, who is discussed in chapter 7) said, "He had one hell of an act. He'd take a piece of clay and make the damnedest things right before your eyes. He'd take that ball of clay and boom, boom, boom you'd have a horsey. Switch it around and have a goat and a pig. He was just amazing" (Taylor and Kotcher 2002, 9, 166, 247–48).

Another oddity of this type was Dickie the Penguin Boy, whose banner by Fred G. Johnson (circa 1960s) shows him with normal arms but short, fused legs so that, as the banner claims, he "Looks and Walks Like a Penguin" (Johnson et al. 1996, 68). An attraction billed as "Mignon the Penguin Girl" was Ruth Davis, who exhibited in the 1930s and 1940s along with her husband, Earl, another "Hoppy the Frog Boy" (Hall 1991, 44).

A very distinctive oddity is that of so-called lobster people, like the one featured on a "Strange Girls" banner painted by Snap Wyatt. The otherwise pretty girl is depicted with red claws and tail like her crustacean namesake. The actual deformity is *ectrosyndactyly,* a congenital condition in which some digits of the hands and feet are missing and the others are fused, producing two opposed "claws" like those of a lobster (*Taber's* 2001; Taggart 1996).

The most famous—and infamous—"lobster" family consists of the ancestors and descendants of Grady Stiles Sr., the "Lobster Man" of American sideshows. The deformity had been known in his family since the 1840s. Nearly a century later, in 1937, Stiles became the father of a boy named Grady Stiles Jr., who at the age of seven began to be exhibited as the "Lobster Boy" (figure 6.4). In time he married a fellow carny, Mary Teresa, who ran a shooting gallery. Their first child, Donna, was normal, but the next, Cathy, began the sixth generation of Stileses with the lobster-claw deformity. The family settled in "Showtown USA," aka Gibtown (Gibsonton, Florida).

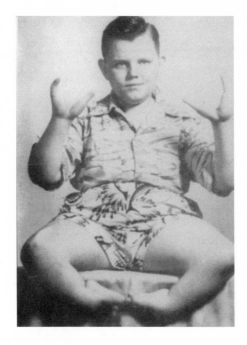

FIGURE 6.4. Grady Stiles Jr., the "Lobster Boy," was an abusive man whose life ended with his murder. (Author's collection)

Grady Jr. was a heavy-drinking, abusive man whose wife eventually left him to marry the "Smallest Man in the World," a midget named Harry Glenn Newman. Stiles retained the children, remarried, and fathered another lobster child, Grady Stiles III. When teenaged Donna became pregnant and told her father that she wanted to marry her lover, Stiles asked to meet the young man. Instead of approving the match, the Lobster Boy pulled out a pistol and shot him to death. Astonishingly, Stiles received probation and, equally astonishingly, after divorcing his second wife, persuaded Mary Teresa to come back to him. She brought her son, Harry Glenn Newman Jr. (who, unlike his father, was not a midget).

Grady resumed show life, framing his own sideshow. It starred him, of course, as the Lobster Boy, and had Grady III and Cathy as backups. It also featured his wife's son Harry as a human blockhead, along with "enough other acts to make it a respectable ten-in-one" (Taggart 1996, 172). The show prospered, but Stiles kept morale low by continuing his abusive behavior. He sometimes appeared drunk in the sideshow and angrily snapped at the spectators with his "claws" (Taggart 1996, 172). Grady continued to beat up Mary

Teresa and once struck his pregnant daughter, "Lobster Girl" Cathy. (An emergency cesarean yielded a daughter, the first of the seventh-generation "lobster" children.)

Finally, after Grady threatened Mary Teresa and her family with a knife, she had her son, Harry, arrange a contract killing of Grady. Subsequently, Mary Teresa was convicted of manslaughter; her son received a life sentence for first-degree murder; and the killer, Christopher Wyant, received a twenty-seven-year sentence for second-degree murder (Taggart 1996). Thus ended one of the darkest chapters in the history of the sideshow.

In addition to this veritable menagerie of human oddities who were imaginatively interpreted in animal terms, there were the Biped Armadillo, the Snake Boy, Koo-Koo the Bird Girl, and Emmitt Blackwelder, the "Turtle Man," who had "only short stubs of arms and legs" (Hall 1991, 23). Others are discussed more fully later, including Percilla the Monkey Girl, the Mule-Faced Woman, and the Elephant Man.

Hirsute Women—and Men

Bearded ladies have long been popular sideshow attractions. Their excessive facial and body hair is due to a condition called *hirsutism*, which is usually caused by overproduction of androgen (*Taber's* 2001).

As mentioned in chapter 1, P. T. Barnum once had the effrontery to have his bearded lady accused of being a man. The hirsute woman, Madame Josephine Clofullia of Geneva, Switzerland, dressed in feminine fashion and wore about her neck a broach with a cameo portrait of her equally bearded husband. She had previously appeared in London, but not before a physician had examined her, declaring her beard genuine and "her breasts . . . large and fair, and strictly characteristic of the female." She gave birth in 1851 to a normal daughter, but the child died before her first birthday. In March 1853 Barnum signed her for his American Museum. During her inaugural appearance, a spectator—secretly hired by the showman—accused Madame Clofullia of being a fake, a male in female dress. He brought a charge of imposture against Barnum, who, feigning annoyance, arranged a medical examination. His three doctors joined Josephine's husband and father and a city physician in certifying her as a genuinely bearded woman. Newspaper stories of the failed suit sent huge crowds to Barnum's museum (Bogdan 1990, 226–28; Harris 1973, 67; Kunhardt et al. 1995, 112).

Annie Jones (1865–1902) was still a baby when Barnum first exhibited her in 1866. Born with long hair and a down-covered face, Annie became the "infant Esau" (after the biblical Isaac's hirsute son). Later she was the "Child Esau" or the "Bearded Girl." She was such a salable commodity that, when an emergency back home in Virginia caused her mother to leave her in questionable hands, a phrenologist made off with the child and tried to exhibit her at a fair. Mrs. Jones had to go to court to reclaim her daughter, which she did when the wise judge let Annie out of an anteroom and she ran not to the phrenologist but to her mother.

A pitch pamphlet, sold at Barnum's museum when Annie was about five, truthfully described her "marvelous endowment of fine silken beard, whiskers, and mustache," while characterizing her otherwise as "altogether as other little girls of her age." When Barnum's Greatest Show on Earth began touring, Annie went with it. Billed as the "Bearded Lady" or the "Esau Lady," she appeared in the circus sideshow during the regular season and then exhibited in dime museums during the winter months—until spring came and she repeated the cycle.

When Annie was sixteen, she secretly married a sideshow talker named Richard Elliott. About 1888 she was photographed by Charles Eisenmann. Brilliantly, he posed her admiring her beard in a mirror; thus, with her back to the camera, he also captured her long tresses, which reached below her knees (Drimmer 1991, 124; Bogdan 1990, 225). After fifteen years of what her mother called a "bad match," she divorced Elliott and wed the show's wardrobe man, William Donovan. They took advantage of her notoriety and successfully toured Europe, at times appearing before royalty. When her husband died several years later, she rejoined the Barnum & Bailey Circus while it was in Europe. Reportedly, "Annie's reunion with the circus was a joyful one. She had many old friends there. Her warmth and eagerness to help were as proverbial in the circus as her skill with her needle. Whenever she came down from her platform after a show she had a steady stream of callers, including many who wanted to chat with her and circus hands who knew they could rely on her to sew on a button or put a patch in a pair of trousers. And she enjoyed hearing herself called by her familiar name, Jonesy, once more." In time, however, Jonesy fell ill with consumption and died at the age of thirty-seven (Drimmer 1991, 120–26).

Although born in the same year as Annie Jones, Clementine Delait of Thaon-les-Vosges in Lorraine was a young woman before she became France's most famous bearded lady. Until then, she had shaved; however, seeing an unimpressive bearded lady at a fair sideshow, she wagered that she could grow a fuller beard. Bets were met with counterbets at her husband's Café Delait. Clementine soon won the contest, and when people began to come from afar to see her, Monsieur Delait renamed their business Café de la femme á barbe (Café of the Bearded Lady). After his death in 1926, Clementine began to exhibit herself, becoming a celebrity on Parisian and London stages. At her death in 1939, as she had requested, her tombstone identified her as "The Bearded Lady of Thaon." Three decades later, her hometown dedicated a museum to Clementine Delait, its most celebrated daughter (Drimmer 1991, 127–31).

Perhaps the longest-appearing bearded lady was Jane Barnell, who was born in 1871 in Wilmington, North Carolina. The daughter of a Russian Jew who repaired wagons and a mother of Irish and Native American heritage, she was born with a down-covered face. Her mother reportedly thought that the child was cursed, and when her husband was away on business, she gave the little girl to the Great Orient Family Circus, a small show with six ox-drawn wagons. Allegedly she toured Europe, where an illness landed her in an orphanage at about age five. "In one way or another," says Drimmer (1991, 135), her father located her and returned her to North Carolina. In 1892, at the age of twenty-one, she joined the John Robinson Circus. Over the years, she appeared in numerous circuses, including Forepaugh-Sells Brothers, Hagenbeck-Wallace, Royal American Shows, and Ringling Brothers and Barnum & Bailey. She was "Princess Olga," then "Madame Olga," and finally "Lady Olga." She married four times and in 1932 appeared in Tod Browning's movie *Freaks*. At that time, she provided the public with some beard-grooming tips, declaring, "Every woman who is lucky enough to have a beard should learn how to take care of it." Her secrets included a weekly milk bath and avoiding too-hot curling irons, which could cause brittleness. A showman once proposed that she dye her hair

FIGURE 6.5. Bearded lady Grace Gilbert appeared as the "Wooly Child" and the "Female Esau" in such circuses as Barnum & Bailey. (Author's collection)

blue so she could be billed as "Olga, the Lady Bluebeard." She angrily rejected the idea but watched her beard turn naturally gray over the years (Drimmer 1991, 132–38).

Among other celebrated bearded ladies was Madame Jane Devere of Kentucky, who was born in 1842 and was still showing her fourteen-inch beard in 1908 with the Yankee Robinson Show. Another was a Mrs. Meyers, who was with Barnum in the 1880s. One of her contemporaries, who toured dime museums from the late 1870s to the early 1880s, offered a pitch booklet, "Brief History of a Celebrated Lady, Namely, Madam Squires, the Bearded Lady" (Bogdan 1990, 227–29; Kunhardt et al. 1995, 260).

Women with beards typically had excessive body hair as well; however, it was usually concealed by the Victorian attire used to emphasize the bearded lady's femininity. Michigan-born Grace Gilbert (1880–1925) was covered at birth with reddish hair (figure 6.5). Circuses such as Barnum & Bailey billed her as the "Wooly Child" and (like Annie Jones) the "Female Esau." According to Drimmer (1991, 138): "In the winter season, when the circus closed down, she would return to her father's farm. She was heavily built, and according to legend she was able to perform a man's work on the farm. Old circus buffs also say that when the roustabouts were erecting the sideshow tent she would take up a sledge and give them a helping hand. Yet, like other bearded ladies, she was famed for her ladylike refinement and her skill with needlework and spent much of her spare time making lace."

More recently there was Percilla the Monkey Girl (figure 6.6)—mentioned earlier as the wife of "Alligator Man" Emmitt Bejano. Born in San Juan, Puerto Rico, and adopted by showman Karl Lauther, the child with the dense, black hair was billed as the "Little Hairy Girl" and then the "Monkey Girl." She performed in Lauther's dime museum and later his midway ten-in-one with a chimp named Josephine. She wore a veil when working the bally. After she and Emmitt eloped in 1938, when Percilla was about twenty, they exhibited in leading carnival and circus sideshows, including Ringling Brothers. Their one child died in infancy, and they adopted a boy, Tony.

For a single-O show they owned featuring Percilla, one of her banners showed her, in bearded-lady fashion, combing her hair in a vanity mirror; another portrayed her in a jungle scene encountering a gorilla; a pair of others each promised "$1,000 Reward if not Real." Away from the sideshow, in public, Percilla pretended to be a Hindu, keeping her face covered. The Bejanos were often billed as the "World's Strangest Married Couple." Showman Ward Hall (1991, 45–46) says that theirs "has been the love story of the century." They celebrated their fiftieth wedding anniversary at the International Independent Showmen's Association headquarters in Gibsonton, Florida, where the Bejanos lived. In retirement, Percilla shaved every couple of days, and she and Emmitt loved to dance together. After he died in 1995, she grieved until her own death, in her sleep, on February 5, 2001 (Taylor and Kotcher 2002, 186–203; *Sideshow* 2000).

FIGURE 6.6. Percilla the Monkey Girl (holding dog) and the Alligator Man were billed as the World's Strangest Couple. (Author's collection)

Other very hairy people were Tirko the Monkey Boy, depicted on a 1970s banner by Snap Wyatt (Johnson et al. 1996, 128), and the remarkable "Wolf Boys," Danny and Larry Gomez. The brothers—covered with black hair from head to toe, including their faces—once appeared in sideshows but now perform in a Mexican circus as trapeze and trampoline artists (*Sideshow* 2000).

Popular hirsute attractions of the nineteenth century were members of Barnum's Sacred Hairy Family of Burmah (figure 6.7), Jo-Jo the Dog-Faced Boy, and Lionel the Lion-Faced Man. Jo-Jo, who reportedly resembled a Skye terrier, with silky yellow hair entirely covering his face, appeared in European circus and fairground sideshows. Brought to the United States in 1884 by Barnum,

155

Figure 6.7. The Sacred Hairy Family of Burmah (one of whom is shown here) was a hirsute attraction introduced by P. T. Barnum. (From a nineteenth-century print)

he was actually sixteen-year-old Fedor Jeftichew, son of a Russian peasant. Barnum billed him as a captured feral child from the Russian forests—a tale invented for his pitch book (Parker 1994, 92; Drimmer 1991, 144–45).

"Lionel" was actually Polish-born Stephan Bibrowsky (1890–1931). His manelike hair, which totally covered his faced, inspired him to frighten his audiences by roaring and snarling at them the moment the curtain was raised (Parker 1994, 92). He appeared widely in Europe and also exhibited at Coney Island. The Lion-Faced Man was with Ringling Brothers and Barnum & Bailey Circus's Congress of Freaks in the mid-1920s (Drimmer 1991, 146–47; Barth 2002, 102, 105).

For sheer quantity of hair, however, we must turn from the odd to the

FIGURE 6.8. The Seven Sutherland Sisters had thirty-seven feet of hair. They appeared with Barnum & Bailey's Greatest Show on Earth and made a fortune selling bottled hair grower. (Author's collection)

normal—if the celebrated Seven Sutherland Sisters can be considered normal (figure 6.8). The daughters of onetime preacher Fletcher Sutherland, they flaunted their hair, which had a collective length of thirty-seven feet. When the young ladies performed their vocal and instrumental concerts—at such venues as the 1881 Atlanta Exposition and, by 1884, Barnum & Bailey's Greatest Show on Earth—Fletcher Sutherland shrewdly observed that the girls' long hair was a greater attraction than their musical ability. This led him to create the Seven Sutherland Sisters Hair Grower, a concoction of alcohol, vegetable oils, and water. The fifth daughter, Naomi, married Henry Bailey, a circus employee, who expanded the family sideline into a business that grossed $90,000 the first year. By the time Naomi died unexpectedly in 1893, business was so good that, to keep up appearances, the remaining sisters hired a replacement for her. The hair-growing business thrived until 1907, then declined slowly over the next decade as the bobbed-hair fad nearly put an end to sales. Overall, their hair grower and related products brought in more than $2.75 million over a

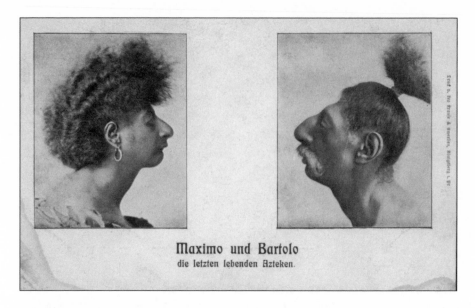

Maximo und Bartolo
die letzten lebenden Azteken.

FIGURE 6.9. The Aztec Children were actually microcephalics, shown here on a late-nineteenth-century postcard. (Author's collection)

thirty-eight-year period, but the septet squandered it on an opulent lifestyle that included personal maids for each, to comb their luxuriant tresses (Lewis 1991).

And More

Many oddities do not fit into a traditional category. Perhaps the best example is the one Barnum billed as "A most singular animal" and "A creature which . . . for want of any name has been designated 'The What Is It?' or 'Man-Monkey!'" Dressed in a furry suit, "It" was actually a black dwarf named William Henry Johnson who had *microcephaly* (an exceptionally small head and mental retardation) (see figure 6.9). Aged eighteen when first exhibited in 1860, he would have a career that spanned more than sixty years, "ultimately making him the most famous 'freak' in the world" (Kunhardt et al. 1995, 148–49). Unfortunately, he was also one of the few oddities who was "Laughed at, pelted with coins, called a 'cross between a nigger and a baboon,' and eventually renamed 'Zip' after the archetypal Southern black figure Zip Coon." Barnum's exhibition of Zip belied his own basic racial tolerance—indeed, he fought for the abolition of slavery—and seems to have had less to do with Johnson's appearance than with his retardation. Johnson appreciated the showman's basic decency and good nature; in turn, Barnum came to see him as a unique individual and gave him an increasing share of the profits.

Sometimes Zip was presented as a mere puzzle, other times as a type of "wild man" who had been "captured by a party of adventurers while they were in search of the Gorilla." Actually, he was American born, probably from Liberty Corners, New Jersey. He was with Barnum and his successors, Ringling Brothers and Barnum & Bailey Circus, until his death in 1926. In the Ringling sideshow he had the number-one platform due to his seniority; reportedly, he guarded the spot with a popgun (Kunhardt et al. 1995, 149; Fiedler 1993, 165–66; Bogdan 1990, 134–42).

Later microcephalics were Schlitzie and his sister Athelia, who were originally from Santa Fe, New Mexico. They were rejected by their parents and taken in as children by showman Pete Kortes and his wife, Marie. They later transferred custody of Schlitzie to George Surtees and his wife. Although always represented as female, insiders like Ward Hall (1991, 21–33) knew that Schlitzie was actually a male. He says: "I would no longer exhibit anyone mentally deficient, due to the criticism of those who would not understand the improvement in the quality of life such as a person would receive in a freak show environment, as opposed to confinement in an institution." He adds: "I have no doubt that Schlitzie enjoyed the trips to Hawaii, Venezuela, Puerto Rico, Mexico, Canada, etc. Attending luaus, holiday dinners and parties where the entire freak show would celebrate. This with the same delight and exuberance of a small child. Once having been rescued from the locked away existence of early childhood, Schlitzie had a comfortable, happy existence for the rest of her eighty plus years."

An interesting category of human oddity exploited by Barnum and his successors is the albino (figures 6.10 and 6.11)—a person suffering from *albinism*, the partial or total absence of pigment in the skin, hair, and eyes (*Taber's* 2001). Barnum brought to America a family of albinos from Holland—the Lucasies—in 1857. In one letter Barnum reported that they were acting "disagreeable" and stated, "I will put them in jail if they don't behave." Later he featured two cute little albino boys among his "living curiosities." They

(Left) FIGURE 6.10. Albinos were popular sideshow performers, like this one featured in a nineteenth-century publicity photograph by celebrated New York photographer Charles Eisenmann. (Author's collection) (Right) FIGURE 6.11. Another albino performer. (Photo by Charles Eisenmann; author's collection)

may have been the same pair—Amos and Charles Gorhen—shown in a later group portrait along with giantess Anna Swan, fat lady Hannah Battersby and her thin-man husband John, and many others. Another lineup, for an 1888 photo of Barnum & Bailey sideshow performers, included two albino girls, the Martin sisters, whose long, pale tresses gave them a striking appearance (Kunhardt et al. 1995, 113, 189, 198–99, 327).

The most famous of the show-business albinos was Unzie the Australian Aboriginal Albino, who normally would have had very dark skin. He had a gigantic white Afro and was sometimes billed as Unzie the Hirsute Wonder. His hair was so fine, however, that he could tuck the whole mass into a silk top hat. "I never tip my hat to the ladies," he would say from the platform. "If I should, they'd think a bombshell had exploded." Suiting action to words, he would remove the hat, whereupon "his incredible white hair would puff out

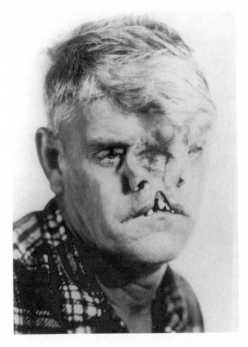

FIGURE 6.12. Bill Durks was billed as the "Two-Faced Man" or (as shown here) the "Three-Eyed Man"—his third eye being gaffed. (Author's collection)

and surround him like an enormous white cloud" (Drimmer 1991, 305–6; FitzGerald 1897).

Ward Hall was friends with another famous oddity, William "Bill" Durks, whom he lured from the Strates sideshow for one season (figure 6.12). Often billed as the "Two-Faced Man," he had an extreme cleft palate that separated the two halves of his face. Durks, says Hall plainly, "looked like he had been hit in the face with an axe." He was married to Mildred, the "Alligator Skin Lady," until her death in 1968; at one time they shared a banner, showing them at their marriage ceremony before a minister and headed "Mr. And Mrs. William Dirks [sic]."

A shy man, Durks was aware of the reaction his appearance could provoke and tried to avoid contact with the world outside the sideshow. For example, when traveling, he often asked his friend Melvin Burkhart (the "Anatomical Wonder"—see chapter 7), to get a sandwich for him from a restaurant. When he did have to go into a public place, he pulled his hat down and turned his collar up. Once in a New Jersey store, a woman approached him and said, "What's the matter with you? Don't you know somebody will think you're trying to rob the place?" When Durks turned to look at her, she gasped, "I'm sorry! I'm sorry!" and ran away (Taylor and Kotcher 2002, 128–41; Fiedler 1993, 210).

Since Durks played the same show route for years, he periodically changed his billing to keep his exhibition fresh. Besides the "Two-Faced Man," he was sometimes billed as the "Three-Eyed Man" (see figure 6.12), a partially gaffed presentation (discussed more fully in chapter 8).

Durks was not the only double-faced oddity. There was also Robert Milwin, who was at the Trenton State Fair in 1954, where he was billed as the "Man with Two Faces." The right side of his face was deformed, appearing almost like a second face in profile. Daniel P. Mannix (1999, 95) says of him, "He could have been a grift (a fake) but I don't think so since I've never seen anything like this before or since, and don't know of any reference to such a deformity." Melvin Burkhart mentioned Milwin while reminiscing about oddities who had passed away (Taylor and Kotcher 2002, 165).

Another oddity with a facial disfigurement was "Mule-Faced Woman" Grace McDaniels (figure 6.13), whose facial tumors gave her a grotesque appearance. One of her sideshow employers, Harry Lewiston, described her in his memoirs, *Freak Show Man* (Holtman 1968). The inside lecturer is speaking:

> "In a minute . . . I'm going to ask Grace to take her veil off so you can see for yourself what she looks like. You won't want to look for long. Instead, you will want to think of yourself, think how lucky you are that you are not like her. Whether you are handsome or homely, beautiful or plain, you can thank your lucky stars you are not Grace McDaniels, 'the Mule-Faced Woman.' . . ."
>
> As Grace lifted her veil, there rose from the audience a tremendous "Ohhhhhhhhhhhhh!" for she was truly a sight to bring on such reactions. It is impossible to describe her accurately. I can only try. Her flesh was like red, raw meat; her huge chin was twisted at such a distorted angle, she could hardly move her jaws. Her teeth were jagged and sharp, her nose was large and crooked. The objects which made her look most like a mule were her huge, mule-like lips. Her eyes stared grotesquely in their deep-set sockets. All in all, she was a sickening, horrible sight.

FIGURE 6.13. Grace McDaniels was as lovely on the inside as she was disfigured on the outside by facial tumors. She was billed as the "Mule-Faced Woman." (Author's collection)

Nevertheless, William Lindsay Gresham (1953, 105–6) spoke for those who knew her when he wrote: "She is one of the best-loved women in the carnival business, a homespun, motherly soul, generous to a fault. After five minutes' conversation with Grace you forget all about the strange contours of her face and are aware only of the warm, courageous heart of the woman herself." Grace married and had a son, who traveled as her manager until she died in 1958 (Drimmer 1991, 321).

One of the most famous human oddities of all time was "Elephant Man" Joseph Merrick (d. 1890). He was exhibited only briefly, reportedly "taken from town to town by itinerant showmen, who exploited him cruelly" (Drimmer 1991, 322). Merrick had a rare affliction that caused his skull and other bones to grow bizarrely, but his condition brought him to the attention of a distinguished medical man, Sir Frederick Treves, in 1884. For the remainder of his twenty-seven years, he was well cared for. However, Merrick's head grew so large and heavy that he was forced to sleep sitting up in bed, with pillows supporting his back and his head resting on his knees. He died in his sleep, his head apparently having fallen backward and dislocating his neck. Treves (1923) believed that he may have tried to sleep like normal people, but his head sank fatally into the soft pillow. "Thus it came about that his death was due to the desire that had dominated his life—the pathetic but hopeless desire to be 'like other people.'" To a greater or lesser degree, that has been the desire of many human oddities.

7 ANATOMICAL WONDERS

AN *ANATOMICAL WONDER* IS A sideshow performer whose freakishness is not readily apparent until it is demonstrated. In other words, he or she is less a *human oddity* (see chapters 4–6) than a *working act* (see chapter 9) but has elements of both.

Contortionists

In the early eighteenth century, a "famous Posture-Master of Europe" performed at various venues, accompanying magician Isaac Fawkes. In 1721, at the Bartholomew Fair in London (as shown by a famous aquatint discussed in chapter 1), a banner depicted him in various contortionistic positions and read, "Faux's [i.e., Fawkes's] Famous Posture Master." The French lad was one of two such prodigies exhibited by Fawkes. A 1723 advertisement for the other described the "Surprising Activity of Body" he performed, including making "a Pack Saddle of his Back," standing "upon his own Shoulders," making "a seat of his own head" (i.e., bending backward to place his head between his thighs), folding "his Body three or four double like a piece of Cloth," and other feats of contorting, tumbling, and dancing, including vaulting and posturing on a slack wire (Jay 2001, 54–57). The young posture master's stunts were described in some doggerel of the day:

> Then with his Legs extended six Foot wide,
> His feet plac'd on two Chairs on either side.
> With what agility we see him rise,
> And vault as if upon a Rope he flies.
> As on the fiddle he's beheld to play
> Such Tunes as ne'er was heard before that day,
> Which being done, to close and make an end.

How from the Scaffold he does
  bend:
And though he's nine Foot high
  beneath it sink,
To rise again by his own single
  Strength.

A nineteenth-century contortionist was billed as Knotella, his real name being unknown. He was remarkably flexible, and one pitch photo (signed "Faithfully Yours, Knotella") shows him bending backward so that the back of his head is touching his calf. He resembled a human hairpin. (Similar contortionists are shown in figures 7.1 and 7.2.)

Knotella and a contemporary *bender* (as they were known in the business) were featured in an 1897 article in Britain's *Strand* magazine. The latter was "a charming young lady" known professionally as Leonora. "Clad in snaky, scaly tights," wrote the author (FitzGerald 1897), "Leonora throws herself into postures." One photographer showed her lying face-down with her legs bent back so her toes touched her chin: "Leonora posing as a human boat," it was captioned.

Lucy Elvira Jones was an American contemporary of Leonora. At age thirteen she performed at the 1894 Texas State Fair.

FIGURE 7.1. A bender (contortionist) strikes some characteristic poses in these nineteenth-century wood engravings.

FIGURE 7.2. The Great Zella ties himself in knots in this publicity composite. (Author's collection)

She was double-jointed and, with her legs bent in the opposite direction at the knees, she "ran around on all fours like a dog" (Mannix 1999, 94).

Benders were among the Ringling Brothers and Barnum & Bailey Congress of Freaks in the 1920s, typically contorting like human pretzels for their group photograph by Edward J. Kelty (Barth 2002, 102, 104–5). In the 1930s, Lorraine Chevalier—of the celebrated Chevalier acrobatic family—amazed audiences by placing her chin on a table, then, grasping the sides, arching her body backward until she was "sitting on her own head" (Packard et al. 2001, 35).

A more recent contortionist was "Bobo the Rubber Man," Francis X. Duggan, who was with the Hall & Christ Show in the late 1960s. A "front bender," Bobo performed a trick in which, bent double, he went through a little barrel. "He had a reputation as a drinker," Ward Hall says, "but being aware of my puritanical feelings, quit his alcohol abuse entirely." Once, he went out on the midway to get a sandwich and did not return. The wind had toppled a sign, which struck him, breaking his hip and other bones. Although it was expected that the injuries would put an end to his career, in a few months he was back working his act. He later received an inheritance and retired to his hometown of Green Bay, Wisconsin (Hall 1991, 36–37).

India-Rubber People

Performers who can stretch their abnormally elastic skin are generally called India-rubber people (figure 7.3). Such people have a condition called *cutis hyperelastica*, or Ehlers-Danlos syndrome, after the Danish and French dermatologists who studied it. This is an inherited disorder in which the skin is characteristically soft and velvety as well as hyperelastic. (The skin is also prone to bruising, and the condition may be accompanied by hyperextensibility of the joints, pseudotumors, calcified cysts beneath the skin, and scarring due to skin atrophy [*Taber's* 2001].)

Many persons with cutis hyperelastica have progressed from amusing their friends to performing in sideshows as an India-rubber man or elastic-skin woman. One such performer was James Morris, who was born in 1859 in Copenhagen, New York. He was a barber who stretched his skin as a diversion for friends, later exhibiting at church socials and Elks' benefits in Rhode Island. Seeing the money that could be made, Morris went on to perform at the dime museum of J. E. Sackett in Providence. Then, beginning in 1882, he signed on with P. T. Barnum for a reported $150 a week.

Morris traveled with Barnum's show, appearing across the United States and later touring Europe. A lineup of Barnum & Bailey Circus sideshow performers in 1888 shows a young Morris—bespectacled and mustached—stretching his upper-chest skin as if it were a pullover. A later photo shows a man pulling down the skin of his left arm several inches (aided by an off-camera assistant). The performer "may be Barnum's own James Morris, wearing a beard to cover up new scars on his face," states one source, although the identification is far from certain. He has also been identified as Carl Haag or Felix Woerhle (Kunhardt et al. 1995, 290, 327).

FIGURE 7.3. An elastic-skin man stretches his chest skin in this 1896 color lithograph. (Author's collection)

In any event, James Morris was reportedly a person of some culture—an intelligent man who learned from his travels. However, he was rumored to have been addicted to drinking and gambling, thus squandering the considerable money he is thought to have earned. As a result, he continued to exhibit himself long after he might have retired. Concludes Drimmer (1991, 308): "There were many other elastic skin men, but Morris was considered one of the best. He was able to pull the skin of his chest up to the top of his head. He could pull out the skin of one leg and cover the other with it. He was able to pull his cheek skin out a good eight inches."

Among several females of the genre was Etta Lake, a heavy-lidded beauty who could stretch her skin some six inches. She flourished in the late nineteenth century. When she was photographed in 1889, she was with the King & Franklin Circus (Mannix 1999, 115).

Another elastic-skin woman was depicted on a circa 1960 banner painted by Snap Wyatt. Headed "Freaks," it shows, along with a leopard-skin girl and a Spidora illusion (see chapter 10), a young, scantily clad woman pulling out the skin of her cheek and side (Johnson et al. 1996, 115).

Another Snap Wyatt banner of about 1965 is for an unidentified "Rubber Skin Man." He is shown stretching the skin from his thighs not by mere inches but by some three feet or more. Although this was obviously an exaggeration, it was an effective, eye-catching dramatization of the very real oddity ticket buyers were about to see—"Alive," as the banner's bullet guaranteed (Johnson et al. 1996, 123).

Some persons have skin that is notably loose, hanging down like that of a bloodhound. For example, at the Chicago world's fair in 1933, Ripley's "Believe It or Not!" show featured Arthur Loose, whose neck flesh hung down in great folds. Billed as the Rubber-Skinned Man, he "pulled out his cheeks eight inches and let them snap back into place." Another was Agnes Schmidt, the "Rubber-Skinned Girl" from Cincinnati, Ohio, who had similar loose folds, especially on her thighs (Mannix 1999, 96, 116). There was also Jack Stretch, who had sagging skin all over his chest and abdomen, as shown in a nude photo from 1964 (Hall 1991, 50, 58).

Today, a young American man named Gary Turner is one of only about ten people worldwide known to have Ehlers-Danlos syndrome. Nicknamed "Stretch," he notes that the more he stretches his skin, the more elastic it becomes. Although he does not perform on a sideshow platform, he did appear on the next best thing—a segment of television's *Ripley's Believe It or Not!* in 2001, where he demonstrated his peculiar ability for a modern audience.

Another modern rubber man is both a contortionist and an elastic-skin man. He is Las Vegas performer Thomas Martin Perez, also known as "Mr. Stretch." He "loves to shock people," states one *Ripley's Believe It or Not!* compendium, "by pulling the skin from his neck over his nose like a turtleneck sweater" (Packard et al. 2001, 35).

Interestingly, an abnormality that contrasts with the elastic-skin condition was exhibited by a vaudeville performer known as Sober Sue. A $1,000 reward was promised to anyone who could make the somber-faced lady smile. Even the professional comedians she appeared with were unable to claim the prize because she suffered not from excessively loose skin but from a rather oppo-site sort of anomaly: the underlying facial muscles were completely paralyzed (Gardner 1962, 136).

Special-Effects Performers

In addition to the benders (contortionists) and those with latex-like skin, certain anatomical wonders have developed the ability to perform remarkable feats with certain parts of their bodies.

Such a person was Martin Joe Laurello, the man with the revolving head, aka the "Human Owl" (Mooney et al. 2002, 12). As described by Percilla "Monkey Girl" Bejano, he "could put his head all the way around" (Taylor and Kotcher 2002, 190). That is, he could rotate his head a full 180 degrees, so that he could look behind him. On occasion during the 1920s and 1930s, Laurello struck a pose for photographer Edward J. Kelty with his fellow Congress of Freaks performers at Madison Square Garden. Standing with his feet planted so that his back was to Kelty, Laurello turned his head to stare directly at the camera (Barth and Siegel 2002, 102, 104, 107).

Laurello's banner heralded him as "Bobby the Boy with the Revolving Head." (As Johnny Meah [1996] interjects, "To add a footnote of sideshow trivia, in the titling of banners, men were always "boys" and women were always "girls" regardless of their actual age.) Supposedly, Laurello "had the ability to dislocate various vertebrae" in order to accomplish his head-turning feat (Meah 1996). Certainly, he had a rare degree of flexibility. Mannix (1999, 112) may be right when he states that "anyone else attempting to do this would have to break at least two neck vertebrae."

Laurello looked nothing like a freak. From head to toe he was ordinary; his hair was neatly combed, his face clean shaven. Wearing a white shirt, sharply creased trousers, and polished leather shoes, he could have stepped out of the sideshow and passed anyone on the street without getting a second glance. That is, of course, unless someone caught his attention and turned to see him looking—and looking and looking—while he continued to walk away.

Laurello used to perform at Hubert's Museum in New York City, located on Forty-second Street, just west of Broadway. When showman Bobby Reynolds was hanging out at Hubert's, starting when he was thirteen, he remembers

Laurello working with such attractions as strongman Charlie Fallon, sword swallower Alex Linton, and others, including the legendary Roy Heckler and his troupe of trained fleas. Like many other sideshow performers, Laurello no doubt found Hubert's a good place to work while the circus was in winter quarters. The museum was on the regular dime museum circuit that included Philadelphia, Newark, Patterson, and other cities (Taylor and Kotcher 2002, 155–56, 219–20).

In 1940 Martin Laurello was photographed—in a side view—striking his head-reversed pose, chin resting on his spine, while chomping on a cigar. He was then with Ripley's "Believe It or Not!" show at the New York world's fair (Mannix 1999, 112).

Not much seems to be known about his background or personal life. However, Percilla Bejano said of him: "He was a Nazi. And he didn't like the American flag. You meet all kinds on the sideshow—worse than me!" she added (Taylor and Kotcher 2002, 190).

Another anatomical specialty was the "eye-popper," who, as Ward Hall (1991, 36) explains, "could control the optic muscles, causing his eyeballs to pop out of the socket on command." Spectators nearly popped their own eyes in reaction. This "had to be one of the best remembered sideshow acts," says Ward.

There were at least two such performers, both known as "Popeye." One was Oscar "Popeye" Noggins, who did the bug-eyed stunt at the 1939 world's fair in New York. He performed with the "Strange as It Seems" show, a congress of strange people who had been cartooned by Ripley rival John Hix (Dufour 1977, 124, 186).

The other eye-popper was an African American from Richland, Georgia, "Popeye" Perry (figure 7.4). He often sported colorful outfits that sometimes included fringe and rhinestones, and one photograph shows him wearing a silver cross on a beaded necklace (Meah 1996; Hall 1991, 53). Mannix (1999, 104) says that Perry's bug-eyed appearance was "a bloodcurdling sight and Perry knew it." He adds: "After the talker had introduced him, Perry would select some squeamish-looking member of the tip—usually a woman—and, thrusting his face toward her, suddenly pop out one of his eyes. The lady usually screamed and retreated back. Then Perry would pop out the other eye. Not

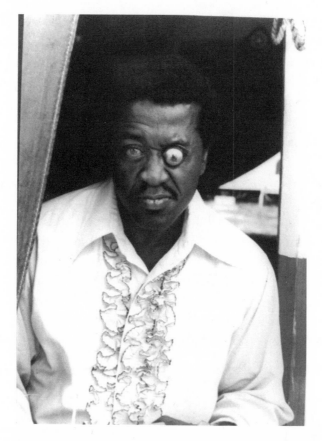

FIGURE 7.4. Sideshow performer "Popeye" Perry got his moniker from his eye-popping ability. (Author's collection)

infrequently, this was enough to make the girl faint. Perry would wait until she had recovered and then, bending over her, pop out both eyes at the same time. Invariably, this was enough to knock the woman out a second time."

Perhaps not surprisingly, Popeye Perry was also a character off the sideshow platform. Percilla Bejano tells about traveling on the road with him:

We used to drive right past [a restaurant], when we saw that Popeye [had] stopped. It was terrible. He'd put his eyes out, you know. Pop his eyes out. They'd come and wait on him, he'd say, "Thank you," and pop his eyes out on them. They'd run back and tell the boss, "There's a man out there losing his eyes!" [The Great] Waldo [discussed in chapter 9] told him not to. He told him, "You're not on exhibition. You don't do that where you eat." One time [a waitress] run out to her car after, run out and drove away! She did. Guess she wasn't going to wait on him again. (Taylor and Kotcher 2002, 191)

Another eye marvel was John Leather, who "could move each eye independently of the other" (Mooney et al. 2002, 12). Leather was among the acts signed up by showman Nate Eagle for the 1939 world's fair "Strange as It Seems" show (Dufour 1977, 124).

Many other individuals have had anatomical stunts or feats that they could perform to the astonishment of others. Some made careers of performing in sideshows, like Laurello and Popeye, while others came to the attention of Robert Ripley or his "Believe It or Not!" successors. For instance, there was Alfred Langevin, who "could smoke a pipe, play a recorder, smoke a cigarette, and even blow up a balloon—through his eye!" (I have seen an old film showing Langevin doing his pipe-smoking feat.) Marguerite Russell "could fold her tongue," Feria Mundial of Mexico City "lifted a chair with his shoulder blades," and Oscar Bradley of Macon, Georgia, walked "on his thumbs and index fingers" (Mooney et al. 2002, 12, 14, 15, 74, 77). There was also "Rubber Face" J. T. Saylors of Memphis Tennessee, who could contort his face so that by lifting his lower lip he appeared to "swallow" his nose (Packard et al. 2001, 33). F. G. Holt of Nashville, Arkansas, had a different use for his facial muscles: he attached little bells to his eyebrows and played various tunes (Mooney et al. 2002, 15).

Then there was Clarence E. Willard (1882–1962), billed as the "Man Who Grows." He was one of "Ripley's Strange People in Person," a group of live exhibits who appeared at the Odditoriums and were booked through the NBC Artists' Service to perform at venues across the United States and Canada. Willard was, according to Bob Considine (1961, 150), "a man who grew before your eyes," who "could stretch out and add six inches to his height." Considine thought that Willard was double-jointed, but noted magician James Randi (the "Amazing Randi") observes that the act became something of "a carnival mainstay" and had a simple explanation: it was a type of illusion (however, since it depended on anatomical manipulation, I included it here rather than in the chapter on magical effects). As Randi (1987, 129) explains:

> In this performance, a man is revealed onstage who seems to fit his clothes well enough. He is seen to go into a "trance" and appears to grow by seven or eight inches, by which time his sleeves are far too short and his pants go to half-mast as well. The gimmick is simple: The man is dressed into a too-small suit, and only has to "scrunch down" while in a standing position. The suit appears to fit him at this point, but as he straightens up and swells out his chest, the bad fit becomes apparent. It is a striking illusion, often enhanced by a popping belt buckle and falling shirt buttons thrown in for further effect.

Mr. Anatomical Wonder

One of the most talented and versatile entertainers ever to have a banner billing him as an "Anatomical Wonder" was Melvin Burkhart (1907–2001) (figure 7.5). As a tall, athletic young boxer with an outgoing, comedic nature, he used to amuse friends with his anatomical stunts at athletic meets. He soon appeared on stage at an amateur show. During the Depression, when times were hard and he was "always getting in trouble," he found work with a small circus, doing a "clown walk-around." That is, he drummed up business in small towns by walking down the main street in a clown costume with a bullhorn yelling, "Big Show Tonight! Conroy Brothers Circus!" He also sold tickets and clowned. Once, when a performer was sick, his boss, Curly Easter, told him to "Go out there and do something" to fill in. Burkhart recalled (interview in Taylor and Kotcher 2002): "And the audience was out there clapping, so I went out there and I took off my shirt and I told them I was going to show them tricks with my body. I didn't know in those days how to present what I do, but I wasn't bad at it. I had the idea. Anyway, I go out there and they are applauding and carrying on. When I go back in there Curly goes, 'I'll be damned. You'll do that next show, too.' That was it."

The act was added to Burkhart's other duties, and he has never labored so hard before or since. "I worked two years with the one-ring circus," he said, "and every time I was with any show, even when I was on Ringling, any time I was

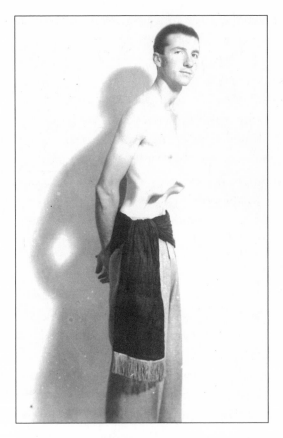

FIGURE 7.5. Melvin Burkhart, the anatomical wonder, performs here in his youth as the "Man without a Stomach"— sucking in his abdomen until it seemed to touch his backbone. (Author's collection)

on another show, it was like taking a vacation compared to the one-ring circus." He taught himself magic, developed a human blockhead routine (see chapter 9), and did other acts, such as the electric chair illusion and, for a blowoff, a snake-wrestling exhibition. He worked the bally, filled in as inside lecturer, and, of course, performed as the "Anatomical Wonder" (Taylor and Kotcher 2002).

One of Burkhart's main anatomical feats, the one he started with as a young man, was sucking in his abdomen to a remarkable degree, so that he became the "Man without a Stomach" (see figure 7.5). Others who did such an act were Rex "Americo" Carson, who was with the Dailey Brothers Circus in the 1940s (Hall 1991, 50, 51), and a later Coney Island sideshow anatomical wonder called "'Isha Voodie' / Man without a Middle!" (Stein 1998, 95). Burkhart performed the stomach feat until, in old age, his doctor told him to quit.

Burkhart describes another feat: "I could breathe through one lung at a time." He would call a young girl up on stage and get her to place her hands on his chest. (He also demonstrated this for an interviewer [Taylor and Kotcher 2002].) "Then I'd say, 'Now let's see if you can do that.' And the girl would start shrieking, 'No! Don't do that!' Big laugh from the audience." He could also do a "rubber neck" effect in which—by tipping his head back and drawing his shoulders down—he could give the appearance of having an elongated neck.

Melvin Burkhart established himself as a major anatomical wonder when he was cartooned by Robert Ripley for his famous "Believe It or Not!" feature, and Burkhart left Hubert's Museum to perform at Ripley's Odditorium in New York in 1939. He also appeared in the cartoon feature of Ripley's rival, John Hix, called "Strange as It Seems." As a result, a furious Ripley replaced him with another anatomical wonder, Ed Hayes, and Burkhart went to work with Ringling Brothers again.

Ripley was especially fascinated by Burkhart's "two-faced man" feat. Unlike the human-oddity version, Burkhart's involved contorting his face so that the right side was "Happy Melvin," with raised eyebrow and upturned mouth, and the other side was "Sad Melvin," with the opposite features (Taylor and Kotcher 2002, 149, 166). Incidentally, according to Ripley's biographer (Considine 1961, 141–42), Ripley hated the term *freaks*, which in any case did not apply to many of his attractions, such as anatomical wonders. He threatened to fire any employee who used the word and substituted *oddities* instead—hence his brilliant term *Odditorium*.

When Melvin Burkhart was in his nineties, he recalled that when he went to work with the James E. Strates carnival in 1956, there had been eighteen sideshow acts, and he was the only one still alive (Taylor and Kotcher 2002). He told a reporter, "You know the way I figure it, yesterday never was, tomorrow will never be, but today is always." He entertained and inspired many. When he died on November 8, 2001, at "Gibtown," his son Dennis, a biochemical engineer, said, "He taught me how to be a rich man. He said a rich man is someone who can make one person smile every day. If I can be half the man my father has been, I will be a great man." His daughter-in-law Jane Burkhart said, "He did what everybody else always talked about doing. He ran away and joined the circus" (Associated Press 2001).

8 CREATED ODDITIES

IN ADDITION TO BORN, BONA fide human oddities, there are what William Lindsay Gresham (1953, 102) terms "'made' freaks." These include tattooed and pierced people and those who otherwise deliberately alter their appearance so that they can be exhibited as curiosities or perform as sideshow working acts. Then there are the gaffed freaks, those whose oddities are partially or completely faked or whose acts are bogus.

Tattooed People

Eighteenth-century explorers encountered native peoples of the South Seas islands, the Far East, and elsewhere who practiced tattooing—the use of a thorn, needle, or other sharp instrument to prick dye into the skin and thus create indelible designs. Tattooing was also practiced in ancient times, being seen in Egyptian mummies dating from 2000 B.C. or earlier (Fellman 1986). The famous Stone Age body discovered in an Alpine glacier in 1991, dating from about 3300 to 3200 B.C., bore several tattooed markings. These were of the familiar blue color, indicating that they had probably been made with soot, and they appear to have had a magical or healing, rather than a decorative, purpose (Spindler 1994). A Chinese chronicle of the third century A.D. describing the "Queen Country," Japan, states that "the men both great and small tattoo their faces and work designs upon their bodies"—a practice that would not be seen in China itself for several centuries (Fellman 1986). (See figure 8.1.)

The art form was popularized in Europe after Russian explorer Georg H. von Langsdorff visited the Marquesas Islands in 1804. He discovered a French deserter named Jean Baptiste Cabri, who had lived there for many

FIGURE 8.1. A Japanese illustrated man is depicted in a nineteenth-century engraving.

years, married a native woman, and fathered several children. He had also been extensively tattooed. Cabri told Langsdorff such elaborate tales of his life among the Marquesans that Langsdorff said, "anyone who heard him relate them would be disposed to think himself listening to a second Munchhausen." Cabri accompanied Langsdorff back to Russia for a brief theatrical career. After spending a year at the Marine Academy at Kronshtadt, where he was a swimming instructor, he went on tour in Europe, attracting the attention of eminent physicians and even appearing before royalty. After a few years, however, his career declined, and he was reduced to being exhibited at country fairs. He died at his birthplace, Valenciennes, France, in 1812, "poor and forgotten" (Gilbert 1996).

Like Cabri, Englishman John Rutherford was tattooed by native tribespeople—in his case, New Zealand's Maoris. He told an extravagant tale of capture and forcible tattooing by two Maori priests during a four-hour ceremony in which he lost consciousness; Rutherford had to convalesce for weeks afterward. Subsequently, the tribe adopted him among their chiefs and offered him many brides. Prudently, he selected two, both of them daughters of the ruling chieftain. After rescue by a brig from the United States, he returned to England, but not before a stopover—and marriage to another native girl—in Hawaii. Rutherford's biographer wrote that he subsequently "maintained himself by accompanying a traveling caravan of wonders, showing his tattooing, and telling something of his extraordinary adventures." These tales were related in a pitch book sold at his appearances. Although some accused him of fictionalizing his story, according to tattoo historian Steve Gilbert (1996, 102), "there is no doubt that the tattooing was authentic Maori work, and that he knew from firsthand experience a great deal about the lives and customs of the Maoris."

The story of being forcibly tattooed by savages has been told by others, including James F. O'Connel, who was reportedly the first such man to exhibit professionally in the United States. O'Connel debuted at Barnum's American Museum after its opening in 1841. He regaled audiences with tales of capture and forcible tattooing by South Seas virgins, one of whom—a beautiful princess, of course—he was obliged by custom to marry (Gilbert 1996). He sold a thirty-one-page pitch book titled "The Life and Adventures of James

F. O'Connel, the Tattooed Man, During a Residence of Eleven Years in New Holland and Caroline Islands," published in 1846. When last heard of, he was with Dan Rice's circus in 1852 (Bogdan 1990, 242–43).

Barnum's greatest tattooed wonder was a Greek, Captain George Constentenus. He was the star of the sideshow with the Greatest Show on Earth in 1876. Since it was America's one-hundredth anniversary, Constentenus was billed as the "Centennial Portrait Gallery." He was covered from head to toe with "388 designs in indigo and cinnabar." The noted physician and author Oliver Wendell Holmes said of the array, "It is the most perfect specimen of genuine tattooing which any of us have ever seen." Barnum added that Constentenus had "over seven million blood producing punctures." His pitch booklet told an elaborate and sensational tale of being raised in a harem in Turkey, having a romantic affair with the daughter of the shah of Persia, and eventually being captured by the "fiendish" khan of Kashgar. Given a choice of being stung to death by wasps, impaled, burned alive, or other fates, including undergoing complete body tattooing, Constentenus chose the last, upon being told that he could go free if he survived. However, the tale was completely bogus: "In actuality, the eccentric Constentenus willingly obtained his own tattoos in a carefully conceived plan to become a self-made curiosity" (Kunhardt et al. 1995, 251).

In 1891 the leading New York tattoo artist, James O'Reilly, patented his electric tattooing machine, and many circus people were among his thousands of customers. After his death in 1908, O'Reilly's apprentice, Charles Wagner, became "the best-known tattooer in America and tattooed over 50 completely covered circus attractions." O'Reilly and Wagner did the work on the first totally tattooed female to be exhibited in a circus sideshow, La Belle Irene. She debuted in London in 1890, and—although her designs included hearts and flowers, cupids and birds, scrolls and sentiments—"Londoners were asked to believe that she had acquired her embellishments in a strange and savage land (Texas) as a protection against the unwelcomed advances of the natives" (Gilbert 1996, 103).

Soon, there appeared a tattooed couple, Emma and Frank de Burgh. Emma's extensive designs included a rendering of *The Last Supper* across her back. One who had admired her and then saw her again years later reported that she had gained so much weight that when he looked at *The Last Supper,* "all the apostles wore broad grins" (Gilbert 1996, 103).

At least one bearded lady, Jean Furella, took a friend's advice and improved both her career and her love life by shaving and having her body illustrated. She was thus reinvented as the "Tattoo Queen" at the Riverside Park in Chicago and enjoyed a happy marriage.

By 1920, several hundred tattooed people were exhibiting in circus and carnival sideshows, some earning up to $200 a week (then a tidy sum). In the competition for ever more extravagant acts, there were soon tattooed fire-eaters, sword swallowers, strongmen, jugglers, knife throwers, dwarfs, fat ladies, and others. Tattoo artists traveled with circuses and carnivals, one of them—Stoney St. Clair (1912–1980)—even having his own colorful banner. Headed "Tattooing by Stoney," it showed him at work illustrating a scantily clad young lady, while omitting the wheelchair to which he was confined due to a childhood attack of rheumatoid arthritis (Gilbert 1996).

Particularly distinctive among the bodily illustrated oddities was Djita the "Tattooed Oriental Beauty," whose skin art was rendered in no fewer than fourteen colors. She claimed that she had been punctured by the tattoo needle 100 million times. Another was Maude Arizona, who was advertised as the "Most Tattooed Lady in the World." She was covered with various figures from her feet up to her neck, where, according to Dick Gardner (1962, 135), "a pearl choker stopped the designs below a singularly attractive face." Ripley's Odditoriums and other enterprises have featured uniquely tattooed oddities. One was Dick Hyland, the "Human Autograph Album," whose body was "signed" by more than 600 celebrities—Robert Ripley included (Mooney et al. 2002, 69).

Probably the most unique of the tattooed men and women was Horace Ridler, a British prep-school-educated ex–army officer who was down on his luck and decided to transform himself into a circus star. His idea was to be tattooed all over with zebra-like stripes. Claiming that he had been forcibly tattooed by New Guinea savages, the "Great Omi, the Zebra Man" eventually became one of the "highest paid circus performers in the world" (Gilbert 1996; Bogdan 1990, 255–56). Ripley was especially taken with the Great Omi, describing him as "the most remarkable-looking person I have seen in traveling to two hundred and one different countries." He was impressed that "the symmetry of the pattern was especially designed to fit the contour's of Omi's face—even the ears are tattooed." Ripley was also amazed by "how close to his eyes the tattooing needle worked." He alleged that the unique blue pattern required "five hundred million stabs" (Considine 1961, 143–44). Be that as it may, Ripley's claim that the work required nine years was an exaggeration— perhaps by Omi. In fact, it took "only" a year.

Omi had successfully toured Europe before coming to America. From Ripley's 1938 Odditorium appearance, he went on to tour with Ringling Brothers and also exhibited at Madison Square Garden, drawing large crowds in his coast-to-coast appearances (Bogdan 1990, 255–56). Omi augmented his extreme tattooing with other freakish elements. He had his teeth filed to points, his nose pierced and fitted with an ivory tusk, and the lobes of his ears pierced and stretched so that the holes measured over an inch across. He had the complete support of his loyal wife. His tattooer was London's best, George Burchett, who wrote: "I have the greatest admiration for these two people. Their devotion to each other was one of the great experiences of my long life, during which I have met many brave and unusual people" (Gilbert 1996, 104).

Reportedly, Omi had once been a British army officer and had seen battle in Mesopotamia with the Desert Mountain Corps. When World War II came, he attempted to aid the American war effort but was judged too freakish to be allowed in the military. Instead, he spent the war years raising money to benefit the troops. "By the time he retired," according to Alan Weiss (1996, 135), "there was no doubt in anybody's mind that The Great Omi had turned himself from an ordinary human into one of the most successful freaks of all time!"

A modern-day Omi is Paul Lawrence, known as "The Enigma" and formerly "Slug the Swordswallower." He has traveled with the Jim Rose Circus Sideshow, a troupe with many self-made freaks who perform in theaters and other venues. The Enigma has been exhibiting as a work in progress. He is tattooed all over with jigsaw-puzzle outlines, and some of the "pieces" have been filled in with the familiar tattoo-blue coloration. He also has surgically implanted "horns" above his forehead. "When not on the road," a bio note reads, "he lives in Texas with his wife Katzen, who is fully tattooed as a cat" (Gregor 1998, 386).

Such full-body tattooing is a permanent, life-transforming commitment. Consider Betty Broadbent, who came from a prominent Philadelphia society family. Intelligent, educated, and privileged, at age seventeen she vacationed at Atlantic City, where she was motivated to obtain some tattoos. Her family's displeasure may have prompted her to have her whole body illustrated, and she became the "Tattooed Lady." Her career included all the leading sideshows in the United States, as well as abroad. She later enjoyed retirement with her third husband at Riverview, Florida. However, Ward Hall (1991, 34) says, "Betty talked little of her early life, but once disclosed to me that she regretted having that first tattoo." (For other illustrated people, see figures 8.2 to 8.5.)

Pierced Ones

Some self-made freaks use body piercings instead of tattoos or, like the Great Omi, combine the two effects. One was Rasmus Nielsen, the 1930s tattooed strongman. An erstwhile California blacksmith of Scandinavian ancestry, he told the obligatory tale of capture and forcible tattooing by South Seas island-ers. The "savages," he claimed, had added to the torture by inserting metal rings through the skin of his chest, placing ropes through the rings, and then dangling him from tree limbs.

In fact, Gresham (1953, 102) describes such a performer, probably Nielsen, as "having a plastic surgeon cut slits in the pectoral muscles of his chest" so that he could lift weights "in imitation of the fakirs of the Orient." Indeed, that is how Nielsen used the torture rings in his act. He inserted an iron bar through the rings; the bar was attached to a chain tied around a large anvil. Leaning back, Nielsen was thus witnessed "lifting 250 lbs by his breasts," according to the caption penned on a photo of the stunt (Gilbert 1996; Mooney et al. 2002, 134). Writes Daniel Mannix (1999, 117): "One day a smart young reporter jumped on Nielsen's platform and shouted that the anvil was wood. Nielsen told him to pick it up. The reporter struggled vainly to lift the anvil while other newspaper men happily took pictures. The resulting publicity made Nielsen one of the best known side-show acts."

A double banner featuring Nielsen was painted by famed banner art-

(Left) FIGURE 8.2. A pretty tattooed girl posed in the buff for this publicity photo, exhibited in Bobby Reynolds's sideshow museum.

(Below) FIGURE 8.3. This "Totally Tattooed" banner graced the front of Bobby Reynolds's International Circus Sideshow Museum & Gallery. (Photo by author)

(Left) FIGURE 8.4. Front of the pitch card of tattooed lady Lorett Fulkerson. It is signed, "Best Wishes / Lorett." She appeared with the Hall & Christ sideshows. (Right) FIGURE 8.5. Back of Lorett Fulkerson's pitch card. (Author's collection)

ist Fred G. Johnson. Still extant in a private collection, it bears the stenciled imprint of Johnson's employer, the O'Henry Tent and Awning Company of Chicago. The upper banner shows the performer—under a scroll-like panel, lettered "Rasmus Nielsen Scandinavian Strong Man"—wearing only shorts to show off his body art and lifting an anvil with his pectorals. In the other scene, Nielsen is lifting a smaller anvil by means of a chain with a hook through his pierced tongue (Johnson et al. 1996, 98–99).

This latter effect is called an *iron tongue act,* in which the entertainer lifts concrete blocks, filled buckets, or the like using a pierced tongue. According to James Taylor (1997, 94), such an act "could be gaffed, with a steel hook 'through' the tongue"; however, "these days, this act is less often gaffed than it is accomplished using genuine tongue piercings." With the current fad of tongue and other body piercings among young people, the act may not seem as impressive as it once was. Nevertheless, such an iron-tongued wonder was with the 2000 traveling ten-in-one sideshow of Hall & Christ. I intercepted the

FIGURE 8.6. An iron-tongued wonder with the Hall & Christ sideshow in 2000 also had pierced nipples fitted with rings, which he used to pull a wagon. (Photo by author)

show on the midway of the York Interstate Fair in York, Pennsylvania, where I obtained the accompanying photo (figure 8.6). The young marvel also had pierced nipples, fitted with rings, with which he pulled a small wagon.

Another type of *human marvel*—one who demonstrates any amazing ability with his or her body (Taylor 1998, 94)—was represented by Harry McGreggor. A 1933 Ripley Odditorium performer, McGreggor "used his eyelids to pull a wagon carrying his wife" (Packard et al. 2001, 30). Another of the genre was R. H. "Sheets" Hubbard, one of the "Strange as It Seems" congress of unusual people presented at the 1939 world's fair in New York City. Showman Lou Dufour described Hubbard as "a young man who would pull weights with hooks passed through his eyelids." Such acts were termed "iron eyelids" (Dufour 1977, 134, 124).

Then there is the iron—well, another part of the male anatomy. The "Amazing Mister Lifto"—Joe Hermann, who performs with the Jim Rose Circus sideshow—has not only pierced nipples but also a pierced penis. He uses the former to do a concrete-block lift before large audiences. As for the latter, published photographs show a nude Mister Lifto with a stretched member lifting a household steam iron (Gregor 1998; Taylor 1998, 10–11).

The most remarkable pierced marvel was no doubt Mortado, who was seemingly crucified during his act. His hands and feet had been pierced surgically, and the holes concealed capsules of "blood" that spouted forth when spikes were pounded through them. As such, he had been the "Sensation of Europe." Later, he claimed to have been "the only living man captured by savages and actually crucified." According to his pitch book, the "savages" had been "a wild tribe of Mohammedans" in the Sahara Desert. Upon encountering him at an oasis, they showed their contempt for a "white Christian" by placing him in a "spread eagle" position and nailing him to a large wooden wheel used for drawing water. Abandoned to his fate, he was fortunately rescued by "some white men" and recovered at an army hospital in Berlin. The piercings, his spiel claimed, prevented him from working, so he was resigned to sideshow life. In a later presentation, utilizing a specially designed chair with plumbing fixtures, the turbaned and exotically costumed performer became Mortado the Human Fountain, with streams of water arcing from the holes in his hands and bare feet.

Mortado made his initial appearance in the United States on April 27, 1930, at Dreamland Circus Side Show, Coney Island. Little is known about his background, except that he claimed to be "a native of Berlin, Germany." A photo in his pitch book, dated 1914, shows him in the uniform of a German junior naval officer at the onset of World War I. He stated that at the time of his alleged capture, he had been "assigned to special duty in Northern Africa" (Mortado n.d.; Barta 1996).

Mortado stayed at Dreamland for years, but the public eventually tired of his act and, says Barta (1996, 161), "When he failed to come up with anything new, his career slowly faded away." Mannix (1999, 119) writes: "Shortly afterwards, I read that a man had been found crucified to a wooden wall of an elevated train station in New York, but when police investigated they found it was a fraud; the man had crucified himself. As it is impossible to crucify yourself, I have often wondered if this was Mortado making a last bid for fame."

All the foregoing acts involve permanent body piercing. A related phenomenon—featuring the impromptu piercings and skewerings of the human pincushion act—is featured at some length in chapter 9.

Other "Made" Oddities

Among the exotic exhibits of the latter nineteenth and early twentieth centuries were "Genuine Monster-Mouthed Ubangi Savages," supposedly the "World's Most Weird Living Humans from Africa's Darkest Depths," according to one circus ad. These were women from the French Congo who beautified themselves by lip enlargement. This was accomplished by slitting a female infant's lips so that wooden discs could be inserted—larger ones being placed in the lower lip. Increasingly bigger discs were used as the girl grew, and her lips were eventually extended ten inches or more, giving the woman "a duckbill appearance" (Bogdan 1990, 193–94; Dufour 1977, 177). Several of the tribal women were originally exhibited in Europe and then brought to the United States to appear in the Ringling Brothers and Barnum & Bailey freak show in the spring of 1930 (figure 8.7).

Ringling sideshow manager Clyde Ingalls introduced them: "Ladies and Gentlemen, from the deepest depths of darkest Africa we present the world's most astounding Aborigines—the 'Crocodile Lipped Women from Congo'— the Ubangis." Actually, the women were not Ubangis. Ringling press agent Roland Butler admitted that he had picked that name from an African map purely for its exotic sound. As he reportedly said, "I resettled them" (Bogdan 1990, 194). After Ingalls introduced them, the "Ubangis" slowly filed in, topless and preceded by men who wore loincloths and carried spears. Naturally, the women's banner art "extended the lips far in excess of reality: in some they appear as if they have turkey platter inserts." Their pitch book was amply illustrated with pictures of the bare-breasted women (Bogdan 1990, 194–95).

FIGURE 8.7. A Ringling sideshow in California featured these "genuine monster-mouthed Ubangi savages" on the bally platform in 1930. (Author's collection)

Another group of native women who deform themselves to achieve their cultural ideal of beauty are the long-necked women of Burma and Thailand. They are the Padaung people, who achieve the look by fitting five-year-old girls with copper necklace rings. More rings are added as they grow, until the desired neck length is reached. The maximum recorded extension is fifteen and three-quarters inches. But there is a drawback: the stretched muscles of the neck are not strong enough to bear the head's weight without the rings, and if they are removed, the woman could suffocate (Packard et al. 2001, 22; Parker 1994, 27).

A ring-necked woman, together with a saucer-lipped "Ubangi" and other female oddities, was depicted on a double banner headed "Strange Girls." Painted by Snap Wyatt, this was for Dick Best's circa 1965 sideshow that featured an all-female troupe of working acts (Johnson et al. 1996, 110, 158).

Whereas the "Ubangis" and the ring-necked women did not deform themselves for the purpose of appearing in sideshows, Fred Walters did. He was, according to Gresham (1953, 103), "one of the weirdest-looking characters of the side-show world." Walters's skin was a strange slate-blue color.

Billed as the "Blue Man," he let audiences think that his was a rare example of abnormally pigmented skin. However, at his death, a quantity of the chemical silver nitrate was discovered among his belongings. Apparently, Walters had begun taking it for some nervous condition, found that it turned his skin blue, and decided to capitalize on the effect, maintaining it through repeated doses (Gresham 1953, 103; Gardner 1962, 135).

Apart from such self-made freakery, there are instances in which a deformity is caused by an accident or the deliberate intent of others. For example, the legless wonder Bill Cole, of Buffalo, New York, was the victim of a railroad accident (Hall 1991, 24). And Captain Callahan, who was sexually mutilated, was a genuine attraction at the 1933 Chicago world's fair, whether or not the tale of how he acquired his deformity was true. Manager Nate Eagle spieled for the blowoff in the African Village (Dufour 1977, 68–69):

Ladies and gentlemen, on the inside of this enclosure you will see and hear Captain Callahan, that brave and durable man who was so horribly tortured by a ferocious group of savages in the Cameroons, who were about to fling his bruised body into a steaming pot of boiling water, after a sadist beast had decapitated his penis and testicles. Please, please, just stop to think—what a terrible, despicable crime! On the inside you will hear from the very lips of Captain Callahan how he was rescued from those ruthless cannibals.

The famous talker continued:

Now, please listen very carefully: everyone is invited to come in, this being the understanding—that the captain will be on an elevated stage. He will remove his robe. And after you see with your own eyes that the captain is absolutely devoid of sexual organs as I am now stating—then, and only then, will you be expected to pay fifty cents to the cashiers as you pass out through the turnstiles.

Falling somewhere between "made" oddities and outright gaffs were the so-called Circassian beauties (figures 8.8 and 8.9). According to mid-nineteenth-

191

(Left) FIGURE 8.8. Alleged Circassian beauties were frequent subjects for photographer Charles Eisenmann. This is the *carte de visite* photo of Barnum's Zoe Meleke. It is autographed on the back. (Author's collection) (Right) FIGURE 8.9. Cabinet-size photo of Zoe Zobedia, another Circassian beauty photographed by Eisenmann. (Author's collection)

century racial theories, the purest and most beautiful examples of the Caucasian race were the Circassians, a tribe from Russia's Caucasus region. Allegedly, Circassian females were often stolen and sold into Turkish harems. P. T. Barnum sought to obtain a "beautiful Circassian girl" in 1864 and soon had one exhibited at his American Museum. She had supposedly been obtained by one of his agents who had disguised himself as a Turk and purchased her from the slave market in Constantinople. However, an alternative story says that Barnum's man was unsuccessful, so a bushy-haired local girl was dressed in Turkish attire and christened "Zalumma Agra, 'Star of the East.'" There followed a succession of such beauties, distinguished by their Afro hairdos and Z-dominating names: Zribeda, Azela Pacha, Millie Zulu, Zoledod, Zuruby Hannum, Zoberdie Luti, Zula Zeleke, Zana Zanobia, and others. "Almost certainly," reports one authority, "all of them were dressed-up local women

CREATED ODDITIES

who were taught to wash their hair in beer, then tease it, for the frizzy look of Circassian exotics" (Kunhardt et al. 1995, 181; Bogdan 1990, 235–38).

Perhaps Barnum's most popular Circassian was a girl renamed Zoe Meleke (see figure 8.8). To disguise the fact that she spoke ordinary Yankee English and knew nothing of her "native" land, the following paragraph was placed in her circa 1880 pitch book, "Zoe Meleke: Biographical Sketch of the Circassian Girl":

Being a very tender age at the time of her exodus from the land of her nativity, her recollections of Circassia are of course very imperfect and obscure; the associations of her far off country seem to her an imperfect and confused dream, rather than reality; and from her long severance from the people of her kind, she has partially, if not entirely lost remembrance of her native tongue; and yet, as has been stated elsewhere in this little sketch, she speaks the language of her adopted land with an ease and fluency that would puzzle the most cunning linguist that was not otherwise informed to discover that she was not a native of America. (quoted in Bogdan 1990, 239)

When interest in the Circassians flagged, there were attempts to exhibit men in the role, but these were unsuccessful. Some Circassian beauties doubled as sword swallowers, snake charmers, or other working acts. When Circassians were dropped as a sideshow feature by 1910, "moss-haired" women and similar bushy-headed oddities took their place (Bogdan 1990, 240). One was "Mlle. Ivy," who was with Barnum & Bailey. She was said to have been "born with a wealth of luxuriant hair, so closely resembling ordinary moss that she is called 'The Moss-haired Girl.' She is a notable and pleasing addition to the army of living monstrosities and living curiosities" (Conklin 1921, 163).

Among these moss-haired wonders were genuine oddities Eko and Iko, who were twin albino blacks. They appeared with the Ringling Brothers sideshow for years, being part of the Congress of Freaks in the 1920s and 1930s (Barth and Siegel 2002, 102–9). Although they sported long ringlets rather than Afros, "the mosslike appearance of their pale yellow hair and beards," says Gresham (1953, 101), made the pair an interesting and popular act. He

193

notes that they were musicians and sat on the sideshow platform, "softly practicing on saxophone and guitar, hour after hour when not called upon by the inside talker to stand up and be seen."

Gaffed Oddities

Human oddities are often gaffed—faked—in whole or in part. We have already seen (in chapter 4) how tricks can be used to make giants seem larger and midgets smaller.

William Durks, the "Two-Faced Man" (see figure 6.12), enhanced his split face to create an alternative sideshow identity and thus enable him to continue on the same show route with fresh billing. Durks, who had an eye and nostril on either side of a growth in the center of his face, later enhanced the effect; he used makeup to add an extra central "eye" (and two more "nostrils"), becoming the "Man with Three Eyes" (Taylor 1997, 40–47).

Bobby Reynolds (2001) recalls that when he solicited Bill Durks to perform in the sideshows at the Flemington, New Jersey, fair, "he was a janitor in his church and they were giving him thirty-five dollars a week and he was sleeping in the basement somewhere." Later, when Durks used a little white makeup to create a third eye, Bobby had a better idea: "I literally wanted to have a plastic surgeon put a real eye in there, a glass glimmer, you know, and . . . he wouldn't go for it. And I had the guy and I set up, and I—you know, it only cost a G-note. I could've had this eye put in there, but he wouldn't go for it. And I said for two hundred dollars more I could've had it wink, you know. But he wasn't going for the plastic-surgeon crap."

The irony is that the "Man with Three Eyes" was actually one-eyed, his other being vestigial. His stepdaughter, Dorothy Hershey, confirms the fact: "Daddy always wore a hat over his one eye because you could tell he only had one." She adds:

> His aunt was there when he was born and the eye came out onto a little thing—it was stuck out and nobody knew what it was. They thought he was dead, and they wrapped him in a little rug and put him underneath the woodstove until the doctor came. And he still wasn't dead when the doctor came, but that eye was ruined. They just

wrapped him up and stuck him under the wood fire until the man could get there and that was the next day.

Then when the doctor come, he said, "This child is still alive!" So they naturally got him back to breathing real good and that's what happened. Bill Durks had a story behind him before he ever entered show business. He had a heck of a time getting into this world. (quoted in Taylor 1997, 46)

Another who altered a genuine deformity was a Texas field laborer named Pasquel Pinon, who had a large tumor protruding from his forehead. This was transformed, by the addition of facial features, into a second, seemingly vestigial, "head." Pinon, who was billed as the "Two-Headed Mexican," appeared in the Sells-Floto Circus sideshow in 1917. His career was brief, however, since Pinon died after only two years—possibly from the cranial tumor (Bogdan 1990, 84–85; Reese 1996).

Among the boldest of the gaffed oddities were bogus Siamese twins, such as Adolph and Rudolph, shown in a circa 1899 photograph. A comparison of their facial features reveals that they lack the close resemblance of identical twins, which conjoined persons always are (their condition resulting from incomplete division of one fertilized egg). In fact, a harness concealed under the young men's specially devised suit held Rudolph so that he seemed to grow from Adolph's waist (Bogdan 1990, 8; Reese 1996, 190).

Vestigial twins were sometimes partially or totally gaffed. Recall from chapter 5 the parasitic twin of Laloo, the Hindu, which was dressed as a female for effect, although it had a rudimentary penis. "Girl with Four Legs and Three Arms was so popular," states Drimmer (1991, 33), "she was widely imitated by fraudulent sideshow operators." He adds, "It wasn't uncommon for an attractive girl to appear before the public with a tiny deformed body of rubber strapped to her shapely torso." Indeed, Gresham (1953, 103) reports: "I saw one cultured old lady displayed in an annex [i.e., blowoff], who was purported to be a double-bodied woman. She was shown in a subdued light and the vestigial twin, revealed when she opened her long cloak, was pretty sad. It was made of rubber, several shades darker than her own skin, and had dust in the cracks of its fingers and toes."

Perhaps the most famous of the gaffed "double-bodied girls" was a veiled woman, Margurete Clark, who had a rubber doll hanging from her midriff. Actually, "Margurete" was Billy Logsdon, an alleged "half-and-half" (or hermaphrodite) (Taylor and Kotcher 2002, 143). Ward Hall (1991, 40) tells of several other female impersonators who transformed themselves into "double-bodied" acts. Among them were Shari Dean, Pinky Pepper, Claude Claudette, and Louise Logsdon, all working for various shows during the same time period, and all using the name Margurete (or Margaret) Clark. He admits: "I wanted one of these fake bodies for use on our own show. An elderly sideshow impresario agreed to make one for a considerable sum. It arrived C.O.D. He had simply removed the head from a toy rubber doll, and sewed it onto a woman's girdle. I took one look and threw it into the garbage can. It served me right for even thinking of fostering such a fake on the public."

As to Billy Logsdon, the reputed half-and-half, the real variety is rare. Medically, a hermaphrodite is "an individual possessing genital and sexual characteristics of both sexes," the clitoris usually being enlarged and so resembling a penis (*Taber's* 2001). Some half-and-half acts have been realistically gaffed. Ward Hall (2004) confided to me how a half-and-half he had exhibited had used a loop of elastic to draw his penis between his testicles to create the folds of a "vulva," the remainder of the penis hanging down as if from a rudimentary organ. At least one physician was fooled by this trick.

However, the showing of genitalia in sideshows was increasingly considered "indecent exposure," thus helping to give rise to a differently gaffed variety. Gresham (1953, 103–4) writes: "The side show half-and-half is usually a man with a very feminine voice which he can, for contrast in the show, lower to a husky baritone. He lets the hair on one side of his head grow long and has it waved, bleaches out the beard stubble on that side of his face, and if very ambitious may exercise the 'male' half of his body with adjustable dumbbells to provide an impressive difference in the muscular development." Such a half-and-half's costume typically continued the split look. For example, Josephine-Joseph, the "Half Woman–Half Man," (figure 8.10) wore a short black dress with plunging neckline and a stocking on "her" feminine side and a strongman's leopard skin on "his" masculine side (Fiedler 1993, 181–83). Thus

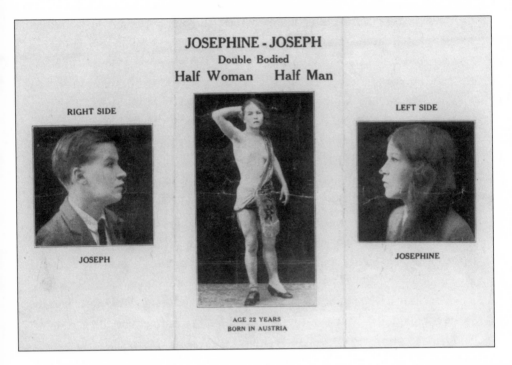

FIGURE 8.10. Josephine-Joseph, the "Double-Bodied Half Woman, Half Man," typified the gaffed presentation. (Pitch folder from author's collection)

styled, the half-and-half could pose and talk as a female facing one way and as a male facing the other way (*Sideshow* 2000).

"Alligator" people represent another type of sideshow oddity that is often bogus. With a secondhand banner, a willing subject, and a secret formula, "a small-time operator lacking the funds to book the real McCoy could manufacture one very inexpensively" (Meah 1996, 120). Famous showman Bobby Reynolds (2001) provided me with the secret recipe: Casco powdered casein glue was obtained from a hardware store, mixed with water, and tinted with "a little bit of McCormick's green [food] dye to get that look." This solution is painted on the hapless show person. After it dries, perhaps assisted by a heater, he or she twists and flexes to help create the cracking pattern that simulates genuine ichthyosis (Meah 1996, 120). Reynolds (2001) described another ingenious touch: While the painted-on coating is tacky, a little sand is sprinkled on to give it a realistically rough texture. Then, during the exhibition, the show's talker would emphasize the effect by striking an old-fashioned kitchen match on the "alligator" person's skin.

Bearded ladies were often gaffed as well. Barnum's Madame Fortune was the genuine variety, but when her son proved to be hairy too, Barnum had an idea: he had the boy exhibited in dresses until the age of fourteen. "This was typical Barnum hokum, reports Mike Parker (1994, 91); "not satisfied with a bearded boy, he did his best to dupe punters into believing that they were actually viewing a bearded girl!"

Then there was Frances Murphy, the bearded lady who worked for the "Strange as It Seems" show at the New York world's fair. Mrs. Murphy lived in uptown Manhattan and commuted by subway. One night she was insulted by some drunken sailors, one of whom gave her beard a tug. She got up and landed a punch that sent him sprawling halfway down the subway car. She gave another sailor a black eye and slammed a third into a metal wall. The incident came to the attention of the police, who decided to look more closely at the assailant. As it turned out, "Mrs." Murphy was a female impersonator who had, according to showman Lou Dufour, "a creditable record as an amateur boxer." Dufour and his partner Joe Rogers were forced to remove the bearded "lady" from their payroll. Their incorrigible sideshow manager and talker, Nathan T. "Nate" Eagle, apparently kept a straight face as he told a newspaper reporter: "I have been completely taken in by this bearded mountebank. Unfortunately, there always is some unscrupulous person who will take advantage of an unsuspecting showman" (Dufour 1977, 124–25).

With such gaffed oddities, it was small wonder that in 1958 the *New Yorker* would characterize Eagle as "a carnival talker of almost unparalleled genius, a man of such deep, legitimate guile and persuasion that, over the past 43 years, with acts too varied and spurious to list fully, he has probably hoodwinked at least half the nation" (quoted in Nelson 1999, 121). Eagle allowed himself to be fooled on another occasion when he was a contractor for the Ringling sideshow attractions at Madison Square Garden. This time, "Brenda Beatty the Bearded Lady" was a fellow named Bernie Rogers. During the engagement, the sideshow was visited by a city vice detective who wanted to know, "Is the bearded lady a female impersonator?" As it turned out, the detective was there as a result of a signed complaint by "Stella the Bearded Lady"—a genuine one whose real name was Betty Macgregor. Eagle alerted "Brenda" and sent her to the hotel while he went to the office to meet the detective. He was accompanied by Dotty Williams, "a beautiful midget lady who had worked a number of years for Nate." Hall (1991, 7–8) picks up the story: "Nate said, 'She looks like a woman, dresses like a woman, and tells me she's a woman. That's good enough for me.' Pointing at Dottie, he continued, 'This little lady has worked for me several years. She looks like a woman, dresses like a woman, tells me she's a woman and during our years together, I have never asked her to raise her dress and drop her panties to show me she's a woman.' Now directing his remarks to the detective he said, 'You look like a man, you dress like a man, that's good enough for me.'" The detective, learning that the alleged bearded lady would be leaving the city in just five days, thought it over. "He then suggested he write to the complainant asking additional information," says Hall. "By the time a return letter could arrive the show would be gone, eliminating the problem."

A few months later, Bernie Rogers was killed in a Nevada traffic accident. Stella Macgregor continued to exhibit as "Stella the Bearded Lady," appearing in the Ringling sideshow in Washington, D.C. in 1973 (the last really big sideshow assembled by Hall & Christ). Shortly afterward, Stella gave up show business for a career as an accountant (Hall 1991, 8).

Gaffing has had its inspired—and ridiculous—moments. Bobby Reynolds once had the idea to create his own "gorilla girl" (rather like "Monkey Girl" Percilla Bejano, discussed in chapter 6). He turned to Carrie Adams, an African American woman who performed a dance act for the bally. Bobby told her, "Carrie, we're going to make you a star." And she replied, "Mr. Bob, when you start talkin' like that it's gonna be bad." But Bobby pacified her and soon was attaching crepe hair with spirit gum all over her face. "And," he says, "I gave her the first Afro that I think ever was." Bobby sat her on the bally platform with a silk scarf over her head and spieled: "Half animal, half human. Her mother was normal; what was her father? These things will be explained on the inside." Inside, the "Gorilla Girl" would lecture on herself, Bobby says. She began:

"My name is Carrie Adams, and dah dah dah." So it's a hot day, and we're working Winston-Salem, North Carolina, or something, and it's really hot, and she was perspiring quite well, and the hair is down like this, on the side, hanging there. And I take the scarf off and there's that, and I put it up with my elbow, and I says, "This is the way we go through life, exactly like this." But she says, "Mr. Bob! Mr. Bob, you gotta put better glue on there. Me a black woman and you a New York Jew, they're gonna kill us down here! They're gonna kill us down here!" I said, "Well, I don't know what to do, Carrie." She says, "I ain't gonna do this no more, honey, unless you give me some real good glue, 'cause I ain't goin' with this stuff, this spirit gum." I says, well, I says, . . . "Oh I'll figure it out." So I got the stuff that we patched the tent with, it's called Brown Bear, and I put that on there and I glue this onto her face, and it held up for the whole day.

Unfortunately, it held better than that: it would not come off! Carrie used alcohol and rubbed and rubbed until her face puffed up, and Bobby decided to seek medical help. He finally found a doctor's office and went inside:

"Doctor, you're not going to believe this." He says, "Try me, son." I said, "Well, I got this lady, I glued hair on her face, and we charge a quarter to see her—half-animal, half-human—and I used this glue and I can't get. . . ." He says, "I'd like to see this. Bring her in." So I bring her in there, and he sits down and gingerly takes the hair off, and puts some salve on, and he says, "Son, I wouldn't be doin' this for at least two or three weeks."

Soon, Bobby had found a new latex adhesive, and he continued spieling "Half animal, half human" until the season ended (Reynolds 2001).

A gaffed presentation reminiscent of Bobby's Gorilla Girl was Lionella the Lion-Faced Girl, a grind show operated by the husband-and-wife team of Jeff and Sue Murray. "Direct from Germany," read one banner; "Stranger than Rosemary's Baby," proclaimed another. In fact, Lionella was the product of "a partial mask that was laboriously glued onto the poor girl's face every day with spirit gum adhesive" (Ray 1993, 35, 45).

Among various other gaffed oddities, one was unique. She was Koo-Koo the Bird Girl, who was with the Ringling sideshow for many years. She posed for the annual Congress of Freaks group photograph during the 1920s and was among the oddities featured in Tod Browning's 1932 film *Freaks*. She is always instantly recognizable, with her diminutive size, big round eyeglasses, feathered costume, and large single plume sticking straight up from the top of her head. Anton LaVey, the "Satanist," who knew her, told Mannix (1999, 119): "She was not a freak at all. She was a gangling, homely girl from New York who dressed in special costumes and learned to exaggerate her worst features. She sucked in her cheeks and popped out her eyes to make herself look grotesque. Otherwise," LaVey adds, "she was a nice, quiet person whom you'd never notice."

Gaffed Acts

There are many other types of gaffs, and here we look at sideshow working acts that were gaffed.

Some acts, although essentially genuine, contain gaffed elements. For example, the previously mentioned tattooed strongman Rasmus Nielsen lifted an anvil allegedly weighing 250 pounds "by his breasts" (Gilbert 1996). Actually, according to anatomical wonder Melvin Burkhart, the anvil was gaffed, being made of aluminum. "It was heavy," acknowledged Burkhart, "but it wasn't a steel anvil" (quoted in Taylor and Kotcher 2002).

Other strongman stunts were exposed by magical authority Walter B. Gibson, who gained fame as creator of the Shadow. (I once spent an enjoyable afternoon talking with Gibson while I was resident magician at the Houdini museum in Niagara Falls, Ontario.) In his delightful book *Secrets of Magic: Ancient and Modern*, Gibson (1967) tells of wooden dumbbells painted to look like they were made of iron, as well as hollow dumbbells that were "weighed on false scales, so that the strong man would appear to be lifting a weight of double size." (See figure 8.11.)

Then there was the veritable Samson, or so he seemed, who could lift a dumbbell that supposedly weighed half a ton. With difficulty, two men wheeled it on stage. Two strong men from the audience were invited up but were unable to lift the great weight, whereupon the performer accomplished the feat to enthusiastic applause. However, says Gibson (1967, 62–64): "During one of his shows, two brawny steel workers stepped on the stage when

FIGURE 8.11. On the midway, in front of an unidentified show's banner line, a strongman hoists a large dumbbell with one hand. (Author's collection)

this modern Samson called for volunteers. They braced themselves, determined to raise the dumb-bell, while the strong man smilingly looked on. As the men raised their shoulders, a strange thing happened. Up came the dumb-bell and the truck with it! As they held the dumb-bell on their shoulders, the truck dangled below. The audience was momentarily stunned—then the truth dawned upon everyone." As Gibson explains: "The dumb-bell was a hollow sham which weighed less than a hundred pounds. It had two slots which fitted into pins in the truck. When the truck was brought on, the dumb-bell was locked tightly in place and could not be lifted. The strong man simply turned it in the right direction, releasing the catches which enabled him to raise the dumb-bell with ease. The truck was so heavy that the average man could only push it, but the combined strength of the powerful steel workers brought the truck up with the dumb-bell."

One type of sideshow exhibit that was "one hundred percent presentation" was the reputed "wild man" or "wild woman" act (Bogdan 1990, 260). Sharing the platform at P. T. Barnum's Second American Museum with the

Two-Headed Girl (conjoined twins Millie-Christine) were the Wild Australian Children. Their pitch book called them Hoomio and Iola and claimed that they had been discovered by explorers, who first mistook them for kangaroos. Described as "long, sharp-toothed cannibals," the pair was suspected of being the "link" between humans and the orangutan. However, according to *P. T. Barnum: America's Greatest Showman* (Kunhardt et al. 1995, 209), "The secret that only showmen back then knew was that in truth, the Wild Australian Children were severely retarded microcephalic siblings from Circleville, Ohio."

In 1880 Barnum exhibited a pair of muscular dwarfs with long hair billed as the Wild Men of Borneo. Named Waino and Plutano, they were described in their pitch books as "so wild and ferocious . . . they could easily subdue tigers." Their "capture" was portrayed in a chromolithographed advertisement showing armed men netting and caging them. Their act included demonstrations of strength and challenges to men in the audience to fight with the diminutive savages. Actually, they were retarded brothers from Ohio, Hiram and Barney Davis, and they continued to be exhibited past the turn of the century (Kunhardt et al. 1995, 270–71).

An 1890s exhibit, the Mexican Wild Man, featured a long-haired man dressed in furs. A circa 1891 photograph by Charles Eisenmann depicts him sitting on a "boulder" and holding up a hand to reveal grotesquely long fingernails (thus making him something of a "made" oddity and not just a gaffed one). His name was George Stall, and he had a successful run, but most of the wild men and women "were so transient that they changed from month to month" (Bogdan 1990, 260–61).

An example of the transient nature of the act comes from circus owner and showman W. C. Coup (1901). He told of visiting a dime museum and seeing a savage fellow with a hairy body and yellowed skin who ravenously ate raw meat thrown to him. He had purportedly been captured from a Kentucky cave, but Coup recognized him as having once been a different act with his own show. "For his new job he had dyed his skin yellow and his whiskers and his hair black. After being a wild man for awhile he resumed his former employment as 'Ivanovitch, the hairy man.'"

Another illustration of the transient nature of the act is this amusing circus anecdote: A young man showed up on the grounds of the John Robinson family circus (in the 1860s) looking for a job. He had long hair and unkempt whiskers and seemed promising as a wild man exhibit. The circus man gave him a dollar to seal the bargain and ordered him to show up for work in the afternoon. But when he returned, he was scarcely recognizable; his hair and beard had been neatly trimmed. Questioned, he explained that he had decided to invest his dollar at the barber's to make a neat appearance for his new job (Bogdan 1990, 69).

Wild men have been portrayed in various ways. Once, to present a troupe of genuine Ubangi saucer-lipped oddities from French Equatorial Africa, showman Lou Dufour enlisted a muscular African American entertainer known as Woo Foo, whose act included fire walking and performing as a wild man. But there were amusingly unintended consequences after an aide to the troupe's aged chief died. As the tom-toms began their beat, says Dufour (1977, 55):

> The gals in the troupe took to Lucas' rhythm in a big way, picking up his motions and whooping it up in general. They seemed happy at last, but he began to get worried. The females were warming up to his body and a few of them had made it known to him that they would like to play house. The old chief was also happy. He started presenting Lucas with presents to show his appreciation for what he anticipated would be genuine aid in his time of need—Lucas realized now that the dead aide had performed all the stud duties in the family. He wanted to quit at once. We jacked up his pay by another twenty-five dollars a day to keep him contented. He was all made up and ready for a show when one of our belles grabbed him and tried to draw him into the grass hut. He screamed, "That's it! That's it!" and vanished, costume and all. His disappearance wrecked the show, proving how ungrateful performers can be when you give them their big break.

Somewhat similar in theme was a 1970s performer styled as an African witch doctor. His banner (by Snap Wyatt) depicted him holding aloft a human skull while dancing on a bed of nails (a sideshow mainstay discussed in the following chapter). A bonfire and an idol-like effigy provided additional atmosphere.

In carny parlance, the wild man or woman was often called a *geek*. In 1903 the Kansas state senate passed legislation forbidding the exhibition of "Glomming Geeks," whom the lawmakers defined as "persons who eat live snakes, rats or other small animals" (McKennon 1972, 1:60). Biting the heads off snakes or chickens was a common geek stunt that turned the stomachs of some and disgusted most of the rest. Often such a geek was an alcoholic who performed in order to indulge his addiction and have a place to sleep (Keyser 2001; Bogdan 1990, 262). Showman Fred Olen Ray, in his *Grind Show: Weirdness as Entertainment* (1993, 14), explains that the act is no longer common, since such people can be seen for free on the street (sadly enough).

Among the female geeks or wild woman acts was Eeka, whose name was an evocative amalgam of *geek, freak,* and *"eek."* Billed as Strange Eeka, she was the brainchild of Chuck and Al Renton, who "were, if not the best, certainly the most memorable Geek Show operators in the last half century" (Meah 1996, 138). Over several years, many women played the title role. A 1970s banner by Fred G. Johnson, headed "Eeka and Giant Snakes," illustrates the interface of different sideshow acts—wild girl, geek, and snake charmer (the last featured in chapter 9). (See figures 8.12 and 8.13.)

Along with Eeka there was Zoma, whose 1950s banners—"Zoma Depraved" and "Zoma the Sadist"—depict her as a fanged savage with a mass of hair as wild as her alleged nature. She is shown alternately headlocking a hapless sailor and using a jagged knife to attack a wild girl rival (Johnson et al. 1996, 140–41).

A sideshow geek was the subject of William Lindsay Gresham's dark study, *Nightmare Alley*. The novel (and subsequent movie) traces the decline of a successful sideshow "mind reader" as he descends into alcoholism and, ultimately, the life of a geek. Transformed by dark grease paint, filthy underwear, a ratty wig, and still more drink, he becomes, states Leslie Fiedler (1993, 345), "a creature disgusting even to his own sodden self," reduced to "gnawing off the heads of chickens for a drink."

The irrepressible showman Bobby Reynolds (2001) once surprised me by saying, "I was a geek for a while." He elaborated: "We used to kill chickens: You did that today they'd carry you away to the SPCA and beat the shit out of you. But we used to take the chicken and we'd grab it and we'd slit its neck

(Above) FIGURE 8.12. Eeka was a wild-woman act featured in this line of banners by Fred G. Johnson, circa 1970s. (Author's collection) (Below) FIGURE 8.13. Eeka was reprised for this Hall & Christ sideshow in Allentown, Pennsylvania, 2001. (Photo by author)

FIGURE 8.14. Single-O exhibit features a wild man who proved not to be wigged out, only wigged. (Photo by author)

and then squeeze it and the blood would hit the top of the ceiling of the tent and rain over and they'd let out this yell, 'Yaaaaaahhhhhhh!' And then you'd reach down and get a rope and throw it into the audience and they thought it was a snake—'cause you're in a pit with all these snakes—and they'd run out of the tent and that was it." Did he actually eat the raw chicken? "No no no. What we did is we killed the chickens and we gave 'em to the cookhouse, and the cookhouse would wash them, clean 'em. We paid fifty cents for the chicken. They would buy 'em for a quarter, they would clean 'em up, and then we would have chicken at the cookhouse." (The cookhouse is a great circus and carnival institution. It is not only the show's dining facility but also the place where show people engage in *cutting up jackpots*—the carny equivalent of "chewing the fat" and "swapping lies" [McKennon 1972, 2:146].)

A modern version of the wild man exhibit—perhaps an indication of how low the genre has sunk—is the single-O show I visited at the 2001 Erie

County Fair in western New York. Its signage proclaimed "WILDMAN / He's Still Alive" but "Condemned to a Living Death" (figure 8.14). Promoted as "An Educational Exhibit," it promised, "See the Horrors of Drug Abuse." Other panels continued the message, with the word "Alive" repeated over and over. A mere 50¢ took one inside to see a swarthy fellow in a fright wig. Chained in a tiny cell, he was responsive to visits by patrons, whereupon he flailed and rattled his chains. Humanely, a small electric fan provided the wild man some relief from the hot weather.

9 WORKING ACTS

APART FROM HUMAN ODDITIES, THE second main category of side-show performers consists of those who exhibit a special skill. Such performers are known in carny parlance as working acts.

Fire-eaters

Fire manipulation is an ancient art, combining skill with danger. One of the earliest of the fire-eating wonders lived in the Roman era—a Syrian called Eunus (d. 133 B.C.). In order to excite his fellow slaves to revolt against Roman authority, Eunus claimed that he had received supernatural powers from the gods, who foretold that he would someday be king. As proof, Eunus exhaled jets of fire, just like the legendary dragon. However, a writer named Florus was skeptical and guessed the secret of the fire-breathing trick. Eunus hid a nutshell in his mouth that contained burning material. The shell had a small opening at each end so that when the fake wizard blew through it, sparks and flames were projected. Eunus's rebellion was initially successful, and he named himself King Antiochus; however, the Romans soon regained control. Eunus was captured and died in prison. (Christopher 1962, 2; *Encyclopaedia Britannica* 1960, s.v. "Eunus"; Gibson 1967, 41).

In seventeenth-century England, a fire-eater named Richardson appeared to dine on various fiery materials. He munched glowing coals, drank flaming liquids, and otherwise attempted to prove that he was unharmed by fire. In the eighteenth century a fire-eater named Robert Powell performed similar stunts at British fairs. Powell supplemented his admission receipts by selling a lotion for the treatment of burns (Gardner 1962, 59). And in the first part of the nineteenth century an Italian woman, Signora Josephine Giardelli, was exhibited in London as the "Fireproof Female." It was advertised that "She will, without the least symptoms of pain, put boiling melted lead in her mouth, and emit the same with the imprint of her teeth thereon; red-hot irons will be passed over various parts of her body; she will walk over a bar of red-hot iron with her naked feet; will . . . put boiling oil in her mouth!"(Dawes 1979, 57).

Giardelli was rivaled by Ivan Chabert (1792–1859), who arrived in London in 1818, his posters proclaiming him the "Fire King" (figure 9.1). He too ate burning materials. As the *Times* reported in 1826: "he refreshed himself with a hearty meal of phosphorous . . . he next swallowed . . . several spoonfuls of boiling oil and, as dessert . . . , helped himself with his naked hand to a considerable quantity of molten lead" (Dawes 1979, 57–60). But it was Chabert's feat of the fiery oven that created the greatest sensation. He entered the oven—actually an iron chest about six by seven feet that had been heated to some 600 degrees Fahrenheit—carrying a thick steak and a leg of lamb. Closing the doors behind him, he remained there, talking with the audience through a tin tube, while the meat cooked. Then he flung open the doors and stepped out in triumph.

Of course, Monsieur Chabert was no more fireproof than other such performers. He merely used magic tricks and simple scientific principles to create that illusion. For example, as magician and writer Walter Gibson (1967, 42) explains: "When he 'swallows' burning oil, the performer does not ladle liquid, but merely lets the spoon become wet. The few drops that adhere will burn for a moment, giving him time to raise the spoon to his mouth. Then he exhales, extinguishing the flame, and immediately takes the spoon in his mouth, as though swallowing the oil." Also, "Chewing of molten metals until they become solid is accomplished by using an alloy of bismuth, lead and block tin, which has a very low melting point. It is dropped upon the moist tongue where it will harden without burning and becomes a solid lump." For the apparent sipping of burning fuel, a wooden spoon is recommended, "because a metal spoon becomes so hot that it burns your lips" (Mannix 1996, 47). As to Chabert's ordeal of the burning oven, that was a magician's trick. First, Chabert placed the thermometer in the fire to give the impression that the oven was very hot. Actually, the temperature was just above 200 degrees. And, because heat rises, the lower portion of the oven remained relatively cool. The fire was lit in the center of the large iron box, and Chabert was able to lie safely on the floor by the doors, his head covered by a protective hood. He could breathe,

FIGURE 9.1. The "Fire King," Ivan Chabert (1792–1859), whose feats included entering an oven heated to 600 degrees and remaining until a leg of lamb was cooked. (Sketch by author)

of course, through the speaking tube. So that the meat would cook quickly, Chabert hung it on hooks directly over the fire. When it was done, he made his dramatic exit from the oven (Gibson 1967, 42).

Some performers have attempted to prove their resistance to fire by walking barefoot across red-hot embers (figure 9.2). This is possible because wood does not conduct heat well and because the time of contact is quite brief. (Experiments show that it is possible to make a short walk across hot coals or a longer walk over cooler embers. As most people know, one can pass a finger

FIGURE 9.2. I walk barefoot over a bed of hot coals. (Photo by Benjamin Radford)

quickly through a candle flame, but drawing the finger slowly through the flame would result in burns.)

Fire eating, however, is the mainstay of sideshow fire acts (figure 9.3). Reports of fire-eating performers date from as early as 1633, and they flourished over the next two centuries. "By then," states Gibson (1967, 41) "the art was gradually relegated to dime museums and circus sideshows, but these survivals of medieval magic still awe and impress spectators today."

FIGURE 9.3. "Fire Eater" is a mainstay among ten-in-one banners, like this one at Coney Island's Sideshows by the Seashore. (Photo by author)

Interesting fire-eaters of the past include a nine-year-old purveyor of the "Chinese fire trick," a Miss Cassillis who toured England as part of a juvenile troupe in 1820. Another was Carlo Alberto, who performed in theaters in England and America as the "Great African Wonder, the Fire King"; an 1843 bill promises that he would also "sing several new and popular Negro melodies." Then there was the great Chinese magician who combined conjuring and fire eating, Ching Ling Foo (b. 1854). He had imitators, notably "Chung Ling Soo," who was really an Englishman, William Ellsworth Robinson (1861–1918). Robinson wore suitable makeup and dress and spoke only through an interpreter—convincing everyone that he was a real Chinaman until he was fatally wounded on stage performing the bullet-catching trick (Houdini 1920, 79–83; Christopher 1962, 169–71).

Among the fire marvels of the 1930s were James O'Satyrdae, a "fire manipulator" at the 1939 world's fair in New York (Dufour 1977, 123), and a Dr. Mayfield, who appeared as a Ripley Odditorium attraction. According to one writer, Mayfield "shaved himself with a blazing blowtorch, later turned the torch on his unprotected eyeball, and finally put the torch directly into his mouth, extinguishing the flame with his tongue" (Considine 1961, 143). The blowtorch stunt (figure 9.4) is accomplished by turning the flame down to minimum heat and keeping the flame moving sufficiently fast (Gresham 1953, 200). Other twentieth-century fire-eaters were Andy Briskey, Pete Terhurne ("Poobah the Fire-eating Dwarf"), Freddy Lulling, Dan Mannix, Bill "The Baron" Unchs, and many others, including, of course, Ward Hall and Bobby Reynolds (Hall 1991, 53; Taylor and Kotcher 2002, 132; Taylor 2001, 57).

The basic equipment for fire eating is the torch—easily improvised by using Elmer's school glue to affix several turns of doubled cheesecloth to a length of coat-hanger wire—and a metal can into which is poured a small amount of fuel. Naphtha or Coleman brand white gas may be used, but lamp oil (a liquid paraffin) is less toxic, burns cooler, and has noncombustible fumes, although it is rather smoky.

Fire eating is not a trick, but there is a trick to it—or, rather, several techniques that the performer relies on. There is no special substance used to coat the mouth, save one—saliva—and it is important that the lips, mouth, and tongue be well moistened with it. Since flames burn upward, to keep them from burning the roof of the mouth, the head must be tipped well back, so that the mouth is aimed straight up. As the flaming torch approaches the lips, the performer breathes out gently and steadily; otherwise, as one carny instructor told a novice (Mannix 1996, 20), "you'll get gas fumes into your lungs, and there'll be an explosion there like in the cylinder of a car. Only your lungs ain't built to take it." Finally, the performer closes his or her mouth, and the flame goes out.

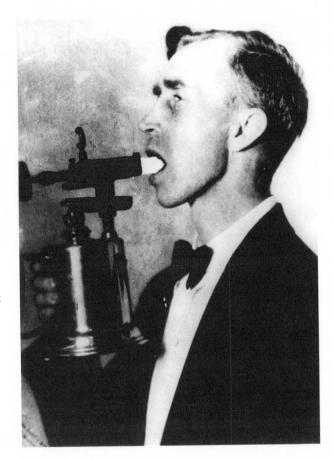

FIGURE 9.4. The blowtorch stunt is demonstrated. (Author's collection)

Of course, there is much more to it than that, as I learned from a book on the subject—*Fire Eating: A Manual of Instruction* (Garth 1993). I also received personal instruction in the art from "Pele the Fire Goddess" (Lynne Couillard), a professional performer who does a complete fire act, performing at Renaissance fairs and other venues. Pele (who takes her name from the ancient Hawaiian volcano goddess) taught me many fine points. For instance, the torch should not approach the upturned mouth vertically (as shown in some illustrations [Garth 1993]), or the rising flames may burn the hand. If the length of the torch makes this unlikely, it is probably too long and may tend to wobble. The torch should instead approach at about a forty-five-degree angle. The tongue is extended to guide the torch into the mouth but then moves to a position with

(Left) FIGURE 9.5. I demonstrate the basics of fire eating. Step 1: Bringing the torch to the mouth at the proper angle. (Right) FIGURE 9.6. Step 2: Using the *wet* tongue to guide the torch into the mouth. (Photos by Benjamin Radford)

the tip touching the backs of the lower teeth. (During practice with an unlit torch, I had a tendency to curl my tongue backward, but Pele warned me that I would be exposing the sensitive bottom of the mouth to probable burning, and I practiced to correct the problem before "lighting up.") The wrapped portion of the torch should not be too long. It must be fully inserted into the mouth, which then closes on the wire beyond, yet it should not go to the back of the mouth. Since the metal part of the torch can get quite hot and burn the lips, it is best to close the mouth by simply "biting" the wire (figures 9.5 to 9.8).

Some fire stunts require a torch sufficiently moistened with one of the more volatile fuels. *Trailing* involves making a swipe along the arm and thus leaving a momentary trail of fire behind (figure 9.9). One presses down on the torch as it initially makes contact with the arm in order to deposit the fuel. Hesitation at this point (as I discovered) can cause a burn. *Fire on the tongue* is a similar feat in which the torch is pressed on the tongue so that when the torch is removed, the tongue remains briefly aflame. (The tongue is well coated with saliva for this feat.) A *transfer from the tongue* uses the flame left in the previous feat to ignite an unlit torch (Garth 1993, 48–55). Garth (1993, 73) describes another transfer—*lighting a cigarette with lit fingers.* The fingers are pressed to a lit, fuel-moist

(Left) FIGURE 9.7. Step 3: Closing the mouth. (Right) FIGURE 9.8. Step 4: Exhaling. (Photos by Benjamin Radford)

FIGURE 9.9. Trailing, as I demonstrate, leaves a momentary trail of fire along the arm. (Photo by Benjamin Radford)

FIGURE 9.10. Poobah the Fire-eating Dwarf (Pete Terhurne) performs alongside the outside talker during a nighttime bally at the Allentown, Pennsylvania, fair, 2001. (Photo by author)

torch, and the transferred flame lasts long enough for the performer to light a cigarette with it. The trick is to accomplish the feat quickly. To facilitate this, an unfiltered cigarette is used so that one can draw harder on it. Also, a little of the tobacco is removed from the end that will be lit; this causes the protruding paper to be easily ignited, which in turn ignites the tobacco.

Safety procedures are essential. One tries to avoid performing outdoors, to keep the wind from blowing flames into the eyes. When working the bally (figure 9.10), however, the professional has to stall until the breeze dies down and tries to turn the body so the wind blows from the back. Fire-resistant clothing, such as blue jeans, is recommended. The torches are kept well soaked in the liquid fuel; otherwise, the fuel would burn off, and the cotton would begin to burn at a hotter temperature. The excess must be shaken off into a bucket, though, so the torch does not drip flaming fuel. A damp rag may be kept handy for the emergency extinguishing of any small fire on the hand or elsewhere

(Garth 1993, 16), although Pele cautions that this method may cause steam burns. She keeps a carbon dioxide extinguisher (the kind that can be used on people) at the ready.

Showman Bobby Reynolds (2001), who has performed an impressive number of working acts, including fire eating, says philosophically: "You know, you burn yourself a little bit, but other than that. . . ." He quips, "The guy that don't know how to do it properly makes an ash out of himself."

Long ago in Toronto I knew Marcel Horne, who sported on each upper arm a tattoo of a fire-breathing god. He performed in the carnivals as "Diablo the Human Volcano." I wrote the accompanying poem in 1970 after watching a performance.

Marcel was a fire-*breather,* that is, one who sips the fuel, then spits it at a torch, thus throwing a great ball of fire across the stage. It is a dramatic effect. It is also a dangerous one. Performers now avoid gasoline and use only less volatile fuels such as kerosene or lamp oil, but the stunt is still dangerous. Failure to spew the liquid as a fine, atomized mist can mean fuel on the performer's face (Garth 1993, 21–22, 61–63). One writer tells in breathless style what happened in one instance: "it splashed from his mouth

The Fire Breather

You step in lit
circles, light
is your
shadow at the core
of fire.
Match
to torch,
your speech
flames,
your name
burns.
You taste,
then wheel and spit
that
thunder-bolt-
shot
light,
that
burnt
shout.
Unknown to us now
how
it is you burn,
our hands
leap up like flames.
The crackling drowns
you out.

and all his face exploded and he ran howling through the crowd in agonized frenzy and afterwards was captured in a state of almost nudity and taken to the workhouse infirmary, where he remains in dreadful condition" (Gardner 1962, 70).

Sword Swallowers

The art of sword swallowing is quite ancient. Itinerant jugglers performed the feat for Egyptian pharaohs, and Marcus Agrippa (63?–12 B.C.) mentioned witnessing the effect in ancient Rome. However, he had been drinking at the time and later attributed what he had seen to the wine. A sixteenth-century writer also witnessed sword swallowing and concluded that it was accomplished with the assistance of demons (Mannix 1996, 49–51).

Witnesses to sword swallowing sometimes suspect trickery. Fake knives and swords do exist, but those with single *retractable* blades must have handles that are longer than half the overall length. And swords with telescoping blades—such as those made by the Parisian magic manufacturer Vosin—are suitable only for theatrical purposes and amateurish demonstrations (Gardner 1962, 76; Houdini 1920, 142–43). The fact is, real sword swallowers swallow real swords (figures 9.11 and 9.12). The important secret is that the performer must conquer what is known as the "gag reflex." According to the great magician Houdini, in his *Miracle Mongers and Their Methods* (1920, 138): "To accomplish the sword-swallowing feat, it is only necessary to overcome the nausea that results from the metal's touching the mucous membrane of the pharynx, for there is an unobstructed passage, large enough to accommodate several of the thin blades used, from the mouth to the bottom of the stomach. This passage is not straight, but the passing of the sword straightens it. Some throats are more sensitive than others, but practice will soon accustom any throat to the passage of the blade."

One sword swallower of the early nineteenth century was Ramo Samee from Madras, India. He was with a troupe of Indian jugglers who performed in England. A playbill dated Friday, August 2, 1822, heralded his appearance at the Royal Coburg Theatre. Among other feats, he was to balance a ten-pound pagoda on his nose and conclude his performance by swallowing a flaming sword. Two decades later, on Monday, July 11, 1842, Samee was still entertain-

(Above) FIGURE 9.11. In this nineteenth-century wood engraving, a performer swallows a sword, flanked by the implements of his art.

(Right) FIGURE 9.12. Illustration from a nineteenth-century *Scientific American* showing the position a sword blade occupies inside the body.

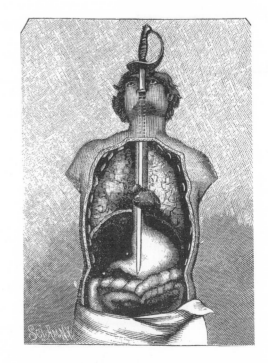

ing, closing his act by "Swallowing a Sword 2-ft. long!!!" "This wonderful feat," according to the playbill, "still continues to astonish the most eminent medical men in London" (Jay 1987, 287–88; 2001, 125).

A later sword swallower, perhaps the first of the great modern ones, was a supposed French-Canadian calling himself Chevalier Cliquot. At the age of eighteen, he ran away with the circus and traveled to South America. In Buenos Aires he watched an elderly man swallow a machete and, inspired, began to practice with a silver wire. He advanced to swallowing a twenty-two-inch cavalry sword and a bayonet weighted with a pair of eighteen-pound dumbbells. Reports Gardner (1962, 75), "The most harrowing moment of his act featured a bayonet fixed backwards to a rifle. He would kneel with the point of the blade directly down his throat, his sister would pull the trigger, and the recoil of the rifle would fire the sword down his gullet."

Once, he satisfied some curious physicians by swallowing a borrowed watch on its chain. The doctors took turns listening to the ticking through Cliquot's belly. One explained: "Poor, outraged nature is biding her time, but mark me, she will have a terrible revenge sooner or later." Indeed, the performer did have some harrowing experiences, such as the time he took his bows while a sword was still lodged in his esophagus. This bent the weapon at an angle, and Cliquot's throat was injured during the removal (Gardner 1962, 74–75; Houdini 1920, 139–41).

Although Cliquot was a genuine performer, shrewdly offering a £500 reward in the event he failed to swallow a sword, he apparently did engage in a deception. According to a writer in *Royal Magazine,* Cliquot was not a French-Canadian at all but one Fred McLane from Chicago (Jay 1987, 289–90).

Cliquot had a host of successors. Houdini (1920, 142) mentions two, the first having studied under Cliquot: "Delmo Fritz was not only an excellent sword-swallower, but a good showman as well. The last time I saw him he was working the 'halls' in England. I hope he saved his money, for he was a clean man with a clean reputation, and, I can truly say, he was a master in his manner of indulging his appetite for the cold steel." Houdini also mentions an Italian magician, Deodota, who combined sword swallowing with conjuring before giving up life as a performer for the "jewelry business" in downtown New York.

A pupil of Delmo Fritz was one of the great women sword swallowers, Edith Clifford. She was born in 1884 in London and began swallowing blades at the age of fifteen. In 1901, when the Barnum & Bailey Circus was on a foreign tour, she joined the show in Vienna. She introduced a number of novelties, including swallowing giant scissors, a saw ("with ugly looking teeth," said Houdini, "although somewhat rounded at the points"), a set of ten narrow blades, and—following Cliquot—a bayonet driven down her throat by a cannon loaded with a ten-gauge shell. Houdini, who visited the show in 1919 especially to see Clifford, spoke highly of her. He noted that she had "perfected an act that has found favor even in the Royal Courts of Europe." She was "possessed of more than ordinary personal charms, a refined taste for dressing both herself and her stage, and an unswerving devotion to her art." Her stage was "handsomely arranged," he said, and "occupied the place of honor in the section devoted to freaks and specialties" (Houdini 1920, 147–51). William Lindsay Gresham (1953, 202) wrote that "the first sword swallower that I ever saw was also the best," describing Edith as "a pretty girl" who performed "gracefully." He bought her pitch book for a quarter and called it "one of the shrewdest angles I ever saw" for a sideshow act: it was an actual instruction booklet. However, Gresham lamented, "I kept that booklet for years but never mastered my gag reflex."

As these examples demonstrate, sword swallowers found many ways to keep their acts from becoming trite. Some, like Clifford, used thin, narrow swords that enabled them to swallow several at once. "Slowly withdrawing them one at time, and throwing them on the stage in different directions," states Houdini (1920, 143), "makes an effective display." Another stunt was to attach a small strong lightbulb to the tip of a narrow cane. With the platform darkened, the audience could watch the light pass from throat to esophagus to stomach—an impressive sight. Houdini (1920, 143) noted, "The medical profession now make use of this idea."

Eventually, this led to the idea of using a neon tube. Ward Hall suggests that a female sword swallower named "Lady Patricia"—Patricia Zerm—was the first to feature the swallowing of a neon tube. "She always wore beautiful gowns," recalls Hall. "It was a beautiful act" (Taylor and Kotcher 2002, 15).

Dan Mannix (1996, 49) tells of a performer he calls Rafael who decided to specialize in neon. "Other men swalla one neon tube," he said. "I only man do all tubes—no swords, no bayonets, no corkscrews." Mannix thus purchased Rafael's collection of blades, which included a giant nickel-plated scissors.

> Rafael told me that he had gotten most of his swords from hock shops. They were old cavalry sabers and lodge swords. He had the blades nickel-plated to make them smooth. He always made sure that the blades were firmly fitted in the hilts. Sometimes after swallowing a sword, the blade falls out of the hilt and the performer really swallows it. Unless he can reach the broken end of the blade with his thumb and forefinger, he is indeed in a predicament. Rafael had had the giant scissors made up specially as a flash item. The bayonet was a standard one he had gotten at an army surplus store.

The blades were displayed on an ornate, heart-shaped stand. It broke down for travel, and the blades were placed in scabbards to prevent scratching or chipping (Mannix 1996, 51).

Mannix learned many lessons from Rafael, such as wiping the sword both before and after swallowing it—before, because "even the smallest particles of dust adhering to the blade could make you retch," and after, to remove the acidic stomach fluids, which corrode the blades' expensive nickel plating (Mannix 1996, 51).

Although sword swallowing is an authentic act, performers have been known to use a trick or two. For example, according to Houdini (1920, 138), "When a sword with a sharp point is used the performer secretly slips a rubber cap over the point to guard against accident." Another safety feature is use of a "guiding tube"—a type of protective sheath that can be swallowed secretly before using a gun to drive down the blade or swallowing a red-hot sword (Gibson 1967, 55).

One dime museum performer did a variation on sword swallowing that was a mixture of genuineness and trickery. He appeared to swallow sharp straight razors. The swallowing was real, but after the blades' sharpness had been demonstrated, the razors were switched for dull ones. This was accomplished by means of a bandana or handkerchief with secret pockets that held the substitute razors. Under cover of wiping the blades, the performer made the switch—not too skillfully when he was being closely observed by Houdini (1920, 143–44).

Some mock advice was offered to would-be sword swallowers in a pamphlet titled "A Text Book on the Art of Sword Swallowing Explaining How to Do It Sixteen Different Ways." It was sold by a husband-and-wife team of sword swallowers who billed themselves as the "Victorinas." Actually, "Joe Van Victorina" was an American, Joseph B. Hallworth (b. 1872), and "Lady Victorina" was Kitty (Fisher) Hallworth. Among the pamphlet's tongue-in-cheek suggestions was a supposedly Chinese method of using opium to dull the senses. Another was to "hire somebody to do it for you, as it may save you much annoyance, and though more expensive is very satisfactory in the long run" (Jay 1987, 290–93). This seems like sound advice.

Mrs. Hallworth may have been the "Victorina" who had a close call at the Chicago Museum in 1902. The incident illustrates why one-piece swords became standard (in addition to the ease of demonstrating their lack of trickery). Victorina was swallowing a thin, dagger-like blade when it separated from the handle. According to Gardner (1962, 76): "Almost fainting with fear, Victorina nevertheless had the presence of mind to drop the handle, constrict her throat and reach down her gullet to catch the butt end of the blade with the tips of her fingers and draw it out. Had she lost it, it might have plunged right through the bottom of her stomach."

Phenomenal Ingesters

In addition to geeks, who may bite the heads off chickens, and fire-eaters and sword swallowers, who have a taste for the dangerous, there are others with seemingly bizarre appetites. Such was a Silesian who appeared in Prague in 1006, who, for an admission price, would swallow up to thirty-six stones the size of pigeon eggs. Six centuries later an Italian stone eater named Francois Battalia was described in a somewhat exaggerated account:

> His manner is to put three or four stones into a spoon, and so putting them into his mouth together, he swallows them all down, one

after another; then (first spitting) he drinks a glass of beer after them. He devours about half a peck of these stones every day, and when he clinks upon his stomach, or shakes his body, you may hear the stones rattle as if they were in a sack, all of which in twenty-four hours are resolved. Once in three weeks he voids a great quantity of sand, after which he has a fresh appetite for these stones, as we have for our victuals, and by these, with a cup of beer, and a pipe of tobacco, he has his whole subsistence.

Several stone eaters performed during the eighteenth century. One could be seen in London in 1788 for a mere two shillings and six pence. His playbill called him "the Most Wonderful Phenomenon of the Age, who Grinds and Swallows stones, etc., with as much ease as a Person would crack a nut, and masticate the Kernel." Another performer, a Spaniard, appeared at the Richmond Theater in 1790, and a later stone eater performed at the Globe Tavern (Houdini 1920, 154–60; Jay 1987, 277–84).

"All of these phenomenal gentry," wrote Houdini (1920, 160), "claimed to subsist entirely on stones, but their modern followers hardly dare make such claims, so that the art has fallen into disrepute." He added: "A number of years ago, in London, I watched several performances of one of these chaps who swallowed half a hatful of stones, nearly the size of hen's eggs, and then jumped up and down, to make them rattle in his stomach. I could discover no fake in the performance, and I finally gave him two and six for his secret, which was simple enough. He merely took a powerful physic to clear himself of the stones, and was then ready for the next performance." Other stone swallowers made use of various substances—such as freshly baked bread or thick cream—to line their stomachs in preparation for their acts (Gardner 1962, 78).

In addition to stone eaters were water spouters, or human fountains, who flourished in the mid-seventeenth century. In contrast to swallowers of swords and stones, they employed the opposite type of glottal control. Their ability was to artfully regurgitate quantities of imbibed liquid. Some used special mouthpieces to eject jets of water high above spectators' heads. Such demonstrations were especially effective outdoors, where sunlight made the arcing streams sparkle (Christopher 1962, 8–10).

Blaise Manfrede, known as the "Maltese Fountain," went on tour across Europe transforming water into wine, beer, milk, and other liquids before spouting it. Such performances combined actual skill with magic tricks (Jay 1987, 296–97). For example, Manfrede's pupil, Floram Marchand, performed in England in 1650 with a water-to-wine feat. He came on stage, drank some thirty small glasses of warm water, then spouted glasses of "full deep claret" (figure 9.13). However, the color became increasingly pale, indicating the secret of Marchand's stunt: he had previously cleared his stomach and swallowed a quantity of red dye (a Brazil-nut solution). Other liquids were produced in conjuring fashion—for example, by deftly switching a glass of water for one filled with rosewater that had been concealed behind his water pail (Gardner 1962, 77–78).

A remarkable ingester was Mac Norton (actually a Frenchman named Louis Claude Delair), who performed in European music halls dressed elegantly in full tails. To begin his act, Norton slowly swallowed a quantity of water, then spouted it in an arching stream into a container twenty feet away. Norton also drank an amazing quantity of beer—some thirty to forty large glass mugs. Actually, however, he secretly made use of his regurgitative skill. Houdini, who saw Norton perform in Nuremberg and was on the same program with him in Berlin, explained how he did it: The filled mugs stood on shelves behind Norton, and he brought them forward a few at a time (grasping two or three by their handles with each hand). When these had been quaffed, he turned for the next batch and took that opportunity to eject the beer into a hidden trough (Houdini 1920, 163; Gardner 1962, 79). Norton's main act entailed swallowing goldfish and half-grown frogs, hence his billing as the "Human Aquarium." Occasionally, however, something could go wrong. Houdini wrote: "I remember his anxiety on one occasion when returning to his dressing room; it seems he had lost a frog—at least he could not account for the entire flock—and he looked very much scared, probably at the uncertainty as to whether or not he had to digest a live frog." At the Oktoberfests in Munich in 1901 and 1913 Houdini saw several frog swallowers but found them most repulsive. "In fact," he said, "Norton was the only one I ever saw who presented his act in a dignified manner" (Houdini 1920, 163–64).

Then there was the "Great Waldo," a German-born Jew who swallowed

FIGURE 9.13. Among the "human fountains" was Floram Marchand, a seventeenth-century performer who drank water and seemingly spouted streams of claret. (From a contemporary print)

watches and rings, coins and lemons, and regurgitated them. He did the same with goldfish. Then he added to his act the thing that made him famous: the swallowing of white mice. Waldo—whose real name was Dagomarr Rochmann—picked up the act by watching other regurgitaters who appeared with traveling carnivals. Once he had learned the technique, he made modest sums by exhibiting at Viennese medical schools. When the Nazis marched on Austria, he fled to Switzerland and was forced to rely on his peculiar talent by performing in nightclubs. In time, an American agent offered him employment in the United States, and he remained there the rest of his life. His 10¢ pitch book bore his photograph. It showed a gangling, bespectacled man attired in formal dress, complete with cape, top hat, and, in his white-gloved hands, a cane. He signed the booklet, "Dr. Waldo" (Mannix 1996, 86–87).

Waldo appeared at Ripley's Odditorium, where he swallowed a goldfish and then regurgitated it moments later into an aquarium. He next swallowed a lemon as the lecturer chanted, "Watch it disappear! Going, going, gone!" As Waldo brought the lemon back, the lecturer noted: "This really is a very dangerous thing to attempt. As you can see, when the lemon is forced back up the throat, it shuts off Waldo's windpipe. His face turns red—from the effort and the shutting off of his wind." He added, "At times, when he attempts this feat without being in tiptop condition, the pressure of the lemon against Waldo's windpipe has caused him to fall on the stage in a dead faint" (Considine 1961, 142–43). Waldo never really fainted, but some in his audience did when he performed his next feat: swallowing a mouse. After extracting one of the white rodents from an aquarium covered with wire mesh, he held it by the tail, took a puff from his cigarette, and blew smoke into the mouse's face. This apparently somewhat anesthetized it and caused it to relax, whereupon, after dusting it with a feather to make sure it was clean, he popped it into his mouth and swallowed it. He usually swallowed a second one, then regurgitated them one at a time and returned them to the aquarium (Considine 1961, 143; Mannix 1996, 107). Mannix (1996, 107), in his novelized memoir, refers to a performer called the "Human Ostrich," who is obviously Waldo, and relates an unfortunate incident that may have actually occurred. One of the mice had not been tranquilized sufficiently by the smoke and grabbed onto the performer's stomach lining. He ended his predicament by drinking a full pitcher of water, causing the mouse to swim for its life; then he regurgitated the water with the mouse.

Percilla the Monkey Girl recalled an incident when Waldo had been performing with the show of her adoptive father, Karl Lauther: She said (Taylor and Kotcher 2002, 191): "He ran everybody out of Pappa Karl's show once. His mice got loose and ran everybody down the hall. A whole box of them. Mice was everywhere. He was next to my stage, right next to me. It made me sick [watching his act]. I told him 'Can't you put them somewhere else?' That's the only time I ever got sick on a show."

Bobby Reynolds (2001), who once worked with Waldo, told me of his tragic end sometime after World War II: "He killed himself, you know. Yeah, he killed himself. He gassed himself. I think he fell in love with somebody, or—I don't know. He was disappointed in life, and he was in a rooming house in New York and he committed suicide."

Some of the gastronomic acts feature less disgusting—and more daring—ingestions. These sideshow performances are akin to "torture" acts—those who ingest toxic substances, eat glass and razor blades, swallow tacks, and the like. Some of these phenomenal ingesters—notably those who swallow acids and poisons—use the same method as the spouters: the ability to regurgitate at will. After sipping the noxious substance, the performer secretly expels it into a handkerchief as he pretends to wipe his mouth. Or he regurgitates it into a glass under the pretense of washing the poison down with a drink of water (Gardner 1962, 78). As preparation, a quantity of "oatmeal mush" is sometimes ingested to absorb the dangerous substance before it is expelled later (Houdini 1920, 166).

The drinking-acid feat can also be accomplished by outright trickery. One way to do this is to use what magicians call a "mirror glass." This is a tumbler, typically fluted, with a mirror cemented in it to form a vertical partition. Even from a short distance, the glass looks empty. The front compartment connects with a reservoir in the bottom of the glass (i.e., a double bottom) that is concealed by a decorative band. Thus, when the acid is poured into the tumbler, it runs into the hidden reservoir. The rear compartment is filled with water, colored to resemble the acid. When the small glass is picked up to be filled with acid, which has previously been demonstrated to be genuine, it is rotated front to back, concealed by the performer's hand. Of course, as a sideshow insider's instructional typescript, "Midway Torture Feats" (n.d.), cautions: "Carbolic acid (phenol) is a deadly caustic, and even a spilled drop or two proves quite painful. The handling of such materials or examination of same by audience must be done with extreme caution." Even with trickery, such acts are highly dangerous. Witness Narishingha Swami, who reportedly licked sulfuric acid and ingested potassium cyanide and other substances, including powdered glass. His techniques are unknown, but in Rangoon, Burma, something went amiss and he "died with tragic swiftness" (Gardner 1962, 73).

Among the sideshow glass eaters was Paul Owen, who crunched expired electric lightbulbs and water glasses. He also munched on razor blades, telling

New York reporters that he had put away some 350,000 since he had acquired a taste for them as a boy (Gardner 1962, 73).

Bernard Leikind, a physicist with whom I taught a 1996 workshop in wonder-workers' feats, has demonstrated the secrets of eating glass. The glass of choice—preferred by sideshow swallowers—is a common lightbulb, which is thin and easily crunchable. Under Leikind's direction, I took a small piece of such glass, placed it flat between my molars, and easily crunched and ground it into a gritty, sandlike powder, which I then swallowed. In an earlier article, Leikind (1995) explains: "Since glass is chemically inert, it is indigestible. If you start with smithereens of thin glass and chew it into tiny pieces it is not likely to produce a cut." For extra protection, showman Bobby Reynolds (2001) told me that "the gaff . . . is . . . that you take a piece of soft white bread and you chew it up and swallow it behind [the glass], and then the whole thing gets mixed together and you pass it out." Some glass crunchers entirely gaff their act, explains Mannix (1996, 88), "by putting chewing gum against their teeth and squeezing the bits of glass into it." Others use the sip-of-water trick and spit the glass out into the tumbler, while still others merely retain the glass in their cheeks.

Many of those who perform swallowing acts in sideshows do just that: they swallow and then have to "digest" whatever they ate. Although ground glass is popularly believed to be a deadly substance if ingested, in fact, when powdered it is about the equivalent of swallowing sand. Performers may cut their mouths occasionally, but that is scarcely fatal, and once the ground glass is swallowed, the performer is "fairly safe" (Mannix 1996, 88). Narishingha Swami used bottle glass, but he had it "ground into powder" before eating it (Gardner 1962, 73).

At our 1996 workshop, I presented a glass-eating feat that I had devised using some basic conjuring principles. I placed an empty soda bottle in a burlap sack and had someone smash it with a hammer. I reached in, picked out a sizable shard of the green glass, popped it in my mouth, and began crunching. Some in the audience began to look horrified, while others, noticing the blood trickling from my lips, laughed nervously, uncertain if I was pulling off another trick. (I had previously performed some feats à la Houdini, including extracting myself from a straitjacket and escaping from a combination of thumb cuffs, handcuffs, and a padlocked wrist chain.) It was indeed a trick. All I had to do was secretly palm a shard of broken green lollipop while the real glass was being smashed and slip a stuntman's "blood" capsule into my mouth. The rest is obvious: After reaching into the bag, I came out with the candy shard, showed it freely, and let it be seen clearly going into my mouth, with no false moves. After crunching the "glass," I bit into the capsule, swallowed all the evidence, and bravely bowed while wiping the "blood" away with a white handkerchief. Magician Mark Edward, who was a special guest of the workshop, made some subtle variations and shared the trick with his advanced magic students (Edward 1996).

Some of the same tricks used by glass eaters can be employed by chewers of razor blades and swallowers of hairpins and tacks. Mannix (1996) cautions that if hairpins are actually going to be swallowed, they should be bent in such a way that they will not stick crosswise in the throat. Gardner (1962, 73–74) reports that "Sebastian Montero, Robert Ripley's storied glutton, ate razor blades, glass, and thousands of carpet tacks, which could be clearly seen in X-ray photographs of his outraged stomach." More bread, Sebastian?

Jim Rose presented a variation on this theme in his Jim Rose Circus Side Show, a troupe of human marvels who performed at indoor and outdoor venues that often hosted rock groups. Rose performed a panoply of feats that included fire eating, lying on a bed of nails, and escaping from a straitjacket. He also performed "internal juggling," namely, "swallowing to the back of the throat, razor blades, then thread, then coughing them back up tied to the thread," according to a playbill (Gregor 1998, 27). Actually, this is a gaffed feat—an old fakir's trick that Houdini learned from his sideshow and dime museum days in the 1890s. The feat originally used needles but later featured razor blades, which could be seen more easily from the audience. The secret is a duplicate set of dull razor blades prestrung on a thread, and the whole thing collapsed into a small packet. This is palmed and deftly switched for the original blades that are supposed to be swallowed (Gibson and Young 1961, 53–64).

Human Pincushions

Various mystics—including Egyptian fakirs and Hindu yogis—accomplished special feats such as stopping their pulses and painlessly thrusting long needles through their arms and cheeks. They claimed that the "mind power" that allowed them to do so was due to occult forces, and scientific observers attributed the effects to autohypnosis, but in reality, a mixture of simple principles and occasional trickery was involved. Hence, explains Walter Gibson (1967, 102), "a host of imitators sprang up who presented most of the same marvels in practically the same style."

In causing his pulse to fade away, the performer uses a simple trick. After a member of the audience places his fingers on the yogi's wrist and notes the strong throb, the mystic gradually eases his upper arm against his side, thereby secretly pressing against a block of wood concealed under his armpit. Alternatively, the fakir may wear a stiff neckband, which he presses down with his chin against the collarbone, thus achieving the same tourniquet effect.

The pulse stopping is merely the prelude to a genuine feat: sticking bodkins and skewers through the flesh and controlling the flow of blood when they are removed. The fakir may first press on the nearest artery to briefly retard the blood flow. Then, relaxing, he thrusts the skewer straight forward through the skin. He may push a thin dagger through his throat by first drawing the flesh forward with thumb and fingers. Thus, the blade pierces only the fleshy part. The fakir may then demonstrate that he can control the bleeding when the skewers are removed, allowing the blood to flow or stop as requested. This is accomplished by either removing the implement quickly, which allows the wound to bleed freely, or removing it slowly, which causes the wound to swell and thus retards blood flow (Gibson 1967, 104).

Gresham (1953, 203–4) provides insight into the human pincushion act:

> Much of the art of the side show lies in the use of little-known natural laws. There are, for instance, areas of the body where the nerves recording pain in the skin seem to be sparser than other spots. The shoulders are one, the inside of the forearm is another. If you take a

hatpin and touch the point of it to the inside of your forearm up near the elbow, pointing away from you, and keep shifting the point a fraction of an inch each way, after a few tries you will find a spot much less sensitive than the others. Now if you give the pin a quick jab it will penetrate the skin, sliding in almost parallel to it. Keep pushing and the point begins to come out the other side, first as a long, slim finger of flesh, then it breaks open with a sharp nip. Leave it there a moment. Now you are a human pincushion.

As to the pain, he emphasizes the advantage of knowing when the piercing will occur and likens it to diabetics giving themselves regular injections of insulin. Of course, Gresham emphasizes that alcohol should be used to sterilize both the arm and the pin. Lifetime sideshow performer Percilla "Monkey Girl" Bejano cautions that the pins should be kept in alcohol "overnight" (Taylor and Kotcher 2002, 191). Gresham (1953, 204) adds that, "To be a happy, carefree human pincushion you have to be one of those people who don't get infections no matter what they do."

One Hindu fakir, whom Mannix (1996, 82) calls Krinko, sometimes allowed his tongue to be nailed to a board by a member of the audience. Of course, the performer had a pierced tongue and guided the nail to ensure that it went through the existing hole rather than making a new one. Krinko also did a stunt that I have seen performed by a magician on television. He swallowed a yard of red ribbon rolled into a ball, then pulled up his shirt, made a cut in his belly with a razor blade, and drew out the ribbon an inch at a time. The secret is that two ribbons are used. The duplicate one is threaded "on a long, flat needle such as women use to run elastic through their panties." The performer grabs a handful of flesh on his side and inserts the needle through the fold so that when the skin is released, the ribbon runs just under the skin. One end protrudes above the navel, and the other emerges from a point nearly at the back and is allowed to dangle down his pants. This part of the ribbon is pulled carefully until the end in the front is drawn just out of sight. Then all the performer has to do to apparently remove the swallowed ribbon from his stomach is make a slight cut in the skin. "Then he could pull the ribbon through as though he were pulling out the string from a pair of pajamas" (Mannix 1996, 82–83).

There have been many variations on the act, with many styling themselves the "Human Pincushion." One was Edward H. Gibson, who entertained vaudeville audiences in the early twentieth century. At each performance, an assistant stuck up to sixty pins into Gibson's face and body (Mooney et al. 2002, 133).

A performer with Ripley's "Believe It or Not!" show at the Chicago Century of Progress fair in 1933 was photographed with needles slipped through the skin of his chest, a safety pin placed like a nose ring, and eight needles arrayed in his cheeks and chin like a porcupine's quills (Mannix 1996, 8). (However, the last look rather like acupuncture needles, with fine wire strands emerging from thin handles. The fineness of the needles would help reduce the pain.)

The "Strange as It Seems" show at the New York world's fair in 1939 featured Ellis Phillips, who pierced his cheeks with hat pins, sewed a button onto his chest, and used thumbtacks to hold up his socks (Dufour 1977, 124). Another 1930s performer was a man named Easler of Lorraine, Ohio, who was photographed with skewers through his cheeks and one inserted diagonally downward from his right upper lip to the center of his chin. He claimed that he was able to do his act "because his nerves did not register pain" (Mannix 1996, 25).

I have witnessed a few such acts. At the 2000 fair at York, Pennsylvania, Dr. Frankestien [sic] was the blowoff act in Hall & Christ's ten-in-one. For an extra fee, one could go into a screened-off area to watch this human pincushion stick a large hat pin through the outside of his forearm, show buttons apparently sewn to his chest (figures 9.14 and 9.15), and lift up his pant legs to reveal socks held up with safety pins. He "lectured on himself" (as showmen would say) and gladly answered questions and posed for pictures.

The most dramatic such act I have seen was that of Zamora the Torture King (figure 9.16). He was formerly with the Jim Rose Circus, where he was billed as Tim the Human Pincushion, before expanding his torture act. His real name is Tim Cridland, and he is a practicing Sunni who lives in California when not touring (Gregor 1998, 27, 386). When I caught Zamora, he was at Malibu Jack's Hideaway in St. Catharines, Ontario, performing with Slimenstra

(Above) FIGURE 9.14. A human pincushion pushes a hat pin through his
forearm. His was the blowoff act in Hall
& Christ's 2000 ten-in-one. (Photo by
author)

Right) FIGURE 9.15. The same human
pincushion shows buttons apparently
sewn to his chest. (Photo by author)

FIGURE 9.16. Zamora the Torture King performs his grueling act at various venues. (Photo by author)

Hymen (who exhibited fire breathing, a bullwhip routine, and a burlesque show). Tim's act was a roster of torture feats that included a fire-eating routine, eating glass from a lightbulb, lying on a bed of nails and a rack of sharp swords, walking on broken glass, chopping onions on his chest with a cleaver, licking a red-hot iron bar, and performing the ribbon-swallowing-and-extracting feat (described earlier). Then, as if all that were merely a warm-up, Zamora began to torture himself in earnest, thrusting skewers through the fleshy part of his right forearm, another into his left biceps, and still another into one cheek and out the other. He even inserted the point of yet another under his tongue and pressed down until it exited from the skin of his throat.

In terms of sheer numbers, Brent Moffatt takes the "pincushion" title, defeating the previous record of 200 needles in the *Guinness Book of World Records*. Moffatt, who works in a body-piercing and tattoo parlor in Winnipeg, Manitoba, pierced his body with 702 surgical needles. To fit them all, he used closely spaced rows down both legs. "The first 500 needles were not too painful because my legs had swelled up. The last two were in my nipples—and they're very sensitive." Removing them was the real pain: "It was excruciating. My legs

237

were covered in blood and people said I was not a pretty picture" (McCandlish 2003). However outlandish Moffatt's feat was, it was accomplished over a period of about seven hours. That scarcely rivals the feats of those who make their livings in sideshows—such as the anonymous performer featured on a 1960 banner as "Pin Cushion Man" (Johnson et al. 1996, 159–60)—putting on several shows a day and living the rough life of a carny.

Although the human pincushion act is typically genuine, there can be gaffs. I recall seeing one method used in a ten-in-one on the midway at the Canadian National Exposition. The performer was a magician friend who did a trick version of the needle-through-the-arm feat. In this version (once sold by magic supply houses), it looks like a large hat pin is pushed through the flesh of the inside forearm. The secret is that, beforehand, an inch-wide stripe of rubber cement is applied across the area. This part of the arm is turned toward the performer, and as he pretends to push the pin through the skin, he simply pinches the cemented area around it. This gives the skin a simulated punctured look. The head of the pin is actually a bulb, and the needle is hollow, so that a drop of "blood" can be squeezed out for added realism. This effect (and its secret) was presented on an NBC special, *Psychic Secrets Revealed*, hosted by Stacy Keach (April 23, 2003).

Blockheads

Often performed by human pincushions, the blockhead act—in which the entertainer pounds a large nail or ice pick into the nostril and apparently into the head itself—looks like the ultimate pincushion effect (figure 9.17). Actually, it is one of the least torturous of the working acts.

Several writers believe that the effect was developed by fakirs of India, possibly centuries ago (Gardner 1962, 32; Mannix 1996, 79). In the sideshows it began as one of an array of torture or pain-proof feats in the acts of such performers as Ellis Phillips. Phillips, the 1930s human pincushion mentioned earlier, would "drive a long nail into his nose" as part of his performance for the "Strange as It Seems" show at the 1939 New York world's fair (Dufour 1977, 122).

Another was "Professor" Leo Kongee. He "obligingly horrified his American audiences by having six-inch nails driven up his nose." One of the few African Americans of the genre, Kongee also did other "painless" feats, including sew-

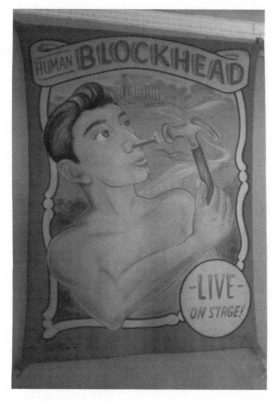

FIGURE 9.17. "Human Blockhead" banner at Sideshows by the Seashore, Coney Island. (Photo by author)

ing a button to his tongue. Still another was a "Peruvian fakir" named Jose Fernandez, who lived in Richmond, Virginia. In addition to swallowing razor blades, he would "drive a 20-penny nail into his head up to the hilt" (Mooney et al. 2002, 134, 135).

The secret of "Driving a Spike in your Head" was one of several contained in a six-page typescript, "Side Show Tricks Explained." Published by A. B. Enterprises, it also supplied instructions for circus and midway shows (such as the "Rope Spinning Act," "100 Clown Hints & Ideas," and "Dynamite Explosion Act"), as well as plans for concessions, rides, and illusions. The instructions called the blockhead feat "another modern miracle" and advised: "Its secret is known only [to] a very few, so help to protect it." The secret is simple: "Perhaps you do not know it, but neither do thousands more like you, that the hole in your nose does not go up between the eyes as most persons believe, but right back over the roof of the mouth to the back of the throat."

It is into this surprisingly long cavity that the nail or ice pick easily slips. Of course, one prepares the spike by filing the tip to smooth it and slightly round the point. The hammering is feigned. The performer firmly holds the spike between finger and thumb and pretends to tap it in but actually only lets it slip forward a little at a time. Done properly, there is little risk—except perhaps an initial tendency to sneeze.

I discussed the feat with Bobby Reynolds (2001), who added, "You cry a lot with the nail in your nose, 'cause it causes a tear duct to get all screwed up, but other than that, no problem." Well, maybe one. Doc Swami—magician, fire-eater, and human blockhead—once failed to pay attention and drove the nail too far, so that it got lost inside. Fortunately, a shake of the head and a hard blowing of the nose dislodged it. "That was the first time that had happened," Swami said, "and I'd been doing the act for 20 years" (Taylor and Kotcher 2002, 168).

One of Bobby's show people, Eddie the Blockhead, kindly demonstrated the act for me in an idle moment. Dressed in a fancy vest and wearing a top hat, he was operating the show's ticket booth. As I readied my camera, Eddie appeared to pound the shaft of a screwdriver into his nose, using the heavy handle of another (see figure 9.18). Apparently seeing me as something of a rube, Eddie explained that, due to a wartime injury, his face had had to be reconstructed, thus leaving a cavity that made the feat possible. His eyes scarcely twinkled. I must say that, although I have seen several blockhead acts, I have never heard that "explanation" before or since.

It was anatomical wonder Melvin Burkhart (discussed in chapter 7) who transformed the act from a torture feat to a comedy routine. And it was Melvin who gave the act its whimsical name, "human blockhead." He had a number of one-liners. When one lady asked if the feat was a trick, he replied, "No, the nail's real. It's my head that's a fake."

Other Torture Acts

Additional working acts of the torture variety are explained below.

Climbing a Ladder of Swords. In ancient times, walking on swords was a Shinto ordeal called *Tsurigi Watari*. However, after Japanese conjurers learned the secret, the Shinto priests abandoned the rite. Later, Far Eastern performers brought the feat to Western audiences (Gibson 1967, 91). Resembling a step-

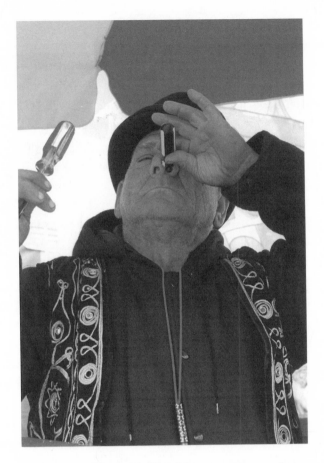

FIGURE 9.18. Eddie the Blockhead demonstrates a popular sideshow feat—pounding a screwdriver into his nose—especially for my camera.

ladder consisting of five to seven rungs of broad swords placed edge upward, the ladder of swords is a sideshow mainstay. The emphasis is usually on the performer rather than the ladder. Wind-whipped banner lines—like the one for Bobby Reynolds's traveling sideshow museum—often include a dramatic "Iron Foot Maiden" banner or some similarly styled act. Bobby's collection naturally includes a classic example of such a "torture rack." A 1954 publicity photo for a young Ward Hall shows the multitalented performer dressed in a sequined costume, his bare feet on the top two blades of a ladder of swords, and juggling.

The secret of the feat is that a sharp edge of a razor, knife, or sword can be pressed against the skin without cutting it, as long as the blade does not slide or turn. "Likewise," notes Gibson (1967, 92), "the sword walker must never lose his balance because the slightest sideward motion of his foot might cause severe injury." Ironically, the illustration accompanying Gibson's explanation is in error, showing the Shinto performer facing the ladder and thus placing his feet *across* the blade. In fact, the feet must be placed lengthwise on the blade edge "and flat," states a typescript of instructions, "in such a way that the pressure is applied [to] the entire length of the foot at once" ("Midway Torture Feats" n.d., 11). In figure 9.19, sideshow torture queen Bambi shows the correct style. Note that her body is turned sideways to the ladder, thus orienting her feet along the blade. (Note also how the inside lecturer has moved close, using his foot to steady the ladder and giving the pretty daredevil a helping hand up.)

Mannix (1996, 83) mentions a possible of way of gaffing (or *grifting*) the ladder-of-swords act: sharpening only a portion of the blade (say, near the handle); that portion could be used later to slice paper as proof of its sharpness. Mannix insists, however, that this was only the occasional spectator's suspicion, at least with Krinko, the sideshow yogi with whom he worked. Krinko had tried passing the swords out for examination, but one man cut himself severely and had to be rushed off for medical attention. In contrast, a set of instructions actually sold to the carny trade (Brill 1957) says to use lodge swords: "These swords are not sharp like a military sword, but you can drag them through paper with a cutting motion. This is good flash."

Walking on Broken Glass. Typically, the "Iron Foot Marvel" act combines climbing the ladder of swords with walking on broken glass. This is shown, for instance, by a tall (eight by thirteen feet), double-panel banner from around 1940 (painted by George Bellis of Sunshine Studios, Wichita, Kansas). The upper panel depicts a scantily clad beauty posing with one foot, on tiptoe, on a nine-blade ladder. The lower panel portrays her walking on broken glass while a satanic figure dumps more shards in her path (Johnson et al. 1996, 44, 156). Similarly, Bambi of the Hall & Christ Show did the ladder-of-swords act, combined with walking on glass and even lying on a bed of nails.

Walking on broken glass involves a wooden box (approximately three feet wide, four feet long, and six inches deep) whose bottom is covered with broken

FIGURE 9.19. With a steadying hand from the inside lecturer, torture queen Bambi demonstrates the classic ladder-of-swords feat in the 2000 Hall & Christ ten-in-one. (Photo by author)

glass. At show time, the performer may break some old bottles and add jagged pieces to the mix. Then, showing that his or her feet are unprepared, the performer walks, possibly jumps, even dances, on the glass—unharmed. According to "Side Show Tricks Explained" (n.d., 4), thick bottles are broken, and the sharp edges are filed or ground down. These pieces are placed in the center of the box, and the freshly broken glass is put only around the edges. The performer avoids the sharp pieces by staying in the center of the box. The feet may also be prepared by soaking them in a solution of alum, drying them, and then rubbing the soles well with powdered resin.

A somewhat different approach is described by physicist David Willey (1999), a friend of mine who has a traveling physics show that has been seen by some 50,000 students. David has also achieved fame as the "resident mad scientist" of the *Tonight Show with Jay Leno*. I once stood off-camera as he demonstrated for a TV documentary not only the glass-walking feat but also his preparation technique, which does not involve grinding the glass fragments' sharp edges (figure 9.20). First, rather large bottles are selected so that the broken pieces will be more gently curved. Any paper labels are soaked off. Then the bottles are placed in a canvas bag and smashed with a hammer (while wearing leather gloves and safety goggles) into relatively small pieces. The box—the bottom made from a piece of half-inch-thick plywood and the sides of two-by-four-inch lumber—is filled to a uniform depth of about three inches. This depth permits the fragments to settle and shift a bit as the foot is slowly, tentatively, placed on them. Then David sorts the glass so that any right-angled pieces (resulting from the juncture of the bottle's side wall and base) are moved to the outer edges, leaving only the flatter pieces of glass in the center. For extra safety, he covers the bed of glass with a heavy cloth and pounds the surface firmly with a cast-iron skillet. This eliminates any jagged points that may have been sticking up.

There is also a technique for walking on broken glass (Willey 1999): "When walking I place each foot slowly, moving it elsewhere if a point or edge is felt, although that is seldom necessary if the bed has been prepared correctly. Care must be taken to brush off any pieces of glass that stick to the bottom of the feet when stepping off the bed." Of course, the sharpness of the glass should be demonstrated to the audience. Willey uses a shard from the glass bed to cut a string holding a weighty object.

Withstanding Molten Lead. One old fakir test is pouring "molten lead" into the ears and even the eyes. "When the hissing lead hit his flesh and began to throw off steam," says Mannix (1996, 83), "people in the tip fainted right and left as though you'd fired a charge of buckshot through the crowd." The fakir would grope about as if blind. But then, with due drama, he would slowly open his eyes, to the relief of the crowd. The secret is that, instead of lead, the fakir uses a similar-appearing compound of antimony. This has an extremely low melting point, so that pouring it over the eyes—which should be closed for the effect—is no more harmful than doing so with candle drippings (Mannix 1996, 83; "Midway Torture Feats" n.d.).

FIGURE 9.20. Physicist David Willey walks on broken glass for a documentary by the Learning Channel. (Photo by author)

Another feat is to dip one's fingers into molten lead—real molten lead. The trick here is to first secretly dip the hand into a bowl of water that is hidden from the spectators' view. Physicist David Willey (1999, 45) explains, "Heat from the lead goes into evaporating the water and hence not into burning the hand, and the resulting steam layer insulates the hand." Willey (under whose tutelage I performed the feat) cautions that the temperature of the lead must be raised well beyond its melting point (327.5 degrees Celsius). "Having lead solidify on one's fingers is not pleasant," he warns.

Lying on a Bed of Nails. This well-known feat comes from the East. According to Robert Ripley (1929, 9), it was common to Sadhus (Hindu ascetics):

> Sadhus who sit on beds of sharp spikes have been more or less featured in the Sunday supplements of our country. This stunt is a popular one in India and I saw half a dozen of them. In Mysore a six-year-old boy was starting out in life by assuming a sitting position on a home-made "Kiddie car" of nails.
>
> One old fellow that I saw in Benares had been on his trundle bed for eighteen years, I was told. After some persuasion, highly emphasized with rupees, the venerable old faquir [fakir] stood up on his spiny mattress and gave me the opportunity to see that there was no fake about it.

The bed of nails was popularized in the United States during vaudeville and became a mainstay in circus and carnival sideshows. One circa 1940 banner headed "Torture of India" depicts a woman reclining comfortably on a wooden bench studded—exaggeratedly—with sharp, pyramid-shaped spikes (Johnson et al. 1996, 42). The secret of the bed-of-nails feat is simply "to have the nails all the same length, and all close together," according to a mid-twentieth-century set of instructions sold to sideshow showmen (Brill 1957). Authorities vary on the correct spacing, with recommendations being one-half inch, one-quarter inch, or two centimeters. ("Side Show Tricks Explained" n.d.; Brill 1957; Willey 1999). All sources agree that pilot holes should be drilled for each nail to prevent the lumber from splitting. In terms of physics, the nails do not puncture the body because if there is a sufficient number of nails to support the body, no one nail will press especially hard (Willey 1999).

Breaking Stone on Chest. This old strongman feat was performed as an act called the "Man of Iron." It was sometimes exhibited in sideshows. The performer lies faceup and raises his body so that it rests on the hands and feet. (Alternatively, his body may be supported by a padded stool beneath the shoulders and another under the buttocks.) A heavy stone or concrete block is placed on his chest and smashed with a sledgehammer, leaving the performer unfazed (Gibson 1967, 101–2; "Side Show Tricks Explained" n.d.; Willey 1999).

The secret is that the heavy stone absorbs the blow, rendering it harmless. Explains Willey (1999):

> When the concrete block is broken, the kinetic energy of the sledge-hammer goes into causing the block's destruction, ultimately warming the pieces, and the momentum of the hammer is passed through the prone person to the earth. The person swinging the sledgehammer needs to hit the block with sufficient force to shatter it, but not so hard that the hammer has a significant amount of energy left after the initial impact.

He cautions:

> It is quite possible for an adult to hit the block too hard, as I found out when an enthusiastic and strong gym teacher hit a block as hard as he could. All the breath was knocked out of me and I had a matrix of puncture wounds on my chest and back. A tetanus shot saw me fine that day, and since then only my wife breaks the block. She practiced just breaking blocks on the ground many times before breaking them on me. Three-section blocks should be placed lengthwise on the top board whereas two-section blocks are best stood on end. I prefer two-section blocks as they shatter nicely.

Willey once broke a block on me, as he had done with Jay Leno. I lay on a bed of nails with another placed on my chest and a concrete block on top of that. I certainly looked like I was a sandwich of torture. However, the block absorbed the blow and I was unscathed, except for a broken piece of concrete that flew in my face. I was glad I had worn a hard hat with a face shield; even so, the impact of the flying concrete broke the safety glasses I wore underneath the shield. I was uninjured but, as I later admitted to some spectators, "surprised."

Electric Marvels

Because electricity and magnetism are invisible powers that can produce dramatically visible effects, they seemed quite magical in earlier times. In 1884 a teenage girl from Cedarville, Georgia, was discovered to be a "human magnet"—or so it was claimed. Certainly Lulu Hurst could attract audiences, packing lecture halls and opera houses in Atlanta, New York, Chicago, Milwaukee, and elsewhere. Crowds came to witness the apparent power of the "Georgia Magnet." In one demonstration, despite the efforts of several people to resist her, Hurst could push them around the stage. Two strong men pressing against a stick she held out were unable to move her from where she stood. And while she held a stick vertically, a man would attempt to push it down to the floor, but the alleged human magnet merely pressed her hand against the stick and prevented the action.

Magnetism? Hypnotism? Some occult force? Actually, Lulu Hurst was using the simple principle of force deflection—as she herself admitted. Having left the stage after only a two-year career to marry her manager, Lulu conceded that her act had involved "unrecognized mechanical principles involving leverage and balance." For example, as the two men pressed against the stick she held out, they pushed *toward* her, while she cleverly directed an upward pressure that effectively deflected their strength. If the men pushed hard enough, and if her deflection were sudden enough and caught them off guard, they might be sent tumbling—much to the amusement of the audience.

Lulu Hurst was not the first such performer (nor the last) to make use of force deflection, along with other physical principles and tricks. In 1846 a French girl, Angelique Cottin, became known briefly as the "Electric Girl" for performing such stunts (Nickell 1991b, 34–40; Gibson 1967, 61–62). However, most "Electric Girls" are attractions at circus and carnival sideshows and dime museums (figure 9.21). The performer is typically called Electra and is, according to the talkers and lecturers, able to withstand strong electrical shocks that would kill an ordinary person. As the act is usually performed, Electra sits in a fearful-looking "electric chair" as the switch is thrown and—claims the inside lecturer—thousands of volts surge through her body. As proof, a mere touch from Electra causes a fluorescent bulb to light or a torch to burst into flame.

A 1976 edition of *A. Brill's Bible of Building Plans,* a catalog of instructional materials for carny showmen and amusement park operators, advertised the "Electric Chair—Sparks Shoot from Her Fingers." Workshop drawings and complete instructions for building the chair were sold for just $5. It was adver-

FIGURE 9.21. Banner art from Bobby Reynolds's sideshow promotes an electric girl as she is typically styled. (Photo by author)

tised as "a simple wood-working project," the "electrical device" being available from an auto parts dealer. "Spectators are told the girl is receiving thousands of volts," said the ad in *Brill's Bible*. The chair "is hot enough to Light a Torch, Cigarettes, Good and Bad Fluorescent Bulbs." The electric girl could also light a torch "from a glass of water" (Brill 1976, 148). The secret was a special transformer, hidden from view, that produced a "high-frequency" current. Though high in voltage, it was low in amperage and therefore harmless to the performer. When Electra pressed her arm against a metal plate mounted on the chair, she received the current but hardly felt it. The bulb that lighted at her touch was one designed for such a high-frequency current; a common incandescent lightbulb would not have worked. One advantage of this working act is that anyone can play the part of Electra—or "Electricia," as a Hall & Christ banner proclaimed during 2000 and 2001.

An interesting variant on the classic ten-in-one Electra act was one featured at the 1935 Exposition Internationale in Brussels, Belgium. There, a man named Floyd Woolsey was hired by Dufour and Rogers' presentation "Le Crime ne Paye Pas" (Crime Doesn't Pay). Styled as an exposé of gangsterism in America, the act involved actors re-creating the "last mile" as the condemned Woolsey was escorted to the electric chair by a priest, prison warden, and witnesses. Lou Dufour (1977, 91–92) recalled: "The lighting and costumes were somber, in keeping with the mood we wanted to present. Woolsey would be strapped in the chair and when the 'electricity' was turned on he would leap, lunge, and twist. He had a real fit in that chair, finally slumping in feigned death. We paid him $100 a week, which was a pretty good salary, but he was worth every dollar. It was his equipment, and he did the stunt ten to twenty times a day. In six months we must have electrocuted him 2,500 times or so."

Snake Charmers

Among the "miracle men" of the East are the snake charmers and handlers who show their power over the feared reptiles. Figure 9.22 is a sketch I made in Marrakech, Morocco, in 1971. I was drawn to the scene by the familiar flute music. The performer was putting on a snake show while his assistant used a tambourine as a collection tray. As shown in the sketch, one of the charmer's stunts was to approach a cobra in a squatting position, one hand on the ground and the other holding a tangle of serpents with which he teased the cobra.

In India the itinerant *Jadu* (magic) performer occasionally does herpetological tricks. For example, he might transform a piece of rope into a snake (after wrapping the rope in cloth and, in the process, making the switch) (Siegel 1991, 186). My friend Premanand, an Indian conjurer and skeptic, knows many such feats. One, described in his valuable *Science Versus Miracles* (1994, 36), is a rod-to-serpent feat like that of Pharaoh's sorcerers related in Exodus (7:9–15). The snake's mouth and tail are held in either hand, and the reptile is stretched straight. Firm pressure on the head with the thumb and index finger causes the snake to stiffen. In this way, it looks like a rod and is so presented until it is thrown on the ground, whereupon it soon recovers and is "transformed" into a snake.

The Indian snake charmer performs in the open air and uses his flute music to cause a deadly hooded cobra to rise and sway in rhythm to the music. A number of additional snakes, released from baskets and jute bags by

FIGURE 9.22. A snake charmer in Morocco teases a cobra with a tangle of snakes. (Sketch by author)

his assistants, may be similarly entranced. When the music stops and the performer extends a stick toward the cobra, it strikes quickly. The snake charmer may even have the deadly reptiles crawling over his arms and concludes his act by dramatically capturing each snake.

Actually, although snakes do have hearing organs, it is the movement of the charmer himself, swaying to the melody, that the cobra follows. By ceasing to pipe, the charmer causes the cobra to poise motionless; then, by extending the stick, he provokes it to strike. In some cases the cobras are drugged or have their venom sacs removed or their mouths sewn shut. But skilled performers can and do handle the most lethal reptiles. From long experience, they understand how cobras behave, know their striking distance, and rely on the snakes' shortsightedness. In concluding his act, for example, the charmer often deliberately provokes the cobra with the movements of one hand; then, as it prepares to strike, he quickly grasps it behind the head with the other. By taking advantage of the snake's natural tendency

251

FIGURE 9.23. Snake charmer Millie Nevello poses with her charges in her Sparks' Show pitch card photograph. (Author's collection)

to hide, he is able to quickly put it in a basket or bag (Gibson 1967, 70–73; Gardner 1962, 51–52).

In the West, snakes are part of circus and carnival exotica. They are often included in menageries (see chapter 11), are featured in single-O and ten-in-one sideshows, and are a regular feature of the latter's bally show (figure 9.23). In fact, a talker exhibiting a snake (as part of what would later be known as the *ballyhoo*) was depicted in an early 1830s print. The scene is European, demonstrating that the practice was not exclusive to American showmen (McKennon 1972, 1:20). Snakes were a regular feature of Barnum & Bailey's circus sideshow bally, as shown by photographs made in 1888. One depicts a "moss-haired" Circassian snake charmer exhibiting a great snake from an elevated position beside a ticket-office stand, with a banner line behind. Another shows what appears to be the same young lady, her snake draped around her, posing for a group picture of sideshow performers (including armless wonder Charles Tripp, bearded lady Annie Jones, and many other stars) (Kunhardt et al. 1995, 325, 327).

The standard bally platform snakes are Indian pythons and Central American boa constrictors. According to Gresham's *Monster Midway* (1953, 141–42).

> These big snakes do not kill their dinners by crushing them to death but by suffocation. They are dangerous only if you let them get a coil around your neck or chest and then only if you are alone and can't find the head or tail. One herpetologist got himself thus entangled and had an unpleasant few minutes until he thought to look in a mirror, find the snake's head, and start unwinding him from there. The girl snake dancers of the carny seldom know anything about snakes except that you have to keep them from extremes of temperature. On days when the thermometer soars above ninety their living props are kept in tubs of water until needed for the show. On cold nights they often take the snakes to bed with them. Boas are mild-tempered for the most part and beautifully colored. Pythons can give you a bad, nonpoisonous bite when startled.

A link with the East was sometimes acknowledged in sideshow snake presentations. A young Indian woman, Saidor A. Isoha, appeared in 1890s publicity photographs by Karl Hagenbeck, whose German circus was among the most important shows in Europe. Isoha reportedly gave up her cobras after watching a man suffer a terrible death from a cobra bite. She once staged public fights, pitting a cobra against a mongoose. Reported William G. FitzGerald (1897) in the London magazine the *Strand*, "This was a little costly, however, for the cobra was always killed." Isoha, who dressed in colorful Indian costumes and wore metal bracelets on her wrists and upper arms, owned six Indian and three African pythons, plus three boa constrictors, all in the eight-to-twelve-foot range. Wrote FitzGerald (1897), "She has a real affection for her snakes, and they for her. One large python will form himself into a living turban about her head."

Most of the European and American snake charmers have been women. The combination of scantily clad ladies and their fang-bearing charges is a subtly erotic, beauty-and-the-beast theme that is irresistible to banner artists. One, by an unknown artist from the Millard and Bulsterbaum Studio, circa 1930s, was headed, "Edna Blanché Snake Charmer" (Johnson et al. 1996, 145). Other banners featured a "Snake Trainer" (like one with the Christiani Brothers Circus-Sideshow & Wild Animals Annex), a "Serpentina" (with the 1968 Hall & Christ Show), and "Eeka and Giant Snakes" (discussed in the previous chapter), among many others (Johnson et al. 1996, 139, 160; Hall 1981, 51). A "Snake Girl" single-O banner, however, featured not a snake charmer but a giant serpent with a girl's head—an illusion show (see chapter 10).

Those doubling as snake charmers have included a Circassian beauty (mentioned earlier with the 1888 Barnum & Bailey sideshow), a tattooed woman (with the 1927 Ringling Brothers Congress of Freaks), and a dwarf, Glen Newman. Newman was with the Hall & Christ Show, whose other snake charmers have included Elise Briskey, Jane and Floyd "Tex" Arnold, Ginger Donahue (see figure 3.9), and, in 2001, erstwhile Coney Island performers Bambi and Bunny Love (Barth and Siegel 2002, 105; Hall 1991).

"Little Pete" Terhurne, aka "Poobah the Fire-eating Dwarf," once did a snake-charmer show titled "The Midget and the Monsters." Actually, there was only one monster, a large boa constrictor. Unfortunately, during one week's run at Toledo, Ohio, the monster died. The show's owners, Ward Hall and Chris Christ, ordered another boa, but money being short, it was decided that "the show must go on." According to Hall (1991, 18–19), Terhurne "took his usual stance with the boa corpse. When people were suspicious, asking if the snake was dead, Pete would cock his head, and with a sly smile, would retort, 'No, it's just sick.'" And so the show went on until the replacement monster arrived.

Knife Throwers

At least in the United States, knife throwing had its origins in the early pioneer period, when two or more competitors engaged in it for recreation (Hibben 1998, 1). In rural areas, like the Appalachia I grew up in, many passed through the rites of boyhood playing Jim Bowie, tossing their hunting knives at targets such as the eye-shaped limb scars on a beech tree trunk.

A number of the sideshow knife throwers were styled in the Wild West tradition. There was "Mexican Pete, Master of the Knives," who was described by Gresham in *Monster Midway* (1953, 81–82). His surname, ironically, was

Pearce. Gresham encountered him at "a firelight vaudeville show, hastily thrown together out of neighboring 'talent' and a variety of show folk who were enjoying the low-budget campsites, that summer of the Great Depression, in the surrounding state park." Gresham recalled:

> I had seen "Mexican Pete" with a circus years before and had never forgotten him. He would start by pinning a cigarette from his wife's mouth to the board with a knife. Next she would hold a poker hand of four aces and he would nail them down with knives through the spots. Then came the "outlining." He placed knives so close to her body that sometimes they pinned her clothes. Then he threw a handful of ice picks. Next came bayonets. He finished up by heaving half-a-dozen small axes. To take her final bow the girl stepped out of a frame of hardware. I thought Mexican Pete was marvelous. I still do.

One might think Mrs. Pearce—correctly billed as "a fearless little lady"—was also wonderful. It took nerve to be so outlined with a frame of hardware, no matter how much confidence she had in her husband's skill.

Another professional knife thrower from the western tradition was "Couteau Gene" Stebbings, who once performed with the Buffalo Bill Wild West Show. An erstwhile rancher, Stebbings was also a "trick gunner and authority on frontier fighting." He went on to manufacture throwing knives and tomahawks for other "impaling act artistes" (Gresham 1953, 84–85).

Although an expert acknowledges that "you can throw any knife" (Hibben 1998, 2), he and other professionals generally advocate the use of specially designed throwing knives. Those seen on the carnival midway in Gresham's day had perfect balance on each axis—length, width, and thickness. In shape, however, the blade suddenly flared near the point to compensate for the handle's weight, as well as to provide a gleaming surface for spectators to see. The steel was plated with nickel or chrome to prevent rust, and the handles were typically painted red to provide "flash" (Gresham 1953, 87).

Longtime professional knife thrower Chris Christ (Ward Hall's partner in the Hall & Christ Shows) told me about the importance of a knife's heft: "You want something heavy. It's kind of like if you ask someone to drive a stake and they look for the littlest hammer you know they never did it before. You want the heaviest hammer. You want it to work for you." Chris suggests a ratio of about an ounce and a quarter per inch, so that a thirteen-inch knife would weigh approximately a pound. He cautions that a lightweight knife will wobble, whereas a hefty one is "going to go right where you put it" (Christ 2001).

As Gresham learned from Pearce, throwers usually hold the knife by the blade, "exactly as you would hold a pencil—if you were going to write with the point held *perpendicular* to the writing surface." The fingers and wrist are kept rigid, and when the arm is straightened in the act of throwing, the knife leaves the fingers due to its own inertia. Gresham (1953, 88) adds: "This is the whole secret of throwing knives: holding fingers and wrist rigid and judging the distance. I have seen many professionals on the midway use a wrist flip, but they simply made it a hundred times harder for themselves." (Some professionals do throw by the handle. For example, Gil Hibben [1998] designs his knives for utility, which means they have sharp blades that could cut the hand. But expert throwers like Hibben are outside the midway tradition.)

The knife thrower always wants to work from the same distance. When held by the blade, the knife will make three-quarters of a turn in a few feet, or one and three-quarters revolutions at a little more than twice the distance. Slightly closer or farther away, and it will not be the point of the knife that strikes the backboard.

When throwing knives to outline a spread-eagled person on a rotating wheel, Christ prefers a smaller, lighter knife (about ten and a half inches long and approximately nine ounces). A heavier knife, he says, will "swing out of there." Hitting the proper spot on a rotating wheel requires timing, so that the knife's trajectory intersects that of the moving spot. "And it's got to be vertical to you when it meets up," he says (Christ 2001). One bit of showmanship in this regard is that, for safety, the knives are aimed a bit farther away from the target person than it appears. While the wheel is moving, it is difficult for the audience to see how far away the blades are, and as the wheel slows to a stop, the person unobtrusively extends his or her arms to make it look as if the knives came closer than they actually did.

What about outright trickery in knife throwing? I asked Christ about a gaffed backboard I had learned about, which was—according to Walter

FIGURE 9.24. Gaffed knife-throwing act using a trick backboard from which knives sprang into view. (Nineteenth-century illustration)

Gibson (1967, 125–26)—"an ingenious mechanical device." It had slits at the supposed strike points, and within each slit was a concealed knife. The knife's point had a spring pivot, which the girl who stood against the board could activate by pressing an arm or other part of her body at the appropriate spot. The knife would instantly spring into view and quiver as though it had just struck there. The area behind the knife thrower was dim, and as he swept his arm backward as if readying for a throw, he tossed the blade behind him, then followed through as if actually tossing the knife. The audience, anticipating the throw, would look ahead to the expected impact. Since a blade then seemed to stick in the backboard, the illusion was complete. Some people actually believed they saw the glint of the blade flying through the air. This clever mechanism was illustrated in a nineteenth-century print (figure 9.24) and featured in a 1920s Broadway show, *Stepping Stones* (Gresham 1953, 90). It was also used, then exposed as a joke, in the 1947 Roy Rogers movie *On the Old Spanish Trail*. It was apparently also used on an episode of *Charlie's Angels* called "Circus of Fear" (October 19, 1977), with Kris Munroe (played by Cheryl Ladd) as the girl against the backboard. More recently, the mechanism was featured on a television exposé of conjuring secrets by the Masked

Magician. However, Chris Christ (2001) says that it was never used on the midway.

Little trickery is employed by circus and carnival sideshow knife wielders. One stunt, however, is to use a sharp knife (the ones used for throwing are dull) to halve an apple placed on the nape of an assistant's neck. With a quick blow, the performer divides the apple, without cutting the assistant. The secret is that the apple was prepared by pushing a large darning needle through it at the bottom, which stops the blade at that point.

Chris Christ (2001) acknowledges that when the knife master performs blindfolded, "obviously, you use a trick blindfold." (There are many different types of blindfolds sold by magic supply houses.) Other than that, knife throwing is a matter of skill. "It's kind of like juggling," he told me. "It's just a matter of practice and certain basic principles."

Of course, as legendary showman Ward Hall sagely observes, "In this type of act, there are occasional mishaps." Hall's first partner was Harry "Leonardo" Leonard, who did a knife-throwing act until his death in late 1964. Hall was often Harry's human target in the act, in which the two men dressed in identical costumes and billed themselves on the banner line as the "Two Leonardos" (Hall 1981, 19, 22). Hall recalls one of their mishaps (1991, 42): "On our opening night with the All American Circus in Oxford, Alabama, I miscalculated a move and received a small cut on the face. My aunt read of it in a trade journal and suggested that I should cease such dangerous endeavors. I didn't quit working the act, but anytime there was a mishap Harry would eliminate that particular stunt from the act. Over the years the act got shorter and shorter." In addition to being a human target, Hall has featured a number of knife throwers in his shows, including Chris Christ (with Connie Kelly among Christ's lovely assistants), John Trower (also with Connie Kelly), Johnny Munroe (with Marilyn and Kathy Munroe), and Bruce Hill (Hall 1981, 57; 1991, 50–55).

Over the years, there have been many attempts to give knife acts new appeal (figure 9.25). One performer had his lovely assistant appear fully clothed. In fact, she was overdressed—in a breakaway outfit. Each knife pinned part of her costume, and after each throw she gave a little twist that left a portion of it on the backboard. Voilà! Knife throwing and striptease combined. (Gresham 1953, 91–92).

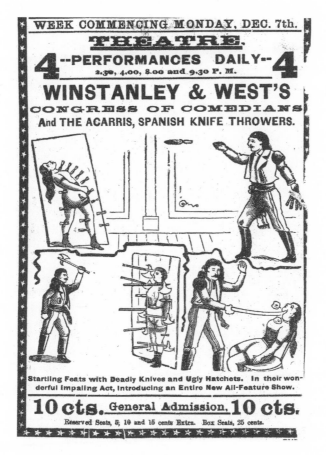

FIGURE 9.25. Vaudeville knife-throwing act featured several interesting feats. (Flyer from author's collection)

Some performers tried other combinations, often pairing knife throwing with another western-style act, such as rope spinning or whip cracking. Mannix (1996, 118) describes the whip-snapping artistry of a cowboy named Bronco Billy who performed such feats as cutting a cigarette from his assistant's lips. "The assistant had to keep his head thrown back and the cigarette sticking out straight," says Mannix. "Otherwise his nose got in the way of the whip lash." A few knife throwers—including Chris Christ and John Trower—are truly masters of the blade, doubling as sword swallowers.

10 ILLUSIONS

∎•∎•
•∎•
∎•∎•
•∎•∎ IN ADDITION TO HUMAN ODDITIES AND working acts, a third major
class of sideshow features is represented by what is known as an
illusion show (figure 10.1). In earlier times, this could mean simply a magic show, particularly one that featured some of the larger effects.
"Illusion shows became popular on midways," says Al Stencell (2002, 139),
"and by World War I they were competing with the new 10-in-1s and holding
their own." Such a show was the Temple of Wonders that operated at Palisades
Park, New Jersey. A 1926 photograph shows banners for a "Prof. of Magic," the
"Burning of She" (a cremation illusion), and many other features, including,
on the bally, a suspension illusion (Barth and Siegel 2002, 54).

The J. L. Cronin Shows, which operated from 1922 to 1931, had a mystery
and illusion show called The Demon of Doom. Billed as the "World's Greatest
Mystery Show," it featured among its small troupe an escape artist who, in
Houdini fashion, wriggled out of a straitjacket (McKennon 1972, 1:101). Another
illusion show had an unusually frank approach. Operated by Dufour and
Rogers at the 1939 New York world's fair, it was dubbed the Fakertorium.
Explains Dufour (1977, 121): "Everything in the show is a fake—illusions, and
so on, with an exposé of how the four-legged girl was presented, etc.—and that
is how the show was sold to the public." More recently, an illusion show might
be just a single-O that features one illusion (Ray 1993, 14). In this chapter, after
first looking at the working acts of magicians and psychic marvels, I describe
several famous sideshow illusions.

Magicians

Among the familiar working acts of the sideshow is the conjurer or stage magician (figure 10.2). The great Harry Houdini (born Ehrich Weiss, 1874–1926)
had his start in such venues. After entertaining at the Chicago world's fair in

260

FIGURE 10.1. Hall & Christ's Wondercade was a type of illusion show. It appeared at the 1981 Ohio State Fair and then went on tour. Note the buzz-saw illusion depicted at right. (Author's collection, gift of Sandy Lesniak)

1893, he performed in dime museums at Coney Island and elsewhere and traveled with medicine shows and the Welsh Brothers Circus sideshow. As the "King of Cards," he did up to twenty platform shows a week for a salary of $12. He later added a handcuff-escape act and became a vaudeville headliner, then progressed to his own full evening show that incorporated magic (including sleight of hand and illusions), dramatic escapes, and exposés of spiritualistic trickery (Christopher 1962, 182–87; Dawes 1979, 193–202).

Many other famous magicians debuted in fairs and sideshows. As noted in earlier chapters, Isaac Fawkes was a major attraction at the annual Bartholomew Fair in the first half of the eighteenth century. His banner proclaimed his "Dexterity of hand." Fawkes performed up to six shows each day at the height of the fair season. Following his death in 1731, his son carried on the

FIGURE 10.2. A magician performing in the Houdini tradition as an escape artist is depicted on this Coney Island banner. (Photo by author)

tradition of fairground conjuring. Still others followed, including a Monsieur Gyngell—"emperor of cards" and exhibitor of "necromancer's powers"—who was at the famous fair in the early nineteenth century.

Like Houdini, the great illusionist Howard Thurston (1869–1936) left home as a youngster and traveled with circus sideshows, performing prestidigitation with cards and doing other small platform magic. He went on to become "an American theatrical phenomenon," presenting an evening show with such features as levitation, a vanishing auto, the East Indian rope trick, and other wonders over some three decades. Thurston's contemporary, Carl Hertz (1869–1924), also toured with a circus before traveling the world with a successful magic show (Christopher 1962, 16–19, 179–90).

Many well-known Canadian magicians likewise had their start in carnival and circus sideshows, among them vaudeville magician Harry Smith of Toronto. I knew Smith and his wife, Sophie, when I was a young magician in the late 1960s and early 1970s and frequently visited them at their Arcade Magic and Novelty Store, where they were in semiretirement. Harry told me that he joined the Steve McGrow Carnival in Pennsylvania at the age of fifteen, where he was a magician, fire-eater, puppeteer, and talker. From about 1920 to 1930 he worked a variety of carnival and circus sideshows, including the Frank West Wonder Shows and Simms Greater Shows (Nickell 1970).

Raymond Lowe was another Canadian magician who did a stint in the carnival, working one year with the Stanger Shows out of Winnipeg. Still another was Bill McClory, who traveled with carnivals throughout his native country as well as the United States. At one time or another, McClory juggled, did rope spinning, rode a unicycle, and played fifteen musical instruments—as well as performing a magic act (Nickell 1970).

One of Canada's most famous magical exports to the United States is Randall James Hamilton Zwinge, now a naturalized American citizen better known as James "The Amazing" Randi. Born in Toronto in 1928, Randi became Houdini's great successor as a sideshow performer, stage magician, escape artist, and nemesis of phony spiritualists, psychics, and similar claimants. (He also became my mentor, colleague, and friend of over thirty years.)

Many now-forgotten magicians enjoyed careers in the sideshows. Photographs of old midway scenes show the banners of some of them. A double banner in the Dailey Brothers Circus Museum (sideshow) banner line, for example, featured a "Master Magician" and promised "Mystery & Fun." Another was headed "Illusionist." A turbaned "Hindu Magician" was depicted on a banner of Happyland's Big Circus Sideshow, with various wonders emanating in a mist from the magus's magical vase. A similar motif was included on a "Master of Magic" banner painted by Fred G. Johnson. And a banner line of a ten-in-one at an unidentified carnival featured a "Prof. De Lenz, Magician" (Johnson et al. 1996, 8, 30, 32, 69).

Sometimes a magician is recognizable as such in an old group photograph of human oddities and working acts. For example, in a 1924 photo of the Harlem Amusement Palace (a dime museum), the house wizard appears, along with a tattooed man, fat lady, living skeleton, snake charmer, man with trained monkeys, musicians, and others; he holds a giant fan of cards in one hand and a magic wand in the other (Barth and Siegel 2002, 53).

Psychic Marvels

Another class of sideshow mystifier is the purveyor of some form of alleged extrasensory power. There are basically two types on the midway: the mentalist and the fortune-teller.

Mentalists are simply magicians who perform mind reading and other "psychic" tricks. In the sideshows they are billed in various ways. For example, there was "Princess Nanna," wife of showman W. D. "Mexican Billy" Ament, who performed at the Midway Plaisance of the 1893 Chicago world's fair. Others were "Mlle. Corina, Mind Reader," "Lady Yava, Mentalist," and many similar performers. Among them was "Madame Bailey, the Girl with a Thousand Eyes," but others were similarly styled, including "Leona LaMar, the Girl with 1,000 Eyes," who worked her act with Hugh Shannon (Stencell 2002, 25–26; Johnson et al. 1996, 32, 33; McKennon 1972, 2:158; Dufour 1977, 49).

LaMar's pitch book (figure 10.3) describes her act, which was a typical one. "The Professor" (her partner) went among the audience and picked out common articles, such as a comb or handkerchief, which the blindfolded LaMar named. She would even call out the date on a coin, the name on a calling card, or the denomination of a piece of paper money, thus supposedly proving that she used "mental telepathy" (LaMar n.d.). Although LaMar performed in lowly state fair midways of the 1920s, the act she and Shannon offered was reportedly "far superior" to that of her rival, Eva Fay, who was herself "a sensation as a mind reader on the Keith Orpheum circuit." LaMar and Shannon were soon signed by Terry Turner (who had taken the teenage conjoined twins Daisy and Violet Hilton out of the Clarence Wortham Shows and onto the vaudeville stage). The duo was soon receiving $2,500 a week (Dufour 1977, 48–49).

Rather than mental telepathy, such acts usually depend on a clever code that the "professor" and "mind reader" have memorized and rehearsed. How the former asks the question signals the category of object. For example, "What is this?" could signify money, while "What am I holding?" might indicate an item of jewelry. An additional phrase, such as "Now concentrate," could provide another piece of information. When the mentalist answers, say, "money," the professor replies, "Good" or "That's right" or some other word or phrase that further identifies the item. Magicians call the routine "second sight."

FIGURE 10.3. Booklet of mentalist Leona LaMar billed her as
"The Girl with 1,000 Eyes." (Author's collection)

The secret is ancient and appeared in print as early as the sixteenth century, when Reginald Scot (1584, 191) debunked all manner of superstitions
and supernatural claims in his *The Discoverie of Witchcraft*. It was subsequently
developed by magicians such as Pinetti in the eighteenth century and Robert-
Houdin (from whom Houdini took his name) in the nineteenth. The renowned
mentalist Julius Zancig performed second sight with his wife, and the couple
was billed in vaudeville shows as "Two Minds with a Single Thought" (Dexter
1958, 187–204; Gardner 1962, 96; Christopher 1962, 162).

A mentalist act need not involve the studious second-sight routine or
even a partner. Numerous tricks that are simple to perform, yet astonishing

to the audience, have long been available. For example, the performer writes a "prediction" on a small pad of paper, then asks a member of the audience to name, for instance, any number under 100. When the person complies, the mentalist shows the pad, on which is written that very number! The secret is a little gimmick called a "nail writer," a device containing a bit of pencil lead that fits on the thumb. To work the trick, the performer initially only pretends to write something. Then, after the audience member states the number, the performer jots it with the nail writer just before revealing it, the pad concealing the thumb's movement (Schiffman 1997, 72–73).

Mentalists often do mind-reading tricks with playing cards. For instance, a spectator is invited to insert his finger into the deck as the mentalist riffles it, remove a card, and concentrate on it. With appropriate byplay—in which the wizard apparently reads the individual's mind—the color, suit, and number of the chosen card are revealed in turn. For this effect, the mentalist uses an apparently ordinary deck, casually flipping through it so the spectators can see that it consists of different cards. In reality, it may be a "forcing" deck, in which every other card is the same and is cut slightly short. Thus, when the deck is riffled, the cards fall in pairs, and the spectator always gets one of the duplicate short cards (Hugard 1980, 272–74).

I demonstrated and sold such "Svengali" decks (as magicians call them) when I was a carny pitchman at the Canadian National Exhibition in Toronto in 1969 (Nickell 1970). Rather than just riffling the cards to show that they were all apparently different, I would spring them slowly from my left hand to my right so that the entire tip could get a look at the cards. Of course, once these decks began to be sold at fairs and carnivals, sideshow mentalists avoided them, using sleight of hand and other methods to accomplish the same and similar feats.

Like mentalists, carny fortune-tellers also take advantage of the widespread belief in psychic phenomena to make a buck off credulous patrons. However, instead of representing a working act and performing before an audience, fortune-tellers operate a concession known in carny parlance as a *mitt camp*. Such fortune-telling booths can be individual enterprises (like the ones I have seen in recent years at some fairground midways) or they can be a screened-off area inside a ten-in-one (like a mitt camp I visited at the Canadian National

FIGURE 10.4. Mitt camp offers palmistry at the 2004 Canadian National Exhibition midway. (Photo by author)

Exhibition around 1970). "Whether the seeress has a canvas banner showing the lines of the hand, or 'mitt,' or whether the sign shows a human head with the bumps identified according to character traits for phrenology," explains Gresham (1953, 115), "it's a mitt camp to the carnies." The same applies to astrology, tarot card reading, or some other form of divinatory or character "reading." (See figures 10.4 and 10.5.)

One canvas banner, by 1930s artist G. M. Caldwell, simply features a giant open hand, displaying the lines and symbols of palmistry and reading "Votre Future." (It has been repainted and once bore the words "Past, Present & Future" and "Man Know Thyself.") Another banner—a double one produced by artist George Bellis of Sunshine Studio, Wichita, Kansas, circa 1940—features a "Mystic Reader" who is alternately studying the skies (for astrological indicators) and gazing into his crystal ball (Johnson et al. 1996, 19, 43).

Some of the mitt camp operators were *gypsies,* a term derived from *Egyptian* due to a mistaken notion about their ancestry. They were actually

FIGURE 10.5. Mitt camp offers psychic readings at the 2004 Canadian National Exhibition midway. (Photo by author)

exiled from northwestern India in the first millennium A.D. and in the Middle Ages sought asylum in Romania, hence their other designation as *Romanies* or (as they prefer) *Roma*. As an ethnic group, they tend to live outside the culture of whatever country they reside in and often treat nongypsies as fair game for such scams as fortune-telling and curse removal (Nickell 2001, 179–80; Randi 1995, 148).

One old gypsy woman advised a young girl of the tribe:

When thou wilt tell a fortune, put all thy heart into finding out what kind of man or woman thou hast to deal with. Look keenly, fix thy glance sharply, especially if it be a girl. When she is half-frightened, she will tell you much without knowing it. When thou shalt have often done this thou wilt be able to twist many a silly girl like twine around thy fingers. Soon thy eyes will look like a snake's, and when thou art angry thou wilt look like the old devil. Half the business, my dear, is to know how to please and flatter and allure people. When a girl has anything unusual in her face, you must tell her that it signifies extraordinary luck. If she have red or yellow hair, tell her that is a true sign that she will have much gold. When her eyebrows meet, that shows she will be united to many rich gentlemen. Tell her always, when you see a mole on her cheek or her forehead or anything, that is a sign that she will become a great lady. . . . Praising and petting and alluring and crying-up are half of fortunetelling. There is no girl and no man in all the Lord's earth who is not proud and vain about something, and if you can find it out you can get their money. (Leland 1882)

Because of unsavory practices, gypsies became unpopular among carnival operators, who sometimes ran ads in *Billboard* reading, "mitt camp, no gypsies." Eventually, most of the soothsayers came to be what the gypsies call *gorgio* (nongypsies). However, Gresham (1953, 116) recalls one "strikingly beautiful gypsy girl" sitting at the table in her fortune-telling concession at a midwestern amusement park. She was bored and leafing through a tabloid, but when he approached, she sprang up with a "swirl of nylon skirts and petticoats," her black eyes taking on the intense "Romany gaze" as she launched into her pitch: "For one hand, one dollar, gentleman. For both hands, two dollars, giving full life reading, telling about future dangers, how to escape them, who you will fall in love with and who will fall in love with you, likewise business enemies for you to watch for."

Whether gypsy or not, the midway fortune-teller relies on some standard methods. One technique—still used by today's "psychics" and "spiritualist mediums"—is called "cold reading." Psychologist Ray Hyman (1977, 22), himself a palmist during his college years, explains how the "reader" first sizes up the client, then,

On the basis of his initial assessment he makes some tentative hypotheses. He tests these out by beginning his assessment in general terms, touching upon general categories of problems and watching the reaction of the client. If he is on the wrong track the client's reactions—eye movements, pupillary dilation, other bodily mannerisms—will warn him. When he is on the right track other reactions will tell him so. By watching the client's reactions as he tests out different hypotheses during his spiel, the good reader quickly hits upon what is bothering the customer and begins to adjust the reading to the situation. By this time, the client has usually been persuaded that the reader, by some uncanny means, has gained insights into the client's innermost thoughts. His guard is now down. Often he opens up and actually tells the reader, who is also a good listener, the details of his situation. The reader, after a suitable interval, will usually feed back the information that the client has given him in such a way that the client will be further amazed at how much the reader "knows" about him. Invariably the client leaves the reader without realizing that everything he has been told is simply what he himself has unwittingly revealed to the reader.

The less skilled pretender to clairvoyant powers, who has not yet mastered the art of cold reading, can fall back on a stock spiel, such as this one (quoted in Hyman 1977, 23):

Some of your aspirations tend to be pretty unrealistic. At times you are extroverted, affable, sociable, while at other times you are introverted, wary and reserved. You have found it unwise to be too frank in revealing yourself to others. You pride yourself on being an independent thinker and do not accept others' opinions without satisfactory proof. You prefer a certain amount of change and variety, and become dissatisfied when hemmed in by restrictions and limitations. At times you have serious doubts as to whether you have made the right decision or done the right thing. Disciplined and controlled on the outside, you tend to be worrisome and insecure on the inside.

Your sexual adjustment has presented some problems for you. While you have some personality weaknesses, you are generally able to compensate for them. You have a great deal of unused capacity which you have not turned to your advantage. You have a tendency to be critical of yourself. You have a strong need for other people to like you and for them to admire you.

Some fortune-tellers convince themselves that they really do have clairvoyant powers, while others rationalize their deceptions and illusions as harmless entertainment or as valuable counseling at a bargain rate.

Torture Box Illusions

A number of sideshow illusions utilize a coffin-size box into which the magician's lovely assistant is placed and then—well, terrible things are seemingly done to her. The box might be sawed in half, intersected with blades, set on fire, or treated to other horrors, but the lady always emerges unharmed. How do they do it? Well, *very carefully,* as the old magicians' joke goes.

Let's start with the classic, sawing a woman in half. An effect similar to it was done by a French conjurer named Torrini in the early nineteenth century, but it properly dates from 1920, when British magician P. T. Selbit performed it in London. Horace Goldin created another version in New York. According to Milbourne Christopher (1962, 190), "During the 1921–22 season the illusion was such a great draw in vaudeville theaters that Goldin sent out six road companies and Selbit toured with nine units."

In the most common version of the trick, two girls are used. The magician's assistant enters the box, sticks her head out a hole in one end, and draws her knees up to her chin. At the same time, another girl (who is concealed in the platform on which the box rests) enters through a trap, puts her feet out two holes in the opposite end of the box, and places her head between her knees. From the spectators' point of view, it appears that a girl has entered the box and that her head and feet are in view. Instead of her being cut in half, the saw blade passes harmlessly between the two doubled-up girls (Hay 1949, 398). A simplified version of the trick requires only one girl. In this case, the box is somewhat short and bottomless, which allows the middle of the girl's body to sag into the platform below, thus being out of reach of the saw (Gibson 1967, 117–18).

The most dramatic version of the illusion dispenses with the box and uses a table and a buzz saw to slice the assistant in two. The secret is that, under her gown, she is wearing a special corset made to retain her shape when her middle sags into a recess in the table. It is this corset that the rotating blade cuts into, with a safety bar to keep it from cutting too deep (Wels 1977, 95–96).

Sometimes a bag of fake blood and gore is affixed to the corset for added realism (as in a version I saw in a live stage show in the 1970s). The buzz-saw illusion was introduced by Horace Goldin and was exhibited on the midway by magicians such as Noel Lester, who used his wife Phyllis in the role of victim on the Strates Shows circuit in the 1950s (Stencell 2002, 130–31).

In another box illusion, the magician's hapless assistant loses her middle. The effect is known variously as the "Invisible Middle Girl," "No Middle Myrtle," and other appellations (Brill 1976, 149, 158). In a wonderful banner illustrating the effect for Bobby Reynolds's traveling sideshow museum (figure 10.6), the box is omitted for exaggerated effect. In reality, the box (figure 10.7) is divided into three vertical sections. The small central section simply hides the girl's midriff by means of two mirrors joined at an angle. Each mirror reflects one side of the box, giving the overall appearance that one is seeing the back of the box and thus making that section look empty.

In an interesting variant called the "Sword Lady" (Brill 1976, 144), the assistant's head extends above a two-section box. The lower section is open, but the upper one has doors that cover her torso. The magician thrusts a number of swords into this area from the sides, and then the doors are opened. Spectators see the swords crisscrossing the space where the lady's torso should be but isn't. In this version, mirrors are unnecessary. Instead, matte-black panels are used, being relatively invisible when the entire interior of the compartment is similarly painted.

One of the most common sideshow illusions is known as the "Coffin Blade Box." Indeed, "No magic or side show should be without this one," states an ad in a showmen's catalog. "We've sold plans of it to all the big shows." The ad continues, "Use it as a stage presentation, a free act on the bally platform, or as a side show act" (Brill 1976, 142). Usually known simply as a blade box, the illusion was especially popular around the end of the nineteenth century and continues to be in use today (figure 10.8). In fact, while doing research for this book, I watched it being presented at Coney Island's Sideshows by the Seashore.

The act involves a young woman lying in the box, which is then intersected by a number of wide blades inserted through holes in the hinged lid. It seems that there is no room left for the lady. Has she vanished, or—? The secret? For that, one pays an extra charge (a form of *aftercatch*, also called a *ding*) to come

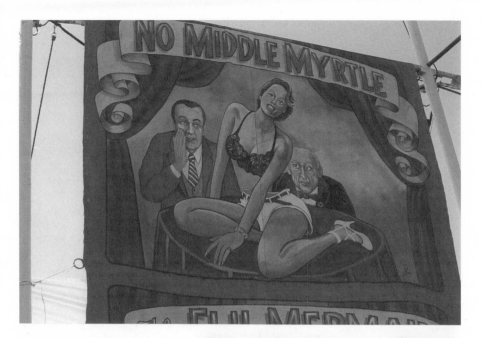

(Above) FIGURE 10.6. "No Middle Myrtle," contrary to its banner depiction, is a magician's illusion (see figure 10.7). (Photo by author at Bobby Reynolds's traveling sideshow museum)

(Right) FIGURE 10.7. The illusion uses a box with mirrors to conceal the young lady's midriff. (Photo by author at Bobby Reynolds's traveling sideshow museum)

FIGURE 10.8. Famed showman Bobby Reynolds exhibits a blade box, long a sideshow feature. (Photo by author)

up on the platform and peer inside. To provide extra incentive, the magician often uses a clever ploy involving his scantily clad assistant. When the blades are being inserted, one seems to catch on something, whereupon the illusionist reaches in and pulls out a bra; the blade then proceeds unhindered. Another blade sticks, and another article of clothing is removed. When all the blades have been inserted, the magician (or talker—often the same person) begins to pitch the aftercatch. Here is the spiel of the late showman Howard Bone (2001, 35–36): "I now invite you to come on stage, up these steps to your right. Walk by the box and look inside to get an eyeful of exactly how she is in there, and then walk down the other set of steps. All this for a small donation of one dime, one tenth of a dollar. If you need change, I'll make it for you. Remember folks, the young lady receives all the money. It all goes to her. [A lie.] Someone start it off and the rest will follow. Thank you ma'am, thank you sir . . . move right along." Of course, the articles of clothing were duplicates, and most people accepted that the joke was on them. They did, however, get to see how the girl's body snaked around the blades; there was room for her after all. From their original vantage point below the platform, spectators could not perceive the depth, so the blades seemed closer together than they actually were.

Not as common as the blade box, but much more dramatic, is the cremation illusion. There are several variants, one of which is called "Flaming Mamie" (Brill 1976, 155). The magician's assistant is helped into the coffin-like box, and then a lighted match is dropped inside. Instantly, real flames leap up and blaze through the length of the casket. Then, suddenly, the sides and ends drop down, revealing only smoldering bones. As an ad for the plans promised, "You use the same girl in the next performance, but it creates a startling illusion" (Brill 1976, 155). The secret is a shallow metal tray, containing a small amount of naphtha or similar fuel, attached on the inside of the lid. After the assistant is placed in the casket, this tray drops down and is stopped by an inner frame. It thus protects the assistant from the brief blaze and conceals her when the box's sides fall down (Wels 1977, 157–59).

With these torture box effects, as with most illusions, it is the magician's assistant—not the illusionist himself—who does the hard work.

Living Heads

A decapitation illusion, probably dating from the Middle Ages and recorded by Reginald Scot in 1584, was sensational for its day. It featured a young boy who was placed facedown on a box. The magician covered the boy's head with a cloth and, reaching underneath with a knife, apparently severed the head, which he then lifted (still covered in the cloth) and placed on a platter at the other end of the box. He removed the cloth and showed the living head before reversing the procedure and revealing the boy fully restored.

The trick actually utilized two boys—the second boy concealed in the box (figures 10.9 and 10.10). The top of the box had a round hole at either end, which could not be seen by the audience, since the box was on a raised platform. After the magician placed the first boy on the box, he picked up the cloth, which contained a dummy head. As the boy's head was covered, the youth ducked it into the hole, while the wizard pretended to decapitate him. When the "head" was carried to the opposite end of the box and seemingly placed on the platter, the hidden boy pushed his head through the hole there (and through the platter's matching hole). The cloth was then pulled away, and the living head was revealed (Gibson 1967, 31–32; Hopkins 1898, 48–50).

A very different type of animated head was inspired by the popularity of spiritualism. Among the "spirit effects" created by magicians in the late nineteenth and early twentieth centuries was a "talking skull." One such version was not only sensational in its own right but was also a prototype for many illusions that followed. Known as the Sphinx, it debuted on October 16, 1865, at London's Egyptian Hall. The exhibitor was a "Colonel Stodare," supposedly "a well educated Frenchman," but in reality, Liverpool-born Alfred Inglis (1831–1866). Stodare entered carrying a small box, which he set on a three-legged table, the emptiness of the area underneath the table being plainly visible. Lowering the box's front, the magician revealed a head of Egyptian appearance, whose eyes he commanded to open. The Sphinx complied and then, following other commands, smiled and proceeded to give a speech. Finally, Stodare closed the box and explained that the magical charm, which had enabled him to revivify an ancient Egyptian's ashes, lasted just fifteen minutes and had expired. When he opened the box again, the head had been replaced by a heap of ashes. Stodare enjoyed great but brief success. He performed the Sphinx for Queen Victoria but succumbed to consumption only one year after the Sphinx was introduced.

The clever illusion depended on the table, which appeared to be empty underneath but actually concealed a confederate. This was accomplished by the use of two mirrors. They filled the space between the table's legs in such a way that they not only hid the accomplice but also reflected the carpeting on either side; thus, audience members thought that they were seeing the carpet beneath the table. The actor could insert his head into the box, withdraw it, and substitute a pile of ashes at the appropriate time (Dawes 1979, 152–54; Hoffmann n.d., 531–32).

A sideshow version of the Sphinx was advertised in *A. Brill's Bible of Building Plans.* For $5 a showman could obtain the secret and the working drawings for constructing the box and "see-thru" cabinet. Brill (1976, 199) promised that construction was "a simple carpentry job" and that the completed cabinet easily broke down into panels for transporting. Another sideshow version was advertised by Brill (1976, 146) as "Ideal for a Grind Show" (recall

(ABOVE) FIGURE 10.9. Dating back to at least the sixteenth century (probably earlier), this decapitation mystery is revealed in figure 10.10. (Nineteenth-century illustration) (Below) FIGURE 10.10. As shown, it requires a dummy head and a second person. (Nineteenth-century illustration)

that a grind show is a continuous presentation). Billed as the "Decapitated Princess," it utilized a "throne" with a living head that rested on the blade of a sword placed across the chair's arms. The "princess" could smile, speak, and otherwise respond to spectators. Once again, a mirror was used, this time concealing the upper portion of the lady's body. The mirror was the width of the chair seat and was placed at a forty-five-degree angle—its bottom edge at the rear, and its top edge concealed by the sword. Thus the seat was reflected, appearing to be the back of the throne, with an apparently unobstructed view under the sword. The girl knelt behind the throne with her knees underneath the seat, pushed her head through a trapdoor in the lower chair back, and rested her chin on the sword (Dexter 1958, 51–52).

An interesting version of the living-head illusion was used by a Syracuse, New York, department store in about 1947. A local newspaper headlined a story on the effect, "Circus Trick in Window Draws Crowds; Sells Hats." Passersby were startled to see, among the several mannequin heads resting atop pedestals, one living head. I obtained the accompanying photo of the display (figure 10.11), a scrapbook news clipping, from an antiques dealer. The display was slyly titled "Fashion Reflections" and utilized two mirrors framed by pedestals (just like those of the three-legged table used in the Sphinx illusion). The bottom edge of each mirror was camouflaged by placing it on a seam of the tile flooring.

When I was resident magician at the Houdini Magical Hall of Fame in Niagara Falls, Canada, from 1970 to 1972, we had a living-head illusion in our big window on Centre Street. The part was usually played by a vivacious red-head, Rusty, whose voice was carried outside by a speaker. She could thus get the attention of passing tourists, gather a tip, and then turn the tip by directing people to the adjacent ticket window.

An elaboration on the living-head illusion was to place the head on the body of a giant spider to create the famous "human spider" or "spider girl" illusion. A. W. Stencell (2002, 136) credits its creation to prolific illusionist Henry Roltair (1853–1910). Roltair transformed his touring stage show into a traveling midway illusion show in 1891, introducing his Palace of Illusions at the Sydney Exposition. He later had shows at the San Francisco Mid-Winter Exposition (1894), the St. Louis Expo (1904), and elsewhere, includ-

FIGURE 10.11. A young lady has her wits about her—but where is her body?—in this living-head illusion. (Author's collection)

SPIDORA

A wonderful bit of the past. An
ILLUSION of the side show from
years ago. The body of a creepy, crawl
spider and the head of a beautiful
girl—sometimes, not so beautiful.

FIGURE 10.12. This Spidora illusion is more effective with a living head, rather than a mannequin one, as seen in this version exhibited in Bobby Reynolds's sideshow museum. (Photo by
author)

ing a spectacular "Creation" show that ran for several years at Coney Island's
Dreamland Park.

The spider girl illusion became a permanent fixture of the midway, eventually becoming known as Spidora (figure 10.12). In 1917 showman James A.
"Fingers" Wallace wrote a letter of complaint to *Billboard* magazine. Wallace
stated that for five seasons he had operated a spider girl show on the midway, but during the present season, showmen were revealing the secret as an
aftercatch for 25¢. Urging that the practice be stopped, he said, "They have no
regard for brother showmen who come in after them" (Stencell 2002, 139).

Nevertheless, Spidora flourished. One embodiment appeared on a 1928
midway as a single-O feature of the Conklin & Garrett Shows. (That western
Canadian carnival was a *gilly show*—i.e., one moving between dates by box-
cars. It was a partnership of J. W. "Patty" Conklin and "Speed" Garrett from
1924 until 1929, when the latter was bought out by Patty's brother Frank.)
At that time, the illusion was in a round top between a ten-in-one and an *at'*

show (a carny term for a show that features athletic contests between wrestlers and boxers traveling with the show and local contenders [Bone 2001, 131]). A single large banner showed a giant, human-headed spider approaching a hapless man. Headed "Spidoro [*sic*]," it claimed in smaller letters, "From Death Valley." Painted on the side of the ticket box was the question, "How Can She Live?" (McKennon 1972, 1:102).

Spidora continued as a sideshow staple for decades. Byron G. Wels (1977, 31, 32), magician and author of *The Great Illusions of Magic*, reminisces:

> Your author first saw this illusion at a Coney Island "Freak Show" on the Midway back in his youth and was completely taken in by the barker's [talker's] spiel.
>
> "Step right up folks, meet 'Spidora,' the Spider Girl. Born with the head and face of a beautiful girl and the body of an ugly spider, she survives in total misery, for no man could love her." He went on to explain that she lived off her earnings by displaying herself in this manner, that she ate flies and other insects. He spoke to her, she answered him, and she was, obviously, very much alive. The barker then closed the curtain and moved on to the next exhibit. The problem occurred when we thought we recognized the same face on a girl who was doing a "cross escape" three exhibits down the line!

There are different versions of Spidora—some apparently manufactured by professional illusion fabricators, others created from workshop plans or improvised from a little behind-the-scenes knowledge. All work on the same basic principle. Spidora is in a cabinet, resting on her web, through which a stair-stepped interior is visible. The illusion works much like the "Decapitated Princess" described earlier, with a mirror concealing the girl's upper torso. The "web" is made of white twine, and it (along with a backing) supports the body of the arachnid, which is fashioned of fake fur (the legs sewn into tubes and filled with lengths of coil spring). The girl can secretly reach up and move the body slightly to impart a bit of "life" to the model (Wels 1977, 31–33).

Some other human-headed monstrosities that were apparently inspired by Spidora are the "human butterfly" and "snake girl" illusions. The butterfly version was among the offerings of an illusion show, the Temple of Wonders, at New Jersey's Palisades Park in the 1920s. The banner promised—correctly, if somewhat tongue in cheek—"Alive" (Barth and Siegel 2002, 54). The human butterfly probably works rather like the snake girl, which is "essentially Spidora with a snake's body substituted for the spider's" (Taylor 1998, 95). A Hall & Christ single-O show featured a "Snake Girl Alive," as its banner promised, with suitable illustrations. More disingenuously, signs proclaimed, "No Arms, No Legs, No Bones in her Body." The illusion did so well that the showmen put a second snake girl on the road (Hall 1981, 97, 100, 111).

Headless People

Complementing the living heads are various "headless" illusions. One of these consists of a coffin-like box that stands vertically and is divided into two compartments: one, for the head, has a door; the other is for the rest of the body, which is in full view throughout the presentation. Called "Where Does the Head Go?" this illusion is similar to the "Sword Lady" described earlier. In this presentation, the door to the upper compartment is closed, swords intersect the chamber, and the door is opened to reveal that the lady's head has vanished. Then the door is closed again, the swords are removed, and the assistant steps out unharmed.

Once again, mirrors are used. They are hinged so that they fold back against the head compartment. A simple mechanism, operated by the illusionist after his assistant is in place, moves the mirrors together to form a wedge pointing toward the audience. To conceal the front edges where they meet, a sword is placed downward through the center of the compartment. Then the other blades follow, all being guided by slots to ensure that they miss the head in its rear compartment (Wels 1977, 251–53). This illusion is excellent for the stage and can be part of an illusion show. However, because it has to be *performed,* a different version—needing only to be *exhibited*—is perfect for a grind show. Known as the "Headless Girl" or—as listed in *Brill's Bible* (Brill 1976, 145)— the "Headless Illusion" (figure 10.13), it has an especially realistic look.

The headless girl illusion was created by Egon "Dutch" Heineman, a refugee from Hitler's Germany. He had exhibited it in Blackpool, England, before com-

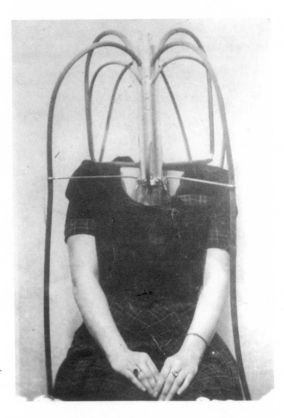

FIGURE 10.13. The headless-girl illusion—like this circa 1940s version—is ideal for a grind show. (Author's collection)

ing to America in 1937 and joining the Goodman Wonder Shows. Goodman's superintendent (and later carnival historian) Joe McKennon (1972, 1:137) framed Heineman's first American show, which was "the big attraction on Depression-era midways." It subsequently became a popular sideshow act and, after World War II, a single-O operated as a grind show (Stencell 2002, 143). What the public saw was "Dr." Heineman and a "nurse"—suitably garbed in hospital attire—attending their remarkable patient. She was seated in full view, with tubes arcing from her neck. Her head was simply missing.

Showmen quickly copied the act. One sold workshop plans for the illusion for $100. Harry Lewiston concocted the story of Olga, a girl from Hamburg who had been partially decapitated in a wreck of the Orient Express. Luckily, Lewiston reported, another passenger was a Dr. Landau, who had been conducting experiments (shades of Dr. Frankenstein) in the life support of

FIGURE 10.14. Advertisement for a decapitated Hollywood starlet "kept alive thru the miracle of science." (Photo by author)

headless bodies. To save Olga, the medical genius had to completely remove her head, the result being viewable for a mere 10¢. "How Long Can Science Keep Her Alive?" asked the sign of one single-O grind show (McKennon 1972, 1:137–38; Stencell 2002, 143, 145–46).

New stories were continually scripted. "Hollywood Starlet Decapitated," read a bogus news story hyping one early 1990s single-O show (figure 10.14). It told how a "showgirl and model was Beheaded when her car ran under a truck." The illusion was billed as "The Headless Woman—Still Alive." More recently, the show was framed as the "Headless Bikini Girl," who had supposedly lost her head to an attacking shark while surfing (Ray 1993, 30).

There were different schematics for the headless illusion, but Brill's (1976, 145) utilized "a special chair" that cleverly hid the head from view. Fred Olen Ray, in his *Grind Show: Weirdness as Entertainment* (1993, 30), notes that the only drawback is that "a living girl with a good figure was required to sit in the illusion for hours on end while the scattered patrons passed by." Sometimes the problem was solved by using two girls, the second one playing "nurse" and the pair periodically switching roles to provide a break from the tedium. The headless girl could not sit entirely motionless, however, lest it be thought that the body was a mannequin, so she would occasionally shudder or twitch to add necessary realism.

Floating Lady

This classic of magic, which appears to defy gravity and suspend a woman in midair, is termed a *levitation*. It is distinguished from a *suspension*, which is the early form of the trick. In a suspension, there is a visible connection between the person and the ground, although it nevertheless seems impossible that he or she could be so precariously balanced. Of course, it is impossible and is actually a trick. The most common sideshow version was the broom suspension illusion, sometimes used as a bally act. According to Brill (1976, 150): "The girl stands on a low stool, [and] rests with a broom under her armpit. The magician makes several magic passes, and she is 'hypnotized.' He removes the stool and lifts her legs, first to a 45 degree angle and finally to a horizontal position. She stays there. . . . Finally she is 'de-hypnotized' and lowered to a standing position, where she walks away." The illusion depended on the girl wearing a special frame made of leather and steel under her clothes, with a ratcheting mechanism that allowed her to be raised and locked into place. The broom was specially made so that its "handle" was actually a disguised pipe that fit into a special flange in the platform to anchor it firmly. The pipe's other end extended upward through the broom straw to engage the mechanism in the harness (Wels 1977, 196–98).

In contrast to suspensions, levitations lack (to use a familiar phrase) any visible means of support. Of course, there is one, but there are various methods of concealing it—mirrors being an obvious one. In the classic floating-lady illusion, the magician's "hypnotized" assistant seemingly becomes lighter than air and floats up and then back down on command. As in the broom suspension, the lady wears a supporting frame beneath the flowing costume. The illusion is conducted close to the curtained back of the stage or platform. From an opening in the curtain, a metal rod—hidden from the audience's view by the girl's body—emerges and engages a socket in the supporting frame.

FIGURE 10.15. The floating lady is a classic magic feat, but it is only an illusion, as shown in this nineteenth-century illustration.

Behind the curtain, another of the magician's assistants operates a crank that raises and lowers the support rod. (A variation—see figure 10.15—simplifies the operation by placing the girl on a supporting platform.)

Brill (1976, 188) said of the mechanism: "It is a simple machine, made like an auto bumper jack, about 9" square, and no part of it over 54" long. It is easily disassembled for transporting. . . . This is not a complicated machine. You can build it with an electric drill and a hacksaw, or you can save time by having most of it constructed in a welding shop where they have power saws for metal. The easy-to-follow plans include 'exploded view.'"

To convince the audience that there are no "invisible wires" supporting the lady (there aren't) or support of any kind (there is), the magician passes a hoop along the length of his "floating" assistant. The hoop would hit the secret lifting rod, except that it has a long horizontal gooseneck in it near the girl's body (Hay 1949, 290–92; Gibson 1967, 114–16).

In his memoir *Side Show: My Life with Geeks, Freaks & Vagabonds in the Carny Trade,* the late Howard Bone (2001, 49–50) gives an idea of the behind-the-scenes problems of the assistant who works the lifting mechanism. The magician's command to the girl to "Rise!" was Bone's signal to begin cranking the mechanism—as smoothly as possible. Once, as he knelt tuning the crank, he saw someone trying to crawl under the canvas to get into the show for free. Bone could neither shout at him nor leave his job at that crucial point, so he used one hand to toss a pair of pliers at the intruder. That caused him to duck back outside, but the magician later complained about the levitation shaking "like an earthquake." "From that point on," says Bone, "I ignored anyone who lifted the sidewall during an illusion."

A sensational version of the floating lady was known as the "Levitation Asrah." In this presentation, the lady lay on a low couch, was draped with a large cloth, rose high in the air, and—when the magician suddenly whisked away the cloth—vanished. The Asrah was performed for years "on the big magic shows, in vaudeville and on state fair midways" (Brill 1976, 189). Sometimes, as a finale, the girl would reappear in a surprising way: shouting, "Here I am!" she would come running down the aisle from the back of the theater or tent.

The trick involved levitating not the girl but a lightweight wire form made to resemble her shape beneath the cloth. The form was hidden on the back side of the couch and brought into place by an offstage assistant using a lifting mechanism and arrangement of cords (made of braided fish line). As the magician lifted the cloth to cover his "hypnotized" assistant, she quickly entered a recess in the couch at the same time that the wire form was lifted from its hiding place. While the magician seemingly caused the girl to levitate, other assistants pushed the couch offstage. This permitted the girl to emerge from the couch, run out the back of the theater or tent, and reenter from the front—with a wink to the ticket seller. (As to the wire form, it never disappeared but was effectively invisible against a "tapestry-figured background" (Wels 1977, 9–10).

Gorilla Girl

Among the most dramatic and dazzling of carnival illusions is the girl-to-gorilla show, in which spectators see Beauty transformed into Beast before their very eyes. I caught the single-O feature in 1969, at the Canadian National Exhibition midway, while on a break from my own work as a pitchman. I joined spectators in the sideshow top to see Atasha the Gorilla Girl standing inside a cage. As a voice chanted, "Goreelya-goreelya-goreelya-ATASHA-GOREELYA!" Atasha's features were slowly transformed into those of a large gorilla. Suddenly, the beast rushed from the unlocked cage and lunged toward the crowd, sending some spectators screaming for the exit, which got the attention of midway passersby and helped draw the next tip (Nickell 1970; Teller 1997). Of course, the apparent metamorphosis was illusory. Often the grinder or talker slyly noted that the Gorilla Girl was in "a legerdemain condition" (*legerdemain* being French for "sleight of hand"), thus indirectly admitting that the transformation was a trick.

The illusion debuted in the 1960s, a presentation of showmen Hank Renn and George Duggan for Carl Sedlmayr's Royal American Shows (Stencell 2002, 142). However, it was a variation on an old effect originally known as Pepper's Ghost. This was an illusion devised by London chemistry professor John Henry Pepper, together with civil engineer Henry Dirks, in 1863. By way of explanation, magician Will Dexter (1958, 34) asks: "Have you ever carried a lighted candle to a dark window, and looked out? What have you seen? Who is that other figure, surprisingly like yourself, carrying a lighted candle on the other side of the glass?" Dexter answers, "*That* is Pepper's Ghost." In other words, the illusion worked on the principle that a clear sheet of glass could—with proper lighting—be transformed from a "window" into a "mirror."

Pepper's Ghost illusion was used for many magical appearance, disappearance, and transformation effects. In Pepper's original presentation, a man who was assailed by specters hacked at one shrouded figure with his sword, which

FIGURE 10.16. The Pepper's ghost illusion uses lighting to turn clear glass into a "mirror" and thus produce eye-catching transformations, as shown in this nineteenth-century illustration.

passed ineffectively through the phantom; then the man collapsed, whereupon the ghost suddenly vanished. Other presentations made possible by Pepper's Ghost were bringing a mummy back to life, turning a living man into a skeleton (figure 10.16), transforming a statue into a lady, and other theatrical effects, including substituting one person for another (Dexter 1958, 33–47; Stencell 2002, 141–42; Wels 1977, 292–94).

Versions of Pepper's Ghost were part of midway ghost shows that became common after Captain W. D. Ament introduced his to North American fairgoers in 1902. The following season, Ament ran his London Ghost Show for thirty weeks with the Robinson Carnival Company, becoming the top-grossing feature. Others hastened to frame their own ghost shows, but Ament observed, "Not one in 50 can run a ghost show after being shown how." Adding to the difficulty of framing and performing such a show, "the hard part," according to

A. W. Stencell (2002, 135–36), "was getting that large plate of glass from town to town safely."

With all these illusions, the method is essentially the same. In the case of the gorilla girl, for example, the glass was set at a forty-five-degree angle across the cage, and there were two sets of overhead lights—one in front of the glass, the other behind. With a gorilla-suited man at the rear of the cage (behind the glass) and "Atasha" (Darleen Lions) in a hidden recess to the side, the stage was thus set (so to speak) for the transformation. With only the front light on, the audience saw Atasha, apparently real but actually a reflection. With someone working the two dimmer switches, the front light began to go down while the rear one came up. As a result, the gorilla began to be seen through the glass, so that the two images were superimposed. The effect was that Atasha began to take on beastly features, much like the effect in the famous movie in which Dr. Jekyll becomes the monstrous Mr. Hyde. Once the front light was completely off and the back light was fully on, the transformation was complete. At this point, the light would flicker off momentarily while the glass was slid back, giving the gorilla an unobstructed path to the front. Suddenly, the "beast" threw open the cage door and lunged forward, scaring the entranced spectators.

Showman Bobby Reynolds (2001) told me about one spectator who was allegedly killed by running head-on into the top's center pole. Stencell (2002, 143) comments on the risk of audience stampede: "They may be skeptical, but when the gorilla charges, they run. That is why the main person on the show is not the girl or the gorilla, but the guy who yanks the curtain on the exit at the right time." He adds, "You don't want the crowd running out through the side wall and falling on stakes or being cut by guy ropes." Reynolds (2001) notes that insurance costs for such a show could be "astronomical."

During one of my several sideshow visits with Bobby—during which we *cut up jackpots* (had a gab session)—I was able to meet a former "gorilla." One of Bobby's helpers, Dave Spencer, had played the part when Bobby ran a show featuring Zambora the Gorilla Girl, who—the tip was promised—"turns from a 110-pound girl to a 500-pound GORILLA!!!" David and Bobby made a sketch of the illusion and went over it with me. Bobby had had the technically demanding job of operating the two dimmer switches, but Dave had the most physically grueling one. It was so stiflingly hot in the gorilla suit that he had to take it off and stand before an electric fan between shows. The show was also demanding in other ways, requiring a large number of workers (Reynolds 2001):

Inside:
  Girl ("Atasha")
  "Gorilla"
  Dimmer-switch operator
  Exit-curtain puller
Outside:
  Second girl (for bally)
  Talker
  Ticket seller
  Roughy (to help set up, take down, collect tickets, etc.)

Nevertheless, Teller—of the magical duo Penn and Teller—is not alone when he states, "Girl-to-Gorilla is my favorite attraction on the midway." He witnessed the metamorphosis of Zahara at the Meadowlands Fair in New Jersey (Teller 1997). The illusion was also featured in the James Bond film *Diamonds Are Forever*.

Girl in the Goldfish Bowl

This illusion features shades of Barnum's Fejee Mermaid, only this time she is "Positively Alive," according to a sign advertising "Myrna the Mermaid: The Little Girl in the Goldfish Bowl." The sign asks, "Were the Old Sailors' Tales Really True?" Banners flanking the show's entrance depict Myrna being caught in a net and displayed in a small fishbowl. "$1000.00 Reward if Not Alive," promises another banner, with appropriate midway cheek. Myrna is the subject of a grind show by Tim Deremer from Canton, Ohio. Deremer, according to Stencell (2002, 147), is "one of the last operators of big illusion shows on midways." Of course, "big" here is relative, since the show is only a single-O, and Myrna is billed as "Only Inches Tall."

    The show is merely the latest embodiment of a long-standing and popular illusion called the "Girl in the Goldfish Bowl." In contrast to Barnum's mummified fake, "later exhibitors have preferred to equip normal young girls with

FIGURE 10.17. The girl-in-a fishbowl illusion is a study in miniaturization, as depicted in this sideshow banner at the 2004 Canadian National Exhibition in Toronto. (Photo by author)

fraudulent fins and green hair, then let them splash about in tanks to keep the 'marks' happy" (Fiedler 1993, 169). But these post-Barnum showmen added the eye-catching novelty of shrinking the bedecked "mermaid" down to goldfish size. "Sure she's not a real mermaid," one ticket-stub holder may acknowledge to another, "but she's so tiny. And look, she's waving at us! She's real!" (See figure 10.17.)

Indeed, she is both real *and* alive, but also illusory. The girl that spectators see only appears to be in the fishbowl; she is actually in an adjoining compartment, and her image is *projected* into the bowl (which is filled with clear mineral oil instead of water). As usual, there are various modifications. Originally, a "reducing lens" was used (Doerflinger 1977, 153). However, the version sold by Brill (1976, 160) was lensless and thus economical. I obtained a 1954 copy of the Brill workshop plans for "Girl in the Fish Bowl." In this embodiment, the bowl rests atop a decorative cabinet that conceals the reclining girl. The interior is covered with black cloth, but the girl is lit with small spotlights, and a mirror reflects her image to the rear of the globular bowl (which fits partly into a hole in the cabinet).

The girl-in-the-fishbowl illusion was shown in a bit of byplay in the 1991 made-for-TV movie *Columbo and the Murder of a Rock Star*. The rumpled detective is seeking an informant, Darlene, at a nightspot called the Aquarium. The bartender indicates that she is the miniature mermaid swimming in the fish tank (which obviously gives the place its name) and tells Columbo to go downstairs. In the cellar he finds Darlene, who is suspended by two cables that enable her to seemingly swim and turn somersaults as if she were in water.

That the "mermaid" is not actually underwater recalls an incident related by Deremer. The girl was smoking a cigarette in her secret chamber. "A guy came out and said, 'If that mermaid is under water, how can she be smoking?' I had to go back and tell her, 'Don't be smoking in there. God, give me a break!'" Deremer ran his fishbowl illusion on the same midways as his girl-to-gorilla show. As a strategy to eliminate the performers' boredom, he says: "What I did with the mermaid and the gorilla show was switch the ape girl with the mermaid girl every two hours. That way, as the mermaid she can relax and get the air conditioning while lying there. When she is the gorilla girl, she has time to stretch her legs, get a drink, go to the bathroom, and walk around a bit behind the tent between shows. So that worked out good" (Stencell 2002, 147).

Brill (1976, 210) also had a "Girl's Head in Goldfish Bowl," which combined the mermaid illusion with a headless-girl effect. "They actually see her head in a fishbowl," the ad promised. "It talks." Brill's 1954 workshop plans for "Girl in the Fish Bowl" also mentioned the possibility of conversation. For the holidays, it was suggested that an elf-like Santa Claus could be used, with a microphone and hidden speaker allowing Santa to speak. So that he could hear the children's questions to him, there would be "a hidden opening in the design of the scrolls on the face of the cabinet." The possibilities are endless.

Other Illusions

Among the numerous other illusions that have been exhibited on midways, one became a staple of the bally platform. Brill (1976, 195) called it "a favorite sideshow bally." Known as the "Cross Escape," it involves an attractive girl being tied to a cross at the neck, waist, and wrists. Suddenly, she walks away! The basic secret is that the ties are made with double (side-by-side) lengths of soft, pliable rope. Each set of ropes has been secretly tied with a piece of fine thread around it. Although the double ropes make the ties seem twice as strong, in reality, the thread permits the ends of the ropes to be switched with a deft move. Thus, instead of two side-by-side lengths, each rope is actually doubled on itself, so that only the thread is holding them together. When the girl is tied, these junctures are hidden at the back of the cross. All the girl has to do is give a hard tug, breaking the thread, and she is free (Wels 1977, 183–85).

Another well-known sideshow illusion is "Shooting Through a Woman," depicted, for example, on a circa 1940 banner by George Bellis (Johnson et al. 1996, 45). One of several versions of this trick is described by Brill (1976, 203) for sale to showmen: "The girl holds a card, preferably the Ace of Spades, to her breast. A sheet of glass is suspended behind her. A shot is fired, the glass breaks, the card has a bullet hole through it—but you use the same girl for the next performance."

This is a good example of how an illusion's effect can be broken down into its components in order to create, modify, or—in this instance—explain the illusion. First, obviously, the girl is not shot; nor would a real bullet ever be fired in a sideshow. Therefore, the gun shoots blanks. The illusion that a projectile passes through the magician's assistant is created by two simple occurrences: the appearance of a hole in the playing card, and the shattering of the glass behind the girl. These are accomplished by switching the card for one with a hole in it and using a hidden spring mechanism that, when triggered, strikes the glass instantaneously (and unnoticeably) before returning to its hidden recess.

A few other sideshow illusions have been created in imitation of certain popular human oddity exhibits. However, they are magic—not gaffed—versions. Evoking such human oddities as Johnny Eck, Jeanie Tomaini, and other "half" people (see chapter 5), the "Living Half Lady" illusion (figure 10.18) has several forms. Originally, it worked on the same principle as the talking-head illusion, in which a lady's head rests on a platter on a table, her body being concealed by mirrors (as discussed earlier). By extending more of the woman above the tabletop, the mirror arrangement conceals only her legs, and the living half-woman is created.

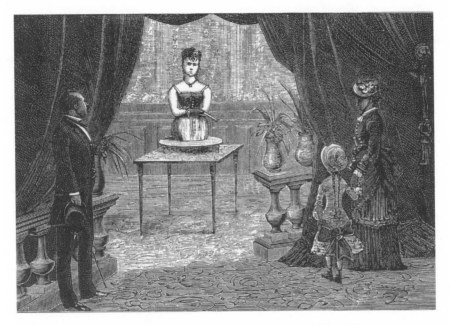

FIGURE 10.18. The living half-lady illusion imitates the human oddity of the same name.

Indeed, the talking-head and half-woman illusions are so similar that they were illustrated in side-by-side diagrams in the April 7, 1883, issue of *Scientific American* (figures 10.19 and 10.20). The magazine headed the double feature "Side Show Science." The magazine also described "a very ingenious improvement" in which a four-legged table was substituted for the old three-legged model. This seemed to eliminate the possibility that mirrors were used to hide the woman's lower body, since the mirrors also would have blocked a view of the table's rear legs. But the mirrors were there nonetheless: The table sat in an alcove, at the front corner of which were two decorative pillars. Behind each pillar, a dummy table leg was hidden so as to reflect in the respective mirror. Thus, spectators on the left saw one on their side, and those on the right saw the other—in each case, appearing as if it were beneath the table's rear corner. Byron Wels (1977, 212–14) comments on the effect of this version:

> There is no way that this girl could live or survive in her present condition, but survive she does; she talks to the magician, jokes with him

FIGURE 10.19. The talking-head illusion invokes the expression, "It's all done with mirrors." (Illustration from *Scientific American,* April 7, 1883, p. 210)

FIGURE 10.20. The half-woman illusion is similar to the talking head. (Illustration from *Scientific American,* April 7, 1883, p. 210)

about her missing nether parts, and the audience can plainly see that she exists only from the top up.

This is another of the old "sideshow" illusions that brought people into the freak show tents off the midway at many an old carnival.

"Step right up, folks!" the barker would holler. "See the world's only Living half lady!"

As an aside to the men in his audience, he would ask, "Who in his right mind would marry a girl like this?"

As might be imagined, however, the viewing angles were critical, making setup difficult. Besides, audiences were growing suspicious of tables—in part due to exposés such as that in *Scientific American*. A new illusion was therefore developed, exhibited as the "Girl in the Swing." In this case, the swing hung trapeze-like in an alcove lined with curtains. To prove that no mirrors were used (they weren't), and to demonstrate that the girl had no lower body (although she did), she would grip crossbars situated between the chains that held the swing and lift herself up so that the magician could pass a sword between her body and the swing seat. He could also pass the blade beneath the seat to prove that there was nothing there. The secret was that, although the lady's head, neck, shoulders, and arms were real, the remainder of her "half-body" was fake. It consisted of "a dummy form encased in a type of corset or foundation garment extending downward from the girl's bust." The rest of her body was in a *prone position* extending directly behind her false front, which blocked her real body from frontal view. To prevent spectators on the sides from catching a glimpse, the lady's body was encased in black tights, which, given the black interior of the alcove, was effectively invisible (Gibson 1967, 112–14). (Magicians call this black-on-black invisibility the "black-art" principle [Hay 1949, 23].) To hold her securely in a horizontal position, the girl's feet were secured to the alcove's back wall. Therefore, "Her smile was the most difficult part of the trick," writes Walter Gibson (1967, 113), "for the girl was in a very strained and uncomfortable position."

Another illusion inspired by real human oddities is the two-headed girl. An illusion show featured it on midways in the 1960s, and Ward Hall was favorably impressed. He believed that it could be a good draw as a single-O if properly framed and given a large front. He and his partner Chris Christ built the show in their backyard. It had beautiful signage depicting a double-headed beauty styled "Elaina Maria." The show debuted at the 1977 Milwaukee Summerfest. Midway passersby were intrigued by the questions painted on the facade: "Heredity? You Be the Judge. . . . Am I My Own Sister?" However, Hall conceded, "In practice the two heads didn't work." Hall & Christ sent the show back "to winter quarters" for a remake. It reopened the following season and was "letter perfect." But there was another problem: "It didn't attract business" (Hall 1981, 91, 97).

Bobby Reynolds also exhibited the two-headed girl illusion. "One of the girls I married was German," he says, "and she brought that illusion with her." He adds, "It's a neat illusion. Both heads talk to each other. It's positively alive." How does it work? Bobby explains, "Piece of glass and lights. Similar to the gorilla show [girl-to-gorilla illusion] but backwards. One laying down and one sitting up" (Taylor and Kotcher 2002, 226).

Many other magic tricks and illusions have appeared in sideshows, dime museums, and similar venues. They are far too numerous to be dealt with here, but interested readers can consult such works as Albert A. Hopkins's *Magic: Stage Illusions, Special Effects and Trick Photography* (1898), Byron G. Wels's *The Great Illusions of Magic* (1977), Nathaniel Schiffman's *Abracadabra! Secret Methods Magicians and Others Use to Deceive Their Audience* (1997), and Herbert L. Becker's *All the Secrets of Magic Revealed: The Tricks and Illusions of the World's Greatest Magicians* (1997).

11 ANIMAL SHOWS

 SOME EXHIBITS FEATURE ANIMALS. ALTHOUGH the premier animal acts are reserved for presentation under the circus big top, midways and carnivals often have animal shows. Like other sideshow features, animal exhibits have a long history.

Menageries

Collections of living animals, wild and exotic, are as ancient as recorded history. In the early twelfth century B.C., a Chinese emperor, Wen, established a "garden of intelligence" wherein animals from the different provinces of the empire were exhibited. Similarly, the ancient Egyptian pharaohs kept menageries as part of their temple complexes, and in the eighteenth dynasty, Egypt's Empress Hatasu sent a fleet of ships to Punt (an ancient land on the African coast of the Red Sea) to bring back leopards, monkeys, and giraffes for her "garden of acclimation." This is history's first recorded expedition to obtain live animals. The ancient Greeks and Romans also established collections of birds and mammals. Although the prevalence of animal collections declined during the early Christian era, in the Middle Ages, menageries and zoos again returned to importance, sometimes as public collections (in Florence, for instance), but more typically as private collections of the nobility (*Encyclopaedia Britannica* 1960, s.v. "Zoological Gardens").

With the increasing popularity of fairs in the seventeenth century and later, animal exhibits became common in Europe. At the Bartholomew Fair in 1784, for instance, there were individual freak animals and menageries (Stencell 2002, 4). In America, menageries also began to thrive (figure 11.1). Previously, exotic animals had been exhibited on occasion, but only as single curiosities. American showmen had to overcome puritanical resistance to entertainment. However, according to Howard Loxton in his *Golden Age of the Circus* (1997,

FIGURE 11.1. Traveling menageries, exhibited in tops (tents),
began to flourish in the first part of the nineteenth century.
(From an old wood engraving)

21): "Menageries, which could be considered educational rather than entertaining, were more acceptable than circuses, though by the 1820s they had also
begun to feature elephants and monkeys performing tricks. They seem to have
travelled farther than the circuses, although large and dangerous animals were
not easy to transport in their cages. Menageries began to make use of canvas
walls to screen their exhibits from those who had not paid admission, and they
used large tents before they were taken up by circuses."

Some menageries began to offer a dramatic feature, following the lead of
showman Isaac Van Amburgh (1805–1865), "who became the first man to enter
a cage full of wild animals." According to Linda Granfield's *Circus* (2000, 66):

His early work with a menagerie developed into a circus routine, and he is credited with creating the first modern trained wild animal act.

What a show it was! Dressed like a Roman gladiator, complete with sandals, Van Amburgh tackled the lion before it could attack him, and used brute force to prove himself the master of the situation. He became famous for putting his head inside a lion's mouth, a trick that was sure to silence the noisiest audience. It's no wonder Van Amburgh was called "The Lion King."

The act caught on and in 1850, for instance, the Hemmings, Cooper, and Whitby Circus made a standard feature of having their lion keeper enter a cage as part of every show.

In 1888 a German trainer named William Hagenbeck invented a circular exhibition cage that was portable yet large enough to permit the animals to run, jump, and form high pyramids on pedestals—another Hagenbeck development. He also pioneered the gentling technique of wild animal training (Loxton 1997, 31; Stencell 2002, 49–50). From such menagerie men, modern circus lion taming was born.

In the meantime, menageries and circuses drew closer together. Loxton points out that sometimes a site would have a circus during the afternoon, followed by a menagerie that evening. In 1817 New York's Theatre of Natural Curiosity combined its menagerie, which included camels and a variety of other animals, with entertainment provided by a group of rope dancers and gymnasts. The first circus and menagerie to be combined in a tour seems to have been the circus of A. J. Purdy in 1832. It also may have been the first *traveling* circus to use a tent. Following the lead of the Theatre of Natural Curiosity, the Zoological Institute converted its menagerie into a circus with a central ring, naming it the Bowery Amphitheater. The institute also sent out a touring menagerie with a circus ring (Loxton 1997, 22).

In his memoir *The Ways of the Circus,* lion tamer George Conklin (1921, 10–19) describes life with a traveling menagerie in the late 1860s. Teamed with the John O'Brien Circus, the show traveled by two wagon trains—one carrying the tents and equipment, the other hauling the menagerie, the performers, and the band. The first train traveled much faster so that it could arrive at the next stand and have the tents set up by the time the second caravan got there. Then they formed a parade to promote the show. Each of the five tents was lit at night by a wooden "chandelier" affixed with some 300 candles and hung from the center pole. Sleep was especially difficult for the menagerie crew, "for it was open to the public nearly all day, and as long as there were visitors we had to watch to see that none of them poked the animals with an umbrella, gave them things to eat, or tried to pat the lion just to see if he was really ugly."

In contrast to circuses like O'Brien's, Barnum's traveling outdoor show of 1851–1853 did not have any ring acts and was, therefore, essentially a collection of sideshows. Styled "P. T. Barnum's Great Asiatic Caravan, Museum and Menagerie," it featured the famous midget General Tom Thumb, several Indian elephants, and museum items by the thousands (McKennon 1972, 1:21). In New York, Barnum's American Museum included—along with its mounted specimens—a zoo, and by the mid-1950s the showman had acquired two giraffes and a unique single-horned rhinoceros (billed as a "Unicorn"), as well as a grizzly bear, Bengal tiger, llama, leopard, and "a den of lions" (Kunhardt et al. 1995, 110). Nor were fish and other aquatic animals neglected. In the Fourth Saloon of the museum was Barnum's "Aquarial Department." There, special tanks exhibited various reptiles, numerous fish, and seals, including the celebrated "Learned Seal," which played musical instruments. In an especially large tank was the "Great Living Whale," obtained from the Labrador coast (Kunhardt et al. 1995, 40, 159).

As mentioned in chapter 1, an 1872 newspaper ad for "The Greatest Show on Earth! Barnum's Magic City" featured a "Menagerie" among its "Separate Colossal Tents." Because these led up to the hippodrome—the big top itself— Barnum's big menagerie tent was clearly a sideshow, as were his museum, fine arts, and other tops, including his living curiosities (a collection of human oddities) (Kunhardt et al. 1995, 224). (For an ad showing some of Barnum's menagerie, see figure 1.3.)

Animal *exhibits* continued to coexist with animal *acts*. When Frank Bostock arrived in the United States from England in 1893, he brought such an admixture, as did the Ferrari brothers, Joseph and Francis, the following year. They soon teamed up, reported *Billboard* magazine (February 10, 1934). The

302

menagerie owners arrived at Coney Island with "a queer mess of show stuff." They had "a small but gaudy animal show known as Noah's Ark in which a boxing Kangaroo, Jolly the elephant, Wallace the untamable lion, a tattooed yak, some performing lions and 'whatnots' were exhibited."

By 1901 Bostock had the touring Bostock Carnival Company and the Bostock-Ferrari Midway Carnival Company, although he traveled with neither. Instead, he spent the entire season with his huge animal show, performing on the Pan American Exposition midway in Buffalo, New York. He thrived and profited, despite a fire that claimed a Bostock menagerie in Baltimore. Relates McKennon (1972, 1:59):

In this late January fire, he lost seventy-four lions and over ninety other animals. He almost lost one of his trainers, Mme. Gertrude Planka in this same fire. This brave young lady went into the blazing arena building and tried to coax the six lions composing her act into shifting dens so they could be rolled out to safety. Crouching in fear, they wouldn't move for their trainer. As burning debris fell into the ring, she tried vainly to lift her huge charges and bodily carry them from the building. The head trainer, seeing that the big cats were doomed, tried to get his fellow worker out of the arena. She refused to leave her pets, and clung to one of her biggest lions as he trembled in fear. Two cage hands finally forcibly pulled her away from the big cat and carried her sobbing from the building as the roof crashed in behind them, stilling the cries and screams of the dying animals.

In time, the old menageries faded from the circuses and carnivals due to a number of factors, including their cost and maintenance, the proliferation of zoos, and the need to protect endangered species. However, vestiges of them remained in the form of other animal exhibitions.

Single-Animal Acts and Exotics

Animal acts were in existence as early as 2400 B.C., and they took numerous forms. During the medieval era, traveling shows of jugglers and other entertainers often included dancing bears or trained dogs.

A popular animal act was the "talking" or "psychic" or "educated" creature. In seventeenth-century France, for example, a famous talking horse named Morocco seemed to possess such remarkable powers—including the ability to perform mathematical calculations—that he was charged with "consorting with the Devil." However, he saved his own and his master's life when he knelt, seemingly repentant, before church authorities. Later in the century, a "Learned Pig" and a "Wonderful Intelligent Goose" appeared in London. The porker spelled names, solved arithmetic problems, and even appeared to read thoughts by selecting, from flashcards, words thought of by audience members. The goose, advertised as the "greatest Curiosity ever witnessed," performed such feats as divining a selected playing card, discovering secretly chosen numbers, and telling time "to a Minute" by a spectator's own watch. Other prodigies were Munito the celebrated dog, Toby the Sapient Pig, and a "scientific" Spanish pony who shared billing with "Two Curious Birds" (Christopher 1962, 8–37; Jay 1987, 7–27).

Investigations of such animals, including two horses—Clever Hans in Germany, and Lady Wonder in the United States—revealed that the acts were accomplished by trainers subtly cueing their performers (Nickell 2002). For example, as a "psychic horse" moved past alphabet cards or blocks, the trainer gave a slight movement of his or her training rod to cause the equine marvel to stop and nudge the indicated letter. Or the animal could be presented as performing mathematical feats by training it to paw the ground continuously—as if to indicate *one, two, three,* and so on—and teaching it to stop when the trainer gave the signal (figure 11.2).

One showman who exhibited a learned pig even published his methodology in 1805. First, a young pig was to be domesticated by making him a house pet, then taught to hold a card in his mouth, using a reward of a piece of apple or a reprimand of a loud shout. Then the pig was to be placed in a circle of alphabet cards and led around by a string until he learned to stop at a given signal and pick up the indicated card (Jay 1987, 16).

Many other animal acts were presented as individual shows. For example, a trained monkey was exhibited in the United States in 1751, and birds, performing dogs, and trained bears were also commonly shown (Loxton 1997, 18–19; McKennon 1972, 1:19).

FIGURE 11.2. Serrano the Psychic Horse was one of a long line of equine marvels. (Author's collection)

In London in 1847, there was even a rivalry between two singing mice. Mr. Palmer, a hairdresser, advertised that his singing rodent was superior to its competitor, in that "it warbles its notes sufficiently loud to be heard across a room for several hours in succession, by day or by night, and continues to do so until weary from exertion." This was attested to by the *Family Herald,* which added, "The notes of this little wonder resemble those of a bird in spring before it breaks into full song, or those of a canary singing himself to sleep" (Jay 1987, 23).

When Frank Bostock and the Ferrari brothers introduced their menagerie shows to Americans in the 1890s, they offered a number of individual animal acts. The Ferraris, for example, booked Fatima the Hoochie-Coochie Bear, as well as their boxing kangaroo, onto dime museum and vaudeville circuits during the off-season. And Bostock had a chimp named Consul that he dressed in a three-piece suit and taught to walk erect. Consul also smoked a cigar, sipped wine, rode a bicycle, and "displayed better manners than many humans" (Stencell 2002, 53).

Many and varied acts followed. In his youth, showman Bobby Reynolds even exhibited a dancing rooster:

I would put Scotch tape on its feet and I would tap dance with this chicken. You put Scotch tape on a chicken's foot and it'll wave its foot one way and then it will wave his foot the other, trying to get the Scotch tape off, and here I am tap dancing along with the chicken. It would walk off stage with me and come back and do the Conga or whatever I was doing. That was my act. No one could remember my name. They would always say, "Where's the crazy kid with the dancing chicken?" I used to go to hotels and I'd have the chicken with me and he'd start crowing. I'd get thrown out of a lot of hotels because of it. I'd put a burlap tobacco bag, a Bull Durham bag, over his head and I'd put black velvet over it and I'd put this over his head and he wouldn't see light and he wouldn't crow. That's why I broke in hens to do this act, so they wouldn't crow. I went around the country like that for a while. (quoted in Taylor and Kotcher 2002, 227)

Often, in contrast to such performances, exotic animals were merely exhibited. (The same is true of animal freaks, which are discussed in the next section.) At its simplest, the exhibition could be a bally show with a snake charmer or talker posing with a large boa or python. This was being done in Europe as early as the 1830s.

In the United States, a "Lyon" was exhibited along the East Coast for a few years beginning in 1719, being shown in Boston, Philadelphia, and New York. (It is the only lion to be mentioned in the newspapers until 1791.) One or another camel was seen in the same cities in the 1720s and 1730s, and a polar bear was in Boston in 1733. The first elephant was exhibited in 1796 (Loxton 1997, 18–19).

P. T. Barnum's American Museum exhibited a number of exotic animals, among them "A splendid specimen of a living Ourang Outang from Borneo," "Black Swans," "The Great Living Whale," "Australian Opossum & Young," "The Living Hippopotamus," "An African Vulture," "Gold & Silver Pheasants," and many more (Kunhardt et al. 1995, i, 159). Among Barnum's exotics was a genuine white elephant from the East. Barnum had long attempted to obtain one of the sacred elephants from Siam but had been rebuffed repeatedly. Eventually, he offered enough money to persuade a Siamese nobleman to get him one, but the elephant, Barnum said, "was poisoned on the eve of its departure by its attendant priests." He finally turned to impoverished Burma and secured one of the rare animals. Alas, when Barnum saw it in March 1884, he was supremely disappointed. Far from being white, the animal merely had a few "pale spots on its body," along with one "pinkish" ear.

Enter Barnum's chief rival, circus man Adam Forepaugh—or "4-Paws," as Barnum called him. He decided to out-Barnum Barnum by having an ordinary elephant whitewashed. He dubbed it the "Light of Asia." In retaliation, Barnum had one of his elephants whitened and billed it as "an exact copy of the other whitewashed elephant." The war of words continued for the season, whereupon Forepaugh's elephant died. "It was dyed already," Barnum quipped. Eventually, the men called a truce and temporarily combined their circuses in 1886 and 1887 (Kunhardt et al. 1995, 295).

Today, exotic animals are still being displayed on the midway. With the decline of the ten-in-one in the 1980s, due to the high overhead, individual animal and illusion exhibits became the mainstay. Such single-O attractions "can work successfully for the Grind Show operator who does not wish to be burdened with the care and upkeep of so much livestock," observes Fred Olen Ray (1993, 25) in his book *Grind Show: Weirdness as Entertainment.*

One such single-O is the "Giant Rat" show. The one I witnessed at the Kentucky State Fair was operated by Lee and Becky Kolozsy (figure 11.3). Similar shows can still be seen on midways. In these exhibits, the giant creature is actually either a capybara or a nutria, both of which are South American semiaquatic rodents. According to showman Bobby Reynolds, who speaks from experience: "I use capybaras; nutrias look better, but they're very vicious. They're very bad, nutrias. You get two of them in there and you could have a blood bath. And they will attack you." He adds: "Capybaras are kind of mellow. You scratch them under the chin once they get used to you." Still, there can be problems. Various regulatory agencies and special-interest groups (Bobby calls their agents "humaniacs") often interfere. "They say, 'You treat this animal bad.' I make a living with them; it would be kind of ludicrous for me to treat them badly." He insists: "The veterinarian sees them every month. They see more doctors than I do. My giant rat has a complete history and they look at him and they check him out. I have to do that for the state, and then I have the

FIGURE 11.3. The "Giant Rat" is a single-O feature on many carnival midways. Note the word "Alive." (Photo by author)

USDA on my ass, the federal one, and then I have the ASPCA. I'm dealing with three people. What do they want?" Bobby continues: "If there's cobwebs they want them down, they want the water changed and they want to know what I feed him. When I tell them Purina Rat Chow, they tell me there's no such thing. There is: It's called 'Laboratory Rat Chow' and it has everything that a rat could use. And then you give them sweet potatoes and lettuce and supplement them with a little sweet feed and you have a little salt and then you throw hay there. It likes hay every once in awhile" (Taylor 1997, 19–20, 93).

Malcolm Garey had similar trouble over feeding live mice to his Giant Flesh-Eating Frogs. (There are several types of these, including the cane toad.) Garey argued that the frogs naturally ate live mice, but the officials were unmoved. He then inquired if he could feed dead mice to the frogs, and when they answered yes, "Malcolm then grabbed a mouse by the tail, swung it around quickly and smacked its head on the edge of the table and proceeded to throw it in with the frogs. The wildlife officials then proceeded to throw Malcolm in jail!" (Ray 1993, 26).

Other exotics displayed in recent years are the coatimundi (a tropical American mammal), sometimes exhibited as the "Crazy Mixed-Up Mystery Animal" and turkey buzzards, presented grandiosely as "Graveyard Scavengers." States Ray (1993, 25), "Something as simple as an Armadillo (cost $25) will often be displayed as Midnight Flesh-Eating Grave Robbers, but," he cautions, "don't try this down South where they are as common as raccoons!"

Freak Animal Exhibits

Because animals are born with deformities more frequently than humans are, and because they are more economical to keep, they have long been exhibited. An animal with a simple deformity such as an extra leg may otherwise be healthy and have a normal life span. However, extremely deformed animals, such as those with two heads, may have other problems and are usually short-lived. Therefore, "Anyone fortunate enough to acquire a healthy two-headed calf can be assured a good steady income for his show" (Ray 1993, 24).

Animal "freaks" include something billed as a "Turkey Horse," standing little more than two feet high, which was exhibited in a box at the Bartholomew Fair of 1631. More than half a century later, in 1692, visitors to the Tower of London saw not only lions on exhibit but also a two-legged dog. Spectators at the 1734 Bartholomew Fair were able to view "enormous pigs" and "double-bodied cows," and in 1790 a six-legged ram was among the attractions (Stencell 2002, 4, 7).

P. T. Barnum exhibited numerous freak animals, both at his American Museum and in show tops with his traveling menageries and circuses. Among them was a "Living Three-Horned Bull," a six-legged cow, and Jumbo the elephant, the largest creature then in captivity (Kunhardt et al. 1995, 278, 327).

Like Barnum's giant elephant, many other animal freaks paralleled human oddities. For example, reminiscent of the Seven Sutherland Sisters (discussed in chapter 6), whose hair totaled thirty-seven feet, was a horse exhibited at Glasgow, Scotland, in the 1890s. It was shown at Fell's Waxworks, although it was quite real and even alive. It sported a blond mane that was nine feet nine inches long, and its tail measured twelve feet eight inches. William G. FitzGerald (1897), writing in London's *Strand*, reported: "There are an extraordinary number of animal monstrosities scattered among the sideshows of the world—the double-mouthed calf, the elephant-skinned horse, the three-legged cow, and such like. There is, however, something more or less repellent about these, and so they have not found a place in these articles. But the long-maned and tailed horse . . . is in no way disagreeable."

Showmen Dufour and Rogers introduced a large show of animal freaks at the 1939 world's fair in New York (along with their "Fakertorium" and other shows). The animal show was presented by legendary talker T. W. "Slim" Kelley, whom Dufour (1977, 119–20) notes "was simply adored by the newspaper and magazine writers." Dufour illustrates how Slim would "dish it out to reporters" by quoting from one of his spiels:

> Adonis is the only bull in the world that has skin like a human's. He has no hair anywhere on his body, and he gets his milk bath every single day, and a cold cream massage every other day. I have him insured with Lloyd's of London for $15,000 and this is no bull. . . . Now, look at this chicken with a human face. She eats hamburger and she's very fond of tuna fish. Her owner sold her because she was afraid of her. And here's my pet, Fanny the radio-movie goose, the only talking goose in the world with a double chin. Fanny won't talk to just anyone, but listen to her talk to me.

Dufour concludes, "Slim knew how to dramatize a freak." The showmen made Slim a partner and framed the show with an elaborate front sixty feet tall.

The Dufour and Rogers—and Kelley—show was called "Nature's Mistakes" and included a two-headed cow, a bull with "elephant feet," a bulldog-faced cow, a "hog without hams," an eight-footed horse, and a six-legged Holstein. In all, reports Dufour (1977, 119–20), "There were seventy freak animals presented in a pit area thirty feet wide, eighty feet long, and four feet deep."

Smaller than "Nature's Mistakes," but nevertheless a huge show of the genre, was that of Al Moody, which toured in the 1970s with Dell & Travers Carnival. It sported "one of the largest banner lines available" (Davies 1996, 65). Indeed, the front consisted of a dozen five-by-seven-foot banners on each side of the entrance, over which was a quadruple-size marquee banner headed "Freak Animals"—with bullets proclaiming "All Alive." They were the work of Fred Johnson, the legendary banner painter. Moody's was a "Continuous Show," according to signs on the flanking ticket booths. Among the features were "Daisy Mae the 2 Headed Cow," which received extra billing. The banners depicted "Sheep with 4 Horns," "Cow with 5 Legs," "Midget Bull," "2 Bodied Cow," and many more (Johnson et al. 1996, 146).

In 1972, at the Canadian National Exhibition in Toronto, I visited an all-animal ten-in-one that included a three-legged sheep, touted as "Nature's Living Tripod," and various alleged hybrids (zebra-donkey, turkey-chicken, dog-raccoon). These hybrids did not match their banner portraits, which showed the front half of one attached to the rear of the other; instead, they merely resembled a blend of features. However, the "1/2 Monkey, 1/2 Squirrel" was nowhere to be seen (I wonder if anyone else noticed?). There was also a ram with four horns, a sheep and a cow with five legs each, and other oddities. The veracity of the "World's Smallest Cow" claim might be doubted, but it was certainly a very small bovine. In addition, the show featured a "Giant Rat," surely a nutria or capybara, demonstrating that the distinction between an exotic and a freak animal is often blurred. In the final analysis, it came down to the manner of presentation. Not all the animals were touted as being "Alive"; as billed, the "World's Smallest Horse" was a "preserved exhibit" (a fetus pickled in a jar), and the "World's Largest Horse" was indeed (as small print had stated) in "photographic form" (Nickell 1972; 1999).

More recently, at the Great Allentown (Pennsylvania) Fair of 2001, Ben Radford and I were able to visit with midway showman Richard Cales and his wife, who were operating a "Freaks of Nature and Pet Zoo" sideshow (figure 11.4). On display was a "4 Wing Goose," a "Giant Chicken," a "3 Legged Duck," and a "Four Horn Sheep," among other "Barnyard Oddities"—all advertised by a colorful front with an array of banners, signs, and flags, plus a ticket booth topped with a hot-pink parasol and operated by Mrs. Cales.

Richard generously waived his posted "No Cameras" policy; he even helped out by giving his "Calf with 5 Legs & 6 Feet" a pitchfork of fresh hay so that it would get up to be petted and photographed (see figure 11.5). I enjoyed petting the freak animals—that is, the ones that were billed on the banner line as "Alive." There were also a number of preserved exhibits, including fetuses of a "Dog with 2 Bodies," a "6 Leg Dog," and other "Freaks of Nature" (figure

FIGURE 11.4. Freaks of Nature and Pet Zoo sports a colorful front with large banners. (Photo by author)

11.6). The Caleses also had at least one exotic presented as a freak, their "Goat without Ears." The animal, which was certainly freakish looking, was actually a La Mancha, a breed of goat that lacks external ears.

We were able to cut up jackpots with Richard, who told us one of those priceless little stories that can only be heard in such a fashion. He explained that although there is a true half zebra–half donkey, termed a "zonkey" (the two species being compatible), he once gaffed such a hybrid by simply painting stripes on a donkey. Unfortunately, he laughingly confessed, when people petted it, the stripes came off on their hands.

In his *Grind Show*, Ray (1993, 24) points out that freak menageries are sometimes filled out with exotics (like the Caleses' earless goat), which he terms "odd-looking but natural creatures." One example he cites is the "Hairless Dog": "Hairless dogs sometimes generate heat because people naturally assume it is an ordinary dog with some kind of disease and therefore inhumane to display it for profit. They are, in fact, a natural breed of dog, the Chinese Crested, that just happens to be hairless, but try explaining that to an irate animal rights activist!"

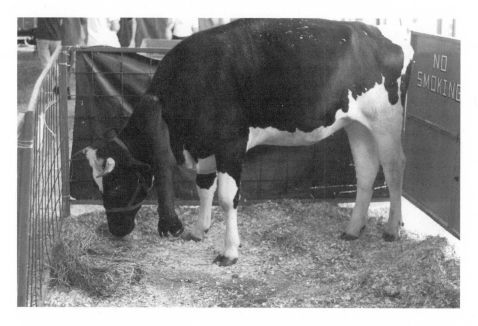

(Above) FIGURE 11.5. Five-legged cow munches hay in an animal sideshow operated by Richard Cales. (Photo by author) (Below) FIGURE 11.6. Preserved exhibits are often included in freak animal sideshows. (Photo by author)

FIGURE 11.7. Among the single-O shows in this nighttime photograph are "World's Largest Pig," "Giant Alligator," and "The Smallest Horse." (Photo by author)

Of course, miniature and giant animals are frequent midway attractions, including "'Porky,' World's Largest Pig," "'Hercules' the Giant Horse," "White Mountain Giant Steer," "Smallest Horse," and "Giant Alligator"—just to mention a few I have personally met (figure 11.7). Ray (1993, 26) found one giant alligator show "impressive" but noted that such a large gator was likely to be lethargic. At the back of the reptile's pen was a sign reading, "This Alligator Is ALIVE—For $10 We Will Make Him Move!"

Flea Circuses

Among the various animal acts, few are more intriguing and humorous than the antics—both real and imagined—of those tiny members of the animal kingdom, the order Siphonaptera, or fleas. Of more than 2,500 species, most trained fleas are *Pulex irritans,* the human flea (Wiseman 2002; Gertsacov 2003).

"Although the flea circus has become part of American culture," observes Ricky Jay (2001, 35), "it inspires skepticism in a wide segment of the populace,

314

for whom the mere notion of a trained, costumed insect-actor is incomprehensible." In fact, I was among those skeptics, and with good reason. As Jay continues, "Their disbelief has been encouraged by specific deceptions: showmen have been known to exhibit preserved fleas cleverly affixed to apparatus or, indeed, to present shows with no fleas at all."

As early as 1578, a London blacksmith, Mark Scaliot, exhibited a tiny coach drawn by a flea secured with a fine gold chain and lock. Other craftsmen followed suit, and a 1656 museum catalog referred to "flea chains of silver and gold," each consisting of 300 links. In the eighteenth and early nineteenth centuries, English, German, and Swiss craftsmen—often clock makers—exhibited flea-drawn coaches and chariots.

In time, exhibitors began to focus less on their craftsmanship and more on the fleas' performance. Military themes were popular. For instance, in 1825 one showman staged sword fights with thirty fleas armed with tiny splinters; he reportedly used a hot coal to animate his performers. A similar exhibition was staged in 1834 by an Italian named Cucciani, who put regiments of uniformed fleas into combat (Wiseman 2002; Jay 2001, 35–37).

The great figure who came to tower over these miniature arenas was the Italian showman L. Bertolotto. His book *The History of the Flea; . . . Containing a Programme of the Extraordinary Exhibition of the Educated Fleas Witnessed by the Crowned Heads of Europe* (circa 1833) promoted flea circuses in several editions over the next few decades. Bertolotto exhibited a number of flea spectacles, including "A first rate man of war, of one hundred and twenty guns, with rigging, sails, anchor and everything requisite in a three-decker, not omitting a numerous crew which, placed on a car of gold, with four wheels, is drawn by a single flea." There were "two fleas, deciding an affair of honor sword in Hand." Bertolotto's show also included four card-playing fleas, a flea orchestra (allegedly playing audibly), and a reenactment of Napoleon's defeat at Waterloo. According to an eyewitness: "Among the most amusing features in the exhibition, we ought to mention the representation of the Emperor of Java, seated under a splendid palanquin, borne by an elephant, and attended by slaves, who fan him as he proceeds. . . . How M. Bertolotto contrives to get his fleas harnessed, and attaches them to the various weapons they wield, is more than our philosophy can comprehend" (Wiseman 2002; Gertsacov 2003).

Bertolotto was imitated by other showmen, not all of whom left a favorable impression. A spectator complained of one, "Never was there such an imposition." The fleas, he reported, "instead of being harnessed . . . were tied by the hindlegs, and the combatants, poor wretches! were pinched by the tail in tweezers and of course moved their legs in their agony" (Wiseman 2002). According to one source, even with Bertolotto, "Unfortunately, many of the fleas he used were cruelly glued to their props and died by suffocation" (Gertsacov 2003).

Nevertheless, the genre flourished in the latter nineteenth and twentieth centuries. An 1885 playbill, for example, advertised flea master S. Jacobs's "Original Cirque des Puces" (Original Flea Circus). It featured "Un carrousel tourné par 1 puce" (a carousel turned by one flea) and two dozen other feats (Jay 2001, 39).

In the United States, "Professor" Roy Heckler became the most celebrated flea circus ringmaster, following his father William, who wrote a book on the subject. For some three decades, beginning in the 1930s, Heckler presented his show several times daily at Hubert's Museum in New York, of which he had become sole proprietor. Jay (2001, 41) recalls the spiel of the outside talker (who was sometimes T. A. Waters, sometimes Bobby Reynolds, and sometimes Jack Elkins):

> Ladies and Gentlemen, downstairs you'll meet Professor Roy Heckler's world-famous trained flea circus. Sixteen fleas, six principals and ten understudies, and they will perform six different acts. As act number one a flea will juggle a ball while lying on its back. As act number two, a flea will rotate a tiny miniature merry-go-round. As act number three, three fleas will be placed on chariots and the flea that hops the fastest will, of course, win the race. But the act, ladies and gentlemen, that most people talk about, the one they pay to see, three tiny fleas will be put in costumes and placed upon the ballroom floor and when the music is turned on those fleas will dance. I know that sounds hard to believe, but may I remind you that seeing is believing, and you'll see it all on the inside in Professor Roy Heckler's trained-flea circus.

Bobby Reynolds (2001) told me about the flea-training methods of Professor Heckler, whom he knew well: "He had a box with a screen and he'd put his legs in there and they'd feed off him. And then he would, you know, rub alcohol on [the bites]. Now, how you train a flea is, you got to get the flea and you put him in a tube, like a test tube. And they keep bouncing, and they jump and hit their head. And once they won't hit their head anymore, or they'll just lay still or dormant or crawl, then they're ready to be tied up." This is a delicate operation using tweezers and a single strand of very fine copper wire. Bobby continued: "You make a loop. Then you put that over the front two legs and behind the neck. Then you take your tweezers and you squeeze that to hold it, then wrap it around the chariots. And then, you know, you kind of tickle 'em. Or they could tickle you more than you could tickle them. And then they'll run across." Since the life span of the flea is only a few weeks, such "training" is time-intensive.

Ricky Jay (2001, 36), who was often at Hubert's Museum as a youngster, points out, "The various acts performed by the insects were imaginatively devised extensions of their natural actions." For instance, "dueling fleas" were in fact frantically attempting to dislodge the splinters fastened to their legs. And the flea "playing soccer" was just kicking away a cotton pellet soaked in a repulsive chemical, giving the illusion of athletic prowess.

Once, when I was cutting up jackpots with Ward Hall (2001) in his trailer just off the midway behind the Hall & Christ Show's ten-in-one, the topic turned to the care and feeding of the miniature performers. Hall interjected:

I've got to tell you a great story about flea circuses. . . . There was a won-derful lady, a good friend, her name was Mimi Garneau. And Mimi was in the sideshow business forever. And she was a lady sword swallower, doing a beautiful act. And I'm going to say this would have been prob-ably mid-sixties. Mimi had, she must have been around eighty at the time, and she had got to the point she didn't want to swallow swords anymore, didn't think she should. And so she built a flea circus, and had a jeweler in Tampa build all the little props, and she got fleas, and did it. Okay? Now, she was booked with Sam Alexander's Sideshow in Belmont Park in Montreal, Canada. They opened early in May. So she went to Canada with her flea circus. It was cold, and immediately before she ever got it opened, before she ever got to working, the fleas were dead.

So she gave the kids that would hang around the park 50¢ to bring their dogs, and . . . she would take the fleas off of them. But kids were bringin' in the dogs that ran around loose [outside], or their pets which had been treated. There were no—it had been a cold winter—there were no fleas. So now she remembered that her next-door neighbor on 120th Street in Tampa had a big shaggy dog that was just lousy with fleas. And so she called her neighbor. If she paid for it, [she asked] would they have a crate built and fly the dog to Montreal, let her take the fleas off the dog, and [she] would fly it right back? And so she spent whatever money it cost her to do this—overlooking one thing: that when it came through Customs coming into Canada, they dipped it [in an insecticide]. And that was just too much discouragement.

Not surprisingly, the real "trained" flea circuses have been almost completely supplanted by the humorously gaffed ones. They seem to have begun as parodies, such as the one by Robert Ganthony (1895) described in his *Bunkum Entertainment*. He offered a skit featuring a card on which a few dots had been drawn:

On this card you will perceive some ten or a dozen students. These I obtained from the orchestra of an east-end music hall [shows card] which I have by dint of enormous patience and assiduity taught a variety of musical instruments; they will now perform the Intermezzo from the opera Cavalleria Rusticana, and I must ask for absolute silence, as it is such a strain on the insects' lungs to play while conversation or other fashionable accompaniment is in progress. . . . The fleas cannot get up and bow as they are fastened to their seats, but they would have appreciated your applause had you given them any.

The first mock flea circus of this type that I recall witnessing "live" took place in Toronto in 1974 and was exhibited by Detroit magician-clown Daren Dundee. He was visiting an informal magic club that convened on Saturday afternoons in a corner of the King Edward Hotel cafeteria, and I was a regular. The show was an elaborate put-on. For example, Daren would place an imaginary flea on a tiny trapeze, which began to swing; then, on command, the "artiste" would "jump," starting a second trapeze swinging. One invisible performer named Goliath was dropped into a cigarette pack and, again on command, began to slowly push a cigarette out of the pack. The pack was then placed on the back of the same flea, who transported it some ten inches across the table. Such effects were accomplished by trick mechanisms, leger-demain, and invisible thread. Daren had two real (but not alive) dressed fleas that he claimed to have obtained years ago in Niagara Falls. The pair—one in a tux, the other a gown—was mounted in a tiny box inside a magnifying cube. He also exhibited miniature living quarters for the fleas, including tiny beds, TV, beer mug, playing cards, and commode; a teeny apple core had been placed so that Daren could comment that one of the girl fleas liked to eat in bed (Nickell 1974).

Nearly three decades later, Ben Radford tipped me to a similar but public exhibition in Toronto, and we drove from Buffalo to see it. Billed as "The Most Minuscule Show on Earth!" it appeared at the Artword Theatre as the "Acme Miniature Flea Circus, Being a Presentation of Trained Fleas ... Performing *Spectacular* Circus Stunts as Seen Before (and on Top of) the Crowned Heads of Europe!" (figure 11.8). A miniature (about four-by-five-inch) poster invited:

THRILL to the Exciting Flea
Chariot Race!
ENJOY the Marvelous Tightwire
Act!
BE AMUSED by the Previously
Unknown True History
of Fleas!
BE AMAZED at the Remarkable
DEATH DEFYING FINALE!!

A similarly small handbill cautioned, "Positively No Dogs Will be Admitted" (figure 11.9). The show promised to put "the Bug Back into Humbug" and quoted from a *Village Voice* review: "Mite-y Feats of Daring-do."

(Left) FIGURE 11.8. The buildup to the Acme Miniature Circus—a flea-bitten operation—includes the sale of T-shirts. (Photo by author) (Right) FIGURE 11.9. The Acme Miniature Circus posts tongue-in-cheek warning signs. (Photo by author)

Presiding over the miniature arena was "the Internationally Acclaimed and World Renowned Authority, Professor A. G. Gertsacov, Psycho-Entomologist & Flea Trainer Extraordinaire" (figure 11.10). The good "professor"—actually professional actor and clown Adam G. Gertsacov, who is a graduate of Ringling Brothers Clown College, among other accomplishments—began the show by humorously hawking a number of pitch items: a miniature program, a little magnifying glass to read it with, small "Save the Fleas!" bumper stickers, and other souvenirs. Our top-hatted ringmaster called this "the Flea Market Before the Flea Circus."

The stars of the show were "Trained Fleas of the Species *Pulex irritans*"—or, as we skeptics thought, *Pulex invisiblis*. Their names were Midge and Madge. Magnifying glass in hand, Gertsacov removed them with tweezers from their miniature trailer and put them through their paces: the chariot race no doubt

FIGURE 11.10. "Professor" A. G. Gertsacov wields a magnifying glass—ostensibly viewing his tiny charges—during the "Most Minuscule Show on Earth." (Photo by author)

depended on a hidden magnet to propel the thumb-sized vehicles; for the tightwire act, the tiny chair and balancing pole were clipped to the wire, which moved on a continuous loop; the "Death Defying Finale" was a flea supposedly shot from a little cannon through a "flaming hoop of death."

Gertsacov kept up a running line of patter. For example, during the tightwire walk he announced: "She's blindfolded herself!" "She's walking backward!" "An astonishing triple split!" Once, one of the imaginary performers escaped, and Gertsacov searched the front row with his magnifier, soon retrieving Midge—or was it Madge?—from the hair of a giggling little girl. The showman entertained his audience well, proving that it is indeed possible to make something out of nothing.

Unfortunately, CTV's *Canada AM* had missed the point. According to the Toronto weekly *Now* (January 23–29, 2003), the producer had considered inviting Professor Gertsacov on the show, "but when told the fleas couldn't leave their hotel room and studio lights would be too hot, the producer bailed, saying a flea circus without fleas is like a magician without tricks." Commented *Now*, "Sheesh."

12 CURIOS

A SPECIAL CATEGORY IS RESERVED for inanimate objects that might be displayed in a sideshow. Since there is no general carny or showmen's term for these, I simply refer to them as curios—that is, objects valued for their strangeness or rarity.

Pickled Exhibits

When neither the banner nor the outside talker promises that an exhibit is "alive," it probably isn't. Many once-living rarities are preserved in some kind of solution, others are mummified, and a rare few are frozen.

Among the first type are what carnies call *pickled punks*—a term never used before the public but reserved for those who are *with it* (in the know). Originally, a pickled punk was a child or fetus kept in formaldehyde or some other preservative. It might be a normal fetal specimen, used in an educational exhibit, or a freak one, such as a two-headed baby or other anomaly (figures 12.1 and 12.2). By extension, the term also came to refer to such specimens of animals or even alleged "aliens" or other entities (Taylor and Kotcher 2002, 247; Keyser 2001).

Although preserved specimens have long been kept for biological and medical purposes (in 2002, I inspected a cabinet of them dating from the eighteenth century in a museum in Saxony), their sideshow value has been exploited in large part by showman Lou Dufour. About 1920, he was impressed by an exhibit of human embryos at the Smithsonian Institution in Washington, D.C. Seven years later, Dufour saw a similar collection of twenty specimens being exhibited by a Dr. Albert Jones at the local fair in Shreveport, Indiana. The lineup at the tent entrance caught Dufour's attention, and—after a few days of effort—he persuaded the doctor to sell the collection to him. Dufour added some other biological exhibits and named the show "Unborn." In 1928 he

FIGURE 12.1. Bobby Reynolds
and his two-headed pickled
punk. (Photo by author)

(Below) FIGURE 12.2. Bobby Reynolds's two-headed pickled punk exhibit was sometimes presented as a blowoff or as a separate grind show. (Photo by author)

opened it with a carnival, the Johnny J. Jones Shows, at Largo, Florida. Dufour (1977, 46–47) would later recall:

> I received an excited call one morning from the fair manager. I had to get over to the grounds at once, to my exhibit. Without getting an explanation, I hurried down. The reason was the quartet of Henry Ford, Thomas Edison, Harvey Firestone, and a Dr. Goodman, who had come to see the "Unborn" Show. I opened up and made my pitch for them. When they expressed approval and enthusiasm I knew I really had something with my assortment of human embryos and fetuses! Edison was deaf so I hollered into the old-fashioned horn he held to his ear. I asked what impelled him to come so early in the day, and Edison explained, "Last night I had these gentlemen to my home as dinner guests and all my wife could talk about was your exhibit. We decided to see for ourselves—and I'm glad we came."

Dufour adds that it took him a day to realize what he had. "If men of above-average intelligence would go to a dusty fairgrounds for the experience," he realized, "it had to be worthwhile." The exhibit proved "a gold mine" for the showman, who soon put together similar exhibits at numerous venues and became, as he said, "the biggest exhibitor of unborn humans in the entire world!"

In part, Dufour's success was due to low overhead. As he noted, all his actors "were bottled in formaldehyde and drew no salaries." At the Century of Progress world's fair in Chicago (1933–1934), Dufour and his new partner Joe Rogers framed two shows. The "Life Museum" began with human fetuses and continued with exhibits on human anatomy, growth, and reproduction; animal life histories; and the evolutionary stages of mankind. The second show was billed as "A Live Two-Headed Baby," but alas, the two-month-old infant died before the show opened. The savvy showmen quickly substituted "another one in a bottle" and dressed a female ticket seller and an inside lecturer in nurse costumes. The former would announce, "It was born alive—you must see the little one." The marquee front pictured a two-headed infant being carried by a stork. By the time the sign's big two-dimensional word "LIVE" had

FIGURE 12.3. Showmen Lou Dufour and Joe Rogers operated a "Real Two-Headed Baby" show at Chicago's Century of Progress exhibition—the central sideshow in this official 1933 postcard of the midway. (Author's collection)

been changed to "REAL," recalled Dufour (1977, 62), "we were well on our way to success." (See figure 12.3.)

Showman Ward Hall calls the Dufour and Rogers exhibit "the original freak baby show" (interview in Taylor and Kotcher 2002). It did launch a thousand tips (so to speak), but it was not the first such exhibit, as shown by classified ads in *Billboard* magazine. In 1921 a California woman offered "two perfect heads on one body. Weighed 19 and three quarters pounds at birth, 10 inches across the shoulders. Preserved in five-gallon jar. For lease by reliable show." Earlier, in 1919, a man had offered to sell showmen genuine two-headed and frog-child infants: "These cost more than paper stiffs [gaffs of paper and wax], but you will not be ashamed to exhibit them. Send 25 cents for descriptions and prices. This small charge is to keep information from moms and children" (Stencell 2002, 152–53).

In any event, the Dufour and Rogers exhibit was soon imitated by others. Fakes began to look more realistic, and because of their rubber (or sometimes soft vinyl) composition, they were called *bouncers* (figure 12.4). Bobby

FIGURE 12.4. Pickled punks are sometimes bouncers (rubber fakes), as in this grind show. The fine print says, "These are facsimiles, created from real live babies." (Photo by Benjamin Radford)

Reynolds—who showed me his genuine two-headed baby (see figure 12.1)—has seen all types: "I've always had something. I've had bouncers. I had one that was wax that looked like a gingerbread boy. Flat wooden thing with water around it. It was horrible. That was the first two-headed specimen I had. The one they had at Hubert's [Museum, in New York]—it was wax—was an exact reproduction of the one I have that's real. I always thought the one they had at Hubert's was real until one time I saw it in the corner and the leg was broke" (interview in Taylor 1997).

The real specimens require some care. Whereas the gaffs can be placed in water (sometimes deliberately clouded with coffee or tea to help disguise the fakery), the genuine specimens are improved by a clear solution. Although this is often called formaldehyde, it is actually quite diluted, since too much formaldehyde can "burn" the specimens. (Aqueous solutions of the preservative are sold under trademark names such as Formalin.) Showmen change the liquid whenever it begins to look cloudy (Stencell 2002, 152–53; Wilson et al. 1996, 192–93).

326

Bouncers are cheaper and easier to acquire than genuine specimens. Another reason for using them is to circumvent legal restrictions. At an Illinois fair in 1977, a former coroner running for sheriff raided the Hall & Christ freak baby show, arresting Chris Christ and charging him with the illegal transporting of human remains. Although a judge eventually ruled that the fetuses were not corpses (there were neither birth nor death certificates) and that it was legal to own them, they had been confiscated and were never returned. Ward Hall never even asked for them back because, "Fortunately, we already had molds of them sitting at the rubber factory. We were only out of business . . . for a week, then we had the bouncers." The candidate for sheriff engaged in his own form of show business: he lined up some fourteen little coffins at a cemetery and—with a priest, rabbi, and Protestant minister in attendance—proceeded to have a burial ceremony for the "carnival babies." The publicity stunt was carried by the wire services, and he won the election (Taylor and Kotcher 2002, 9).

Hall and Christ encountered more trouble in Ohio. There, the operator of their freak baby show, Henry Valentine, attempted to appease a fairgrounds inspector by showing him that the genuine fetuses had been replaced with rubber ones. Unfortunately, as the inspector explained, Ohio law is "very specific. You cannot have any made-up freak. Now if you had the *real* ones there'd be no problem. You'd get the license, but I can't license these because they're fake" (Taylor and Kotcher 2002, 8).

Because many people find the *baby shows* (aka *bottle shows*) repulsive, and some carnival owners reject them on their midways, a few grinders have taken a new tack. For example, Jeff and Sue Murray framed a "Horrors of Drug Abuse!" show, attempting to give the exhibit a moral tone and some educational value. It utilized a traditional show tent, in contrast to most of the newer trailer-constructed grind shows. Depicting a cyclops-eyed baby, the marquee banner proclaimed, "Man-Made Monsters," "Mother Nature's Mistakes," and "Children Born of Addiction" (Ray 1993, 21–22). Jeff stored his bouncers dry, putting them in special jars on opening day and adding water and a splash of coffee. It created, states Ray (1993, 22), a "disturbing effect": "At a date in Selmar, California, one Mexican woman staggered out of the tent on a particularly hot day, grabbed the ticket box for support and promptly leaned over and

FIGURE 12.5. A mummified prospector was actually embalmed—or is this Canadian sideshow exhibit only a replica? (Photo by author)

threw up. While not exactly an ideal situation it did serve as great publicity and helped sell a lot of tickets to marks whose curiosity had been set on fire."

As noted in the previous chapter, preserved animal fetuses are also exhibited. For instance, Jeff and Sue Murray operated a "Mystery Museum" grind show that included pickled freak animals among its varied exhibits.

Other Preserved Exhibits

Another major type of preserved exhibit is the mummy (figure 12.5). Most of the dried, emaciated figures that have found their way into sideshows and similar exhibits were not naturally preserved—as sometimes alleged—but are the result of embalming.

One such figure was the former Elmer McCurdy, an erstwhile soldier and miner who became a bank and train robber. He was killed by a sheriff's posse after an attempted train heist in Oklahoma. Locally embalmed with arsenic, the body was claimed in 1916 by some shrewd showmen from the Great Patterson Shows, who took it on tour. McCurdy's mummified body went from carnival to carnival, once being forfeited as security for a failed $500 loan. It was thus acquired in 1922 by policeman-turned-showman Louis Sonney, who exhibited the outlaw's mummy in his "Museum of Crime" sideshow and other venues off and on during the 1930s and 1940s. For example, McCurdy's mummified remains were exhibited in theater lobbies during showings of the film *Narcotic* (1933).

In 1968 McCurdy's body was acquired by the Hollywood wax museum, which later sold it to the "Laff-in-the-Dark" fun house at the Nu-Pike Amusement Park in Long Beach, California. When a scene was being filmed there for *The Six Million Dollar Man* (1976), what was thought to be a fun-house mannequin, painted fluorescent orange, fell off a hook, and the crew discovered a protruding arm bone. An autopsy turned up a bullet wound in the abdomen as well as a tag reading "Property of Louis Sonney." The owners then "grudgingly" released the mummy, and Elmer McCurdy was finally laid to rest in an Oklahoma graveyard next to fellow outlaw Bill Doolin (Taylor and Kotcher 2002, 205; Stencell 2002, 215–16; Miller 2003).

One of the most famous mummies was that reputed to be Abraham Lincoln's assassin, John Wilkes Booth (1838–1865). Following his demise, some forty people, usually shortly before their own deaths, "confessed" that they were Booth (claiming that the assassin had somehow escaped and lived a secret life). One person, David E. George, who committed suicide in 1903 at Enid, Oklahoma, even confessed posthumously. His long unclaimed but remarkably embalmed body was obtained by Memphis lawyer Finis Bates, who identified the man as "John St. Helen" and claimed that St. Helen had confessed that he was really Booth. Bates published an account of this "true" story, *The Escape and Suicide of John Wilkes Booth*, and for many years the mummy was exhibited in carnival sideshows. Although it superficially resembled the actor-turned-assassin, even bearing fractures and wounds similar to Booth's, the mummy was investigated in 1910 by the *Dearborn Independent* and debunked (Nickell 1993). Initially, Bates had only rented the mummy to showmen on occasion, but after the lawyer's death, it was sold and returned to the entertainment circuit. Its whereabouts have been unknown since World War II, although current researchers still hope that it will turn up for DNA and other testing (Taylor and Kotcher 2002, 210).

Still another sideshow mummy was that of notorious Utah nightclub entertainer Marie O'Day. She was stabbed to death by her common-law husband in 1925 and, according to legend, her body was dumped in the Great Salt Lake. The salt preserved her corpse so that, when it turned up on shore a dozen years later, Marie still had her red hair and even the "corn upon her toe," according to promotional literature. Marie's mummy was exhibited by a number of showmen in thirty-eight states. At one time she was shown in a special "Palace Car" (actually a semitrailer divided into a sleeping quarters for the operator and an exhibition room for Marie). Later she was exhibited by "Palace of Wonders" grinder Captain Harvey Lee Boswell, who died in 2002 (Taylor and Kotcher 2002, 211; Stencell 2002, 150).

Not all sideshow mummies are genuine. "Big Cleo, World's Tallest Girl"—who reportedly stood nearly eight feet tall and weighed 460 pounds—was a fabricated mummy. The single-O show was framed with large pictorials depicting Cleo as a bikini-clad beauty. One featured her towering over two tropical explorers saying, "Take Me to Your Leader" (Ray 1993, 17).

In addition to pickled punks and mummies, other preserved exhibits include the products of taxidermy. For example, when P. T. Barnum acquired John Scudder's American Museum in late 1841, he inherited its resident taxidermist along with its collection of stuffed birds and small mammals. Barnum began adding larger mounted animals, such as lions, zebras, wolves, grizzly bears, and even huge stuffed elephants (Kunhardt et al. 1995, 110).

In the late 1860s the John O'Brien Circus had, as part of its menagerie, an "aquarium," which was actually a wagon with a glass front. An assortment of stuffed fish was arranged on a wood panel just behind the glass. The aquarium thus took up only about a foot of the wagon's four-foot width, leaving a three-foot compartment to be used for other purposes, such as sleeping quarters for the driver or his relief man (Conklin 1921, 21–22).

Many freak animals are short-lived and thus become taxidermic exhibits. In 2002 in Waldenburg, Saxony, I visited a small natural history museum that had several such curios, including two-headed and double-bodied calves. A little twin-headed calf is displayed at the Farmers Museum in Cooperstown, New York (placed near the Cardiff giant, discussed later in this chapter).

Some freak animal shows include taxidermic exhibits. In his traveling

FIGURE 12.6. This two-headed goose in a sideshow exhibit looks suspiciously like an example of the taxidermist's art. (Photo by author)

International Circus Sideshow Museum & Gallery, Bobby Reynolds displayed a stuffed five-legged calf. Once, when we were talking about why he was no longer operating a live show, Bobby gestured across the tent to the calf and observed, "It doesn't eat, shit, or talk back." Another time, he expounded on the practicality of such exhibits, saying, "See, this way you can put 'em in a truck; you could lock the truck up." In other words, they require no care or thought (Reynolds 2001). Bobby's worry-free menagerie includes a "real" two-headed goose (figure 12.6) and a humorous "hippy chicken" sporting a 1960s peace symbol dangling from its neck.

Bobby's collection also includes shrunken heads (figure 12.7), which are akin to mummified and taxidermic exhibits. Bobby gave me some pointers on distinguishing between genuine and gaffed shrunken heads; for example, fine nose hair is one feature of the authentic ones. (Gaffed shrunken heads

FIGURE 12.7. Showman Bobby Reynolds (left) poses with me—and another "shrunken" friend. (Photo by author)

are widespread, with many being sold to showmen by Tate's Curiosity Shop of Phoenix, Arizona. See Taylor 2001, 66–69.) I learned more about the subject from one of the world's foremost authorities on shrunken heads, Bill Jamieson (2001). I also inspected his impressive collection at his Toronto home.

Shrunken heads were prepared by the Jivaro tribes of the Ecuadorian and Peruvian Amazon, and the practice dates back to pre-Columbian times. The heads were taken from enemies as trophies, and the preparation was intended to keep the enemy's spirit from taking revenge in either the present life or the afterlife. The head-shrinking process began with a downward slit through the skin at the back of the head. The skull (which would not shrink) was removed and discarded. The eyes were sewn shut, and the lips were held closed with thin wooden pegs (these were later removed and replaced with string). The head was then boiled for up to two hours, resulting in its shrinking to about a third of its original size. Next, the skin was turned inside out and scraped to remove any adhering flesh. It was then returned to its original position, and the slit at the rear was sewn closed. Final shrinking was done by filling the skin sack with hot stones, which seared the interior skin, followed by hot sand, to reach the finer crevices and cavities. This treatment was later applied to the outside, and the head was finally suspended over a fire, which hardened and blackened it.

Still another type of preserved exhibit is the frozen animal. An example is "Little Irvy—The 20 Ton, 38 Ft. Whale" once exhibited by Jerry and Charlotte Malone. Harpooned on July 1, 1967, Little Irvy was promptly frozen with some forty tons of liquid nitrogen pumped around and inside the carcass. The frozen sperm whale was kept in a glass tank in a Thermo King refrigeration truck, accompanied by a sign reading, "This Exhibit Is Dedicated to the Preservation of Whales"—a punning, ironic claim, given that the whale was actually killed for exhibition. "See the Giant from the Pacific," read a sign on the side of the truck. Some customers complained that they had been misled and urged Malone to add the words "DEAD WHALE" in large letters. Malone retorted that he would not do so "for the same reason that Banks don't put '12½% INTEREST' [on loans] in big letters on their front windows" (Deford 2001).

Bogus Creatures

Sideshows are repositories of numerous allegedly paranormal entities—ranging from the Fejee Mermaid of Barnum's time to today's preserved extraterrestrial corpses. Approximately 100 percent of these are fakes.

Hoax mermaids, for example, date back to the sixteenth century. Known as "Jenny Hanivers," such manufactured mermaids were typically produced by joining parts of two different species—the upper half of an ape (such as an orangutan or monkey) and the lower portion of a fish (such as a salmon). Such a fake was exhibited in 1822. Two decades later, P. T. Barnum acquired it from the original owner's descendants and exhibited it as the "Fejee Mermaid" (see chapter 1). When Barnum's fake was publicly challenged in South Carolina, he and his partner in the venture, Moses Kimball, discussed suing the accusing naturalist for libel (Harris 1973, 65–67). Instead, Barnum just had the mermaid shipped back to his American Museum, where it presumably perished when the museum burned in 1865. "It has been claimed," however, "that Barnum's original mermaid found its way back to Moses Kimball in Boston and thence to the Peabody Museum" (Kunhardt et al. 1995, 43). The one at the Peabody is actually known as the Java Mermaid, "one of the many imitations that appeared in rival exhibits across the country." According to the *Harvard Gazette* (Early 1996), many of its type were cheaply manufactured:

> For years experts believed that the "mermaids" were made by sewing together the head of a monkey and the tail of a fish. But in 1990, Peabody conservator Scott Fulton conducted a full-scale examination. Fulton ran starch tests on the Java Mermaid's front section. "We discovered that it is made of papier-mâché molded to resemble the limbs of the creature," he says. Then he showed the creature to Karel Liem, professor of ichthyology, and Karsten Hartel, curatorial associate in ichthyology at the Museum of Comparative Zoology. "It was the ingenuity of the thing, the way it was put together that I remember," says Hartel, who confirmed that the creature's [composure included real fish parts. According to Fulton's] records, the mermaid's teeth, fingernails, and fins, are nothing more than the jaws and the teeth, spines, and fins of a carp and a porgy-like fish, "placed liberally."

I have seen several of these "originals"—fakes of Barnum's fake! The old showman would have been delighted at the homage. One is displayed at the Ripley's Believe It or Not! Museum in Hollywood. Its display card, headed "World's Greatest Fake," implies that it is Barnum's own: "*Believe It or Not! This* curious object was once exhibited as a genuine mermaid. Incredible as it may sound, thousands of people paid 25 cents in 1842 to see P. T. Barnum's 'Fejee Mermaid.'"

Another is at Coney Island's Sideshows by the Seashore, which bills it as "P. T. Barnum's 'Figi [*sic*] Mermaid' circa 1842 / on loan from the Barnum Museum / Bridgeport, Connecticut." Be that as it may, it does not match the illustration of the original that first appeared in the *New York Sunday Herald* and that Barnum termed "a correct likeness" (Kunhardt et al. 1995, 42).

Bobby Reynolds's traveling sideshow museum featured a version of the proliferating fake, with a banner proclaiming it "Real" (figure 12.8). Actually, inside the show tent Bobby had *two* of the fakes—one labeled a hoax "by P. T. Barnum and Bobby Reynolds," the other billed as the real McCoy (figure 12.9). I once questioned Bobby about its authenticity, given the original's apparent demise in the 1865 fire. Without missing a beat, the showman informed me

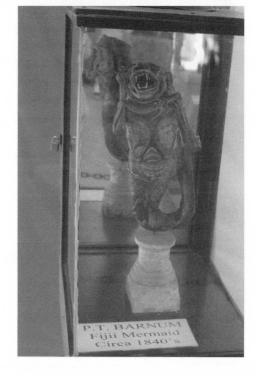

(Above) FIGURE 12.8. The Fiji Mermaid—a "real" exhibit—appears to gaze at Bobby Reynolds from her banner. (Photo by author) (Right) FIGURE 12.9. The Fijii (*sic*) Mermaid—Barnum's lost original, or one of many spoofs? You decide! (Photo by author)

FIGURE 12.10. A "Jenny Haniver" is a manufactured mermaid—in this case, one made
by altering a devilfish. (Photo by author)

that the curio had apparently been rescued by a fireman and passed down in
his family. "And you believe that story?" I asked, good-naturedly. Bobby—
whose eyes will still be twinkling when he's dead—replied that since he had
paid several thousand dollars for it, he *had* to believe it.

One type of manufactured mermaid was created by making alterations
to a devilfish (Stein 1993, 260–61). One of these was exhibited in the Hall &
Christ sideshow (figure 12.10); another is in my personal collection.

Among other taxidermic fake creatures are the humorous American jackelope and the German Wolpertinger. The jackelope is a jackrabbit with an antelope's antlers (figure 12.11). It supposedly inhabits the American Southwest.
The Wolpertinger is the product of several animals combined by taxidermy,
typically including a raccoon's tail, a bird's wings, and a duck's feet.

More serious offerings are the "devil baby" exhibits. These are gaffed freak
creatures, usually made to look like mummified specimens and displayed in
small coffins. They typically sport horns, hoofed feet, claws, and fangs (Taylor
and Kotcher 2002, 243). I investigated one of these in a curio shop in Toronto

FIGURE 12.11. The jackelope is a taxidermist's fake, a jackrabbit fitted with antelope antlers. (Photo by author)

in 1971. Supposedly purchased from an Irish museum a dozen years before, it appeared to be a papier-mâché fake, although it used real horns and hooves. The hair had been glued on (Nickell 1995, 114).

A photograph of a similar figure appears in a book titled *Vampires, Zombies, and Monster Men* (Farson 1976). Actually, it is a pair of figures, with arms folded as if in the repose of death. A sign mounted in the creatures' coffin states that they are "Clahuchu and his Bride." It goes on to explain that "these shrunken mummified figures were found in a crude tomblike cave on the island of Haiti in 1740 by a party of French marines. They are supposed to be the remains of a lost tribe of 'Ju-Ju' or Devil Men—who, after death followed a custom of shrinking & mummifying their dead." The sign concludes: "Are they real? We don't know, but . . . *X-Rays showed skin, horn & hooves human!*" There was, astonishingly, no mention of a skeleton. Painted beneath the sign were these mumbo-jumbo words: "YENOH M'I DLOC." Suspicious of the inscription, I soon discovered that reading each word backward in turn yields the prankish message, "Honey I'm Cold!"—an indication of how seriously we should take such "devil figures" (Nickell 1995, 114–15).

Showman William Nelson, who once managed the show wagon of the Pawnee Bill Wild West Show, began to sell "mummified curiosities" in 1909. These included a "Devil Child" that sold for "$15 cash" or, "with 8 × 10 banner, $35.00." Other "mummified" (papier-mâché) entities sold by Nelson were a "Gigantic Moa," a "Two-Headed Patagonian Giant," and a "Big Sea Horse"—the latter advertised as "six feet long and made to ship in a box." The ad explained: "It is a mummified subject with a big natural horse's skeleton head and two legs with slit hoofs" (Stencell 2002, 39–42).

Today, an elaborate figure of this genre is "Devil Man," a touring figure owned by James Taylor. Its accompanying leaflet, "Certain Facts Concerning the Devil Man" (1998), states: "Some purport him to be really real. Others claim he is really fake. We just say he is really cool." But, reading further, one learns that Devil Man is the creation of sideshow banner painter and "gaff artist" Mark Frierson, who fashioned it from papier-mâché, pieces of bone, and craft supplies.

Taken much more seriously was the "Sasquatch" that toured as a carnival single-O exhibit and was billed as "safely frozen in ice." It debuted in 1968 as the Minnesota Iceman. Partially obscured by the foggy surface of the block of ice, the figure attracted two famous cryptozoologists (those who study legendary animals such as the Loch Ness Monster). One thought that the creature was "most probably" a Neanderthal man who had been dead for less than five years. Alas, the creature was a fake, crafted by top Disneyland model-maker Howard Ball. I saw the creature when it was exhibited on the midway at the 1973 Canadian National Exhibition. It was lying in a freezer-like tank, but some of the ice had melted away, exposing part of the body. I reached in and felt it; not surprisingly, it was rubbery (Nickell 1995, 230).

Sideshow gaff artist Doug Higley also touted alleged Sasquatches with his grind show "Bigfoot Museum." A sign promised "15 Authentic Exhibits Explore Myths, Monsters, Wonders, and Humbugs." Among other items of evidence were casts of Bigfoot tracks, accompanied by photos of the late anthropologist and cryptozoologist Grover Krantz, an arch–Bigfoot promoter. Doug told me that he exhibits such material in a "spirit of fun and tradition," and he disparaged "the gullibility of some eggheads like Grover Krantz" (Higley 1999).

In contrast to Bigfoot, a supposed man-beast from our evolutionary past, are the sideshow extraterrestrials that typically appear as futuristic versions of ourselves. Their morphology has become quite standardized, and they are typically represented as small, big-eyed, big-headed humanoids (Nickell 2001, 160–63). The notion that alien beings were recovered from a flying saucer that crashed near Roswell, New Mexico, in 1947 has become part of American folklore and fakelore. It has been revealed that the crash debris was from a "weather balloon" (actually, a secret spy balloon intended to monitor sonic emissions from anticipated Soviet nuclear tests). However, popular books continue to spread rumors and hoax tales about the retrieval of crashed saucers and their alien occupants. The Roswell myth has been fueled by forged "MJ-12 documents," bogus accounts by con men and dishonest UFOlogists, faked diary entries, and even a hoaxed "alien autopsy" film in 1995, followed the next year by a Roswell "UFO fragment"—all spread by media hype and hoopla. It is no wonder that showmen have hijacked the Roswell bandwagon and sidetracked it to the back end of the midway.

In 2000, Bobby Reynolds debuted his "Alien Bodies" exhibit, advertised as "Direct from Roswell" (figure 12.12). "See a Real Space Creature," promised a sign, "inside this show now!!!" Of course, the creature was "real"—real rubber. I had bought an identical alien from Bobby the year before and exhibited it at my workplace, the Center for Inquiry in Amherst, New York, where I told visitors it was "from the distant planet Latex."

I visited the trailer-framed grind show at the 2000 Erie County Fair, accompanied by two friends. With a straight face, Bobby accepted the three wooden nickels I tendered for his big sideshow, then escorted us to the nearby single-O feature. Inside was a duplicate of my rubber humanoid, together with a fake alien fetus in a jar and a curiously deformed little extraterrestrial displayed atop some metal "wreckage." I lowered my voice and commented about the latter, "That looks like Doug Higley's work." Bobby replied, "Yes, I got that from Doug." Later, further around the midway, we came upon another alien single-O (figure 12.13). By dropping Higley's name and offering my wooden-nickel business cards, we were given a free guided tour by the friendly woman running the show. Inside the small tent was one of Higley's "real" aliens, exhibited in a wooden crate stenciled "Top Secret." It was accompanied by some documents sporting charred edges and a "Confidential" rubber-stamp impression (just like the one on Doug's letters to me).

FIGURE 12.12. The "Alien Bodies" grind show at the 2000 Erie County Fair in New York spoofed the Roswell conspiracy theories. (Photo by author)

Higley does not say much about his technique for producing Fejee Mermaids, chupacabras, Amazonian pygmy mummies, an "iguana boy," aliens, and other "real entities." In a booklet he declares: "Not rubber. My secret process is best!" One clue comes from a sign in Bobby Reynolds's alien show: "This exhibit is made possible by the use of space age polymers to preserve the specimen . . . preventing further deterioration and odor." Doug himself admits that his "secret" is "polymer clay" (Higley 1999), and Fred Olen Ray (1993, 36) describes the final step in the process, noting that one of Doug's creatures was "baked in his kitchen oven."

A fellow showman dubbed Doug Higley the "Phantom of the Midway" because, since the creatures are exhibited as "real," the existence of the artist is unknown; his is a phantom presence. In an article titled "Truth or Fiction" in *Circus Report,* Higley (1998) asks, "When Warner Bros. does a movie featuring a Lost Jungle City, do they put on the poster, 'Not real! Untrue! This is Fiction!'? Do the Universal [Studios'] monsters get promoted with 'Showgoer

FIGURE 12.13. This "real" alien is made of real polymer clay. (Photo by author)

beware! The monster is rubber!'?" Of course not, says the Phantom: "I look at every show I do or every gaff I create for others as my own little movie. The fiction is the fun, the mystery is the value, the fantasy is the goal. Each is designed to work the brain—crinkle the brow and crack a smile, and, yes, in some cases even educate and inform."

Other Curios

An interesting variety of other curiosities have appeared as exhibits in dime museums, sideshows, and similar venues. Among "Over 10,000 Curiosities!" advertised by Barnum's museum were "Geological Conchological and Numismatic Collections, Specimens of Natural History, Wax Statuary, Paintings, Historical Relics, Etc." There were "3,000 Specimens of Native Birds," as well as other stuffed wildlife, including lions, zebras, bears, and elephants. Barnum exhibited Indian costumes, automatons, and Civil War artifacts, including Fort Sumter "relics," a secession flag, and slave shackles (Kunhardt et al. 1995).

Following World War I, midway war shows proliferated, featuring photo-graphs of battle scenes, along with actual gas masks, grenades, trench mines, uniforms, helmets, guns, and similar battlefield items. However, incidents of exploding gas canisters and ammunition led to government restrictions on the display of potentially dangerous artifacts. World War II spawned another round of such war shows, featuring military paraphernalia, wax figures of Nazi leaders, and various Hitler cars (Stencell 2002, 83–89).

Crime shows began to flourish in the 1930s following the deaths of such notorious gangsters as John Dillinger (1903–1934). Dillinger's father appeared in one such show wearing his son's clothing and holding a wooden gun that the outlaw had used for a sensational jail escape. Showmen Lou Dufour and Joe Rogers set up a hugely fronted "Crime Never Pays" show at the California Pacific Exposition of 1935 in San Diego. It featured "Dillinger's Bullet Proof Limousine," along with the gangster's personal effects. Another feature was a gruesome wax-figure scene from Chicago's famous St. Valentine's Day mas-sacre (Stencell 2002, 212–13; Dufour 1977, 182).

There were numerous crime cars, including several billed as the "original" bullet-riddled auto in which outlaw couple Bonnie and Clyde were gunned down (figure 12.14). I saw one of these on the midway of the Canadian National Exhibition in the 1970s. It may have been the genuine one; report-edly the sedan was acquired in the 1960s by showman Ted Toddy. He won an injunction against other claimants and offered a "$10,000 Reward if This Is Not the Real Death Car." It was sold in 1973 to a Nevada casino owner for $175,000 (Stencell 2002, 219–21). (A photo of the Toddy car appears consistent, in terms of model and arrangement of bullet holes, with a 1934 Associated Press/Wide World photo of the car [Newton 2002, 25].)

In 1972 I saw a curio that directly evoked P. T. Barnum. At a ten-in-one at the Canadian National Exhibition was a banner for the "Cardiff Giant—10 ft. 4 ins." The portrait depicted a very tall man, and the talker promised, "He's a big son of a gun!" However, fine print on the banner stated, "The original, Farmers Museum, Cooperstown, N.Y." Still finer print admitted, "This is a fac-simile." Inside the tent—at the end of a long platform, following a rubber man, a fire-eater who doubled as a sword swallower, and some illusions and other acts—was the giant: a concrete statue. Like the copy once made by Barnum, it

FIGURE 12.14. Gangster cars now on exhibit at a Las Vegas casino include Bonnie and Clyde's bullet-riddled Ford (once a sideshow attraction) and the Lincoln owned by Al Capone and Dutch Schultz. (Advertising postcard)

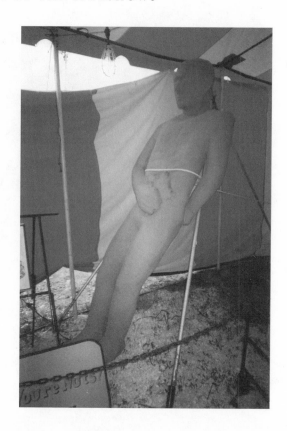

FIGURE 12.15. The Cardiff giant is a replica of the notorious giant hoax. (Photo by author)

was a fake of the original 1869 fake. It resembled (or was it the same as?) one I had photographed in 2001 at Bobby Reynolds's sideshow museum at the Erie County Fair in Hamburg, New York (figure 12.15).

As these examples demonstrate, almost anything can be exhibited in a sideshow—whether genuine or merely "real"—as long as it has some claim to the strange or exotic. Not surprisingly, therefore, as Ray (1993, 36) points out, "The museum format show has always been an old standby in the Grind Show business," from Barnum's American Museum to such modern examples as Jeff Murray's "Mystery Museum Show," Doug Higley's "World's Smallest Side Show" (an interesting twist), and Bobby Reynolds's "The World Famous International Circus Sideshow Museum."

13 THE EGRESS

LADIES AND GENTLEMEN, DON'T MISS THIS special feature: the wonderful, surprising—the Egress! Please, step this way.

As described in chapter 3, Barnum's "Egress" signs—seemingly leading to a major exhibit—were actually directing patrons to the exit. Here we approach the egress of our tour of the sideshows. Sadly, we also come to another egress: the end of the sideshow era. Long ago, circus sideshows disappeared, and now the century-long run of carnival sideshows—certainly the large, traditional ones—is all but over.

The circus sideshows declined for several reasons. In earlier times, people would mill about the lot, both during the day and after the circus performance had ended at night, so there were always customers for sideshows. As times changed, people began to arrive more or less on time for the performance. If they were early and visited the sideshows, by the time they made their way to the big top, the best seats had been taken. "And so as a result," explains Ward Hall (2001), "sideshows just don't work on a circus today." He concedes that he knows of one, but it is a little three- or four-banner museum-type show. "So it's not really a circus sideshow either, but that's it. That's why there's no [circus] sideshows."

But what about the carnivals? Sitting in his trailer behind the Hall & Christ ten-in-one at the 2001 Allentown, Pennsylvania, fair, Hall spoke of the situation today (figure 13.1). He acknowledges that midway crowds are still plentiful and that they can be persuaded to spend money. He notes that he and his partner Chris Christ have enjoyed a greater income in the last fifteen years than he did in any of the previous forty years. I remarked on the irony, given the decline of the sideshows, and he replied that popular interest had been sparked by a number of television specials, including the Learning Channel's *Sideshow Alive: On the Inside,* a two-hour documentary that has aired dozens

345

FIGURE 13.1. Great showman Ward Hall in his trailer just off the midway. (Photo by author)

of times. There has also been a spate of books and magazines waxing romantic about the disappearing shows (see, for example, *The Last Sideshow* by Hanspeter Schneider).

Hall states that the decline of sideshows began in the mid-1950s with the advent of the big rides—many of them from Europe. He says, "They were like a vacuum cleaner. They'd just suck the money up off the midway." Midway space began to be given to such money-making rides, leaving less and less space for shows. The big shows—the girl revues, black minstrel shows, and the like— were the first to go. In the 1960s the carnival sideshows started dropping off at an accelerated pace due to the lack of choice locations and a rise in salaries. So as old showmen died or retired, Hall and Christ bought many of their shows.

(Hall stops his analysis to interject that when Chris Christ became his partner in 1967 at age nineteen, "He was the youngest sideshow operator in the United States." Now, some three and a half decades later, he is still the youngest.) As to the shows they bought, Hall states:

> We were not continuing to operate them. Most of them we just took off the road and absorbed their attractions into our existing shows, because we were eliminating competition. And it got to the point where we would go to the fairs convention in Las Vegas and I used to always wear a white suit so that they could easily see us. Chris would wear, you know, bright colors or something. We would just go stand in the lobby. And these guys would come up: "Hey, can you play such-and-such a fair with me?" "Will you come over to my fair?" "Will you come over to my carnival?" . . . Because we . . . had the shows and they knew we had to feed 'em . . . we had the greatest routes. . . . . Even into maybe the early fifties, if you had a big show, you booked with a carnival, and you stayed there all year. You played their good ones [locations] and their bad ones. There were only a couple of shows that were able to hopscotch and pick out the fairs they wanted. . . . In 1967 we ended up on Gooding's Million-Dollar Midways, and we had shows there for ten years. And they had, undoubtedly, the best route in the United States at that time. And then also, as time went along—and with each one of these there's a story—but we ended up with the big-gest, biggest fairs. And so we would keep one show with Gooding, and the big show with Chris would hopscotch around.

As time went on, the number of excellent rides grew, and they were all trailer-mounted and easy to set up and tear down. In addition, these rides were all owned directly by the carnival. "They're not getting 40 percent and giving 60 percent to some operator; they're getting 100 percent," Hall observes. "So it's a matter of economics: 'Why the hell should I give up 400 feet of my valu-able space to five or six shows? I can take that same 400 feet and I can put seven rides in there'" (Hall 2001).

As to the future, he paints a bleak picture:

FIGURE 13.2. Showman Chris Christ relaxes at the home he shares with Ward Hall in Gibsonton, Florida. (Photo by author)

Oh, there'll be some single-Os, but even they're disappearing. . . . Today there is one motordrome working occasionally at fairs. There are no revues, no girl shows; there are two animal shows working— Ricky [Richard Cales] that's here, and Dennis York. There are two sideshow-type things—that's Bobby Reynolds, who doesn't have a live performance, and we still have a so-called ten-in-one. And of the grind shows, there are maybe—maybe—fifty or sixty left out of a thousand. So the whole back-end business, it's the same thing. It doesn't matter if you have a grind show or if you get a bigger show. [The question] is: where do you go that they're willing to relinquish space to you?

Chris Christ (2001) (figure 13.2) echoes his partner's assessment, stating, "We're fighting an economic monster that's bigger than anything we've had to go up against." Will the economy be the final blow to the sideshows? "Oh, I think it's going to be the final nail, it will probably be the final nail in the coffin. But I think it's going to be the final nail in the coffin for a lot of people." He adds that while they might be making a good living with their show equipment, all of which they basically made with their own hands, the situation is "getting more marginalized all the time."

Both Hall and Christ, and others I talked with, discount political correctness as a major factor in the decline of sideshows. It is true that when the decline accelerated in the 1980s, the exhibition of human oddities had begun to provoke complaints from some members of the public. For example, as mentioned in chapter 6, Otis the Frog Boy's act was closed in 1984 after a woman lodged a complaint regarding the display of disabled people. (He moved to Coney Island, where he restyled himself as a working act, the Human Cigarette Factory.) However, such confrontations had no real effect on the decline in sideshows.

"Political correctness had absolutely nothing to do with it," says Bobby Reynolds (2001). Agreeing with Hall and Christ, he states: "It's all economics. The guys that buy these million-dollar rides need all the room they can get so they can make the payments. . . . All you'll have out here eventually is very big, noisy rides, fun houses that are not so funny, and somebody hustling you for a teddy bear. And the sideshow will be gone. It'll be diluted like the rest of our country."

Reynolds's sideshow museum approach represents a cutback in the overhead. As to Hall's show, he says: "You notice he charged two dollars where I'm charging a dollar? That's to make up the difference for the midget [dwarf Peter Terhurne] and the fat guy [Bruce Snowden]." Hall could not let go of them, Reynolds explains, because they are friends. "So Pete has been around him for what, forty years? So what the hell is he gonna do, throw Pete out? So he has to keep him."

Since I interviewed these showmen, all have closed their shows. Bobby Reynolds ceased to be on the midways in 2002, and in October 2003, Ward Hall and Chris Christ followed suit, finally closing the flaps of their World of Wonders show. Having decided to retire, they planned a last show the weekend before Halloween at Florida's Guavaween Festival. With an anticipated 120,000 people in attendance, according to Pele the Fire Goddess, "Ward got a sequined outfit and planned to give the crowds the bally of his life. Unfortunately, that is not what happened. The show was set up directly across from the heavy metal music stage. Ward didn't even go out and talk because no one could hear him

FIGURE 13.3. Sideshows by the Seashore at Coney Island keeps the carny ten-in-one tradition alive. (Photo by author)

over the driving music." He just played the tape of his standard spiel, and even though little Pete worked the bally eating fire, "even that didn't help much. Of all those thousands of people, only roughly 500 passed through the entrance of the tent. It was such a sad, sad day for the history of sideshows. What was supposed to be a crowning moment in esteemed careers ended up being over-washed in the waves of guitar-ridden teen angst." Pele adds, "The end of an era has truly seemed to occur" (Pele 2003). The World of Wonders show was put up for sale. Hall invited his many friends to visit him and Christ at Gibsonton and "to take us out for lunch or dinner" (Sideshow Central 2004).

Nevertheless, Coney Island showman Todd Robbins has continued to keep the magic of sideshows before the public. He has worked at the last ten-in-one, Sideshows by the Seashore in Coney Island (figure 13.3), and he is dean of the Coney Island Sideshow School, which continues to teach fire eating and other essential arts and secrets of the ten-in-one era. More importantly, he has created an off-Broadway show called *Carnival Knowledge* (figure 13.4), which

FIGURE 13.4. Todd Robbins's *Carnival Knowledge* presents "The Twisted World of the American Sideshow" to theater audiences. (Advertising folder)

FIGURE 13.5. A broken-down show truck—a detail of a mural by Bill Browning (in the Showtown Bar & Grill in Gibsonton, Florida)—seems a fitting image to close with. (Photo by author)

features Todd swallowing swords and doing the human blockhead act, actually using the hammer and wearing the hat of the late Melvin Burkhart, who made the act famous. Other features of Robbins's show are Madame Electra (doing an electric chair act), Twistina (in the blade box illusion), the Flying Ebola Brothers (from the Moscow Circus), a dwarf, the snake charming Pythonia, the sensational girl-to-gorilla transformation, and more. The show even sports banner art by the great Johnny Meah.

Elsewhere, of course, there are single-O shows at some midways, and intrepid performers are seeking new audiences at Renaissance fairs, trade shows, the university circuit, nightclubs, and other venues. In addition, television documentaries, movies, journals such as *Shocked and Amazed,* and a succession of books—including this one—continue to keep alive the tradition, the entertainment, and the wonder that was the sideshow. Perhaps it is not yet time to fold the last tent (figure 13.5). In the meantime, we ask you to please step this way. The egress is just ahead.

REFERENCES

Associated Press. 2001. "Melvin Burkhart: 'Blockhead' Wowed Circus Crowds." *Albuquerque Journal*, November 13.

Barnum, P. T. 1927. *Barnum's Own Story*. New York: Viking Press.

Barta, Hilary. 1996. "Mortado." In Wilson et al. 1996, 1259–61.

Barth, Miles. 2002. "Edward J. Kelty and Century Flashlight Photographers." In Barth and Siegel 2002, 12–19.

Barth, Miles, and Alan Siegel, eds. 2002. *Step Right This Way: The Photographs of Edward J. Kelty*. New York: Barnes & Noble.

Becker, Herbert L. 1997. *All the Secrets of Magic Revealed: The Tricks and Illusions of the World's Greatest Magicians*. Hollywood, Fla.: Lifetime Books.

Bogdan, Robert. 1990. *Freak Show: Presenting Human Oddities for Fun and Profit*. Chicago: University of Chicago Press.

Bone, Howard. 2001. *Side Show: My Life with Geeks, Freaks & Vagabonds in the Carny Trade*. Northville, Mich.: Sun Dog Press.

Brill, A. K. 1957. *Side Show Stunts*. [Peoria, Ill.: A. B. Enterprises].

———. 1976. *A. Brill's Bible of Building Plans*. 2nd ed. Peoria, Ill.: A. B. Enterprises.

Brouws, Jeffrey T., and Bruce Caron. 2001. *Inside the Live Reptile Tent*. San Francisco: Chronicle Books.

"Certain Facts Concerning the Devil Man." 1998. Baltimore, Md.: Dolphin-Moon Press.

Chandler, Gary. 2002. "All Aboard for Last Carnival Train." *Buffalo News*, August 18.

Christ, Chris. 2001. Interview by Joe Nickell and Benjamin Radford, Allentown, Pa., September 1.

Christopher, Milbourne. 1962. *Panorama of Magic*. New York: Dover Publications.

Conklin, George. 1921. *The Ways of the Circus: Being the Memories and Adventures of George Conklin, Tamer of Lions*. As told to Harvey W. Root. New York: Harper & Brothers.

Considine, Bob. 1961. *Ripley: The Modern Marco Polo.* Garden City, N.Y.: Doubleday.

"Cotton Candy." 2003. http://www.gti.net/mocolib1/kid/foodfaq1.html.

Coup, W. C. 1901. *Sawdust and Spangles.* Chicago: Herbert S. Stone. Quoted in Bogdan 1990, 260–61.

Davies, Glen C. 1996. "Memorial to the Milestones." In Johnson et al. 1996, 63–66.

Dawes, Edwin A. 1979. *The Great Illusionists.* Secaucus, N.J.: Chartwell Books.

DeBurke, Randy. 1996. "One-and-a Halfs." In Wilson et al.1996, 49–53.

Deford, Frank. 2001. "More Tales of a Whale." In Taylor 2001, 84–91.

Dexter, Will. 1958. *This Is Magic.* New York: Bell Publishing Co.

Doerflinger, William. 1977. *The Magic Catalog.* New York: E. P. Dutton.

Dorson, Richard. 1959. *American Folklore.* Chicago: University of Chicago Press.

Drimmer, Frederick. 1991. *Very Special People: The Struggles, Love and Triumphs of Human Oddities.* New York: Citadel Press.

Dufour, Lou, with Irwin Kirby. 1977. *Fabulous Years.* New York: Vantage Press.

Earle, Jack. 1952. *The Long Shadows.* San Francisco: Haywood H. Hunt.

Early, Andrea. 1996. "The Little Mermaid?" *Harvard University Gazette,* October 17.

Edward, Mark. 1996. Personal communication, April 15.

Encyclopaedia Britannica. 1960. Chicago: Encyclopaedia Britannica.

Farson, Daniel. 1976. *Vampires, Zombies, and Monster Men.* New York: Doubleday.

Fellman, Sanndi. 1986. *The Japanese Tattoo.* New York: Abbeville Press Publishers.

Fiedler, Leslie. 1993. *Freaks: Myths and Images of the Secret Self.* New York: Anchor Books.

FitzGerald, William G. [1897]. "The Fabulous Creation." *Strand* (London). Reprinted in Taylor and Kotcher 2002, 90–113.

Ganthony, Robert. 1895. *Bunkum Entertainment.* Quoted in Jay 2001.

Gardner, Dick. 1962. *The Impossible.* New York: Ballantine Books.

Garth, Benjamin. 1993. *Fire Eating: A Manual of Instruction.* New York: Brian Dubé.

Gertsacov, "Prof." A. G. 2003. Performance and accompanying materials of the Acme Miniature Flea Circus, Artword Theatre, Toronto, Canada. Interview by Joe Nickell and Benjamin Radford, January 25.

Gibson, Walter. 1946. *The Bunco Book.* Holyoke, Mass.: Sidney H. Radner.

———. 1967. *Secrets of Magic: Ancient and Modern.* New York: Grosset & Dunlap.

Gibson, Walter B., and Morris N. Young. 1961. *Houdini's Fabulous Magic.* New York: Bell Publishing Co.

Gies, Joseph, and Frances Gies. 1981. *Life in a Medieval City.* New York: Harper Colophon Books.

Gilbert, Steve. 1996. "Totally Tattooed: Self-Made Freaks of the Circus and Sideshow." In Johnson et al. 1996, 101–5.

Gould, George M., and Walter L. Pyle. 1896. *Anomalies and Curiosities of Medicine.* New York: Bell Publishing Co.

Granfield, Linda. 2000. *Circus.* Toronto: Groundwood Books.

Gregor, Jan T. 1998. *Circus of the Scars: The True Inside Odyssey of a Modern Circus Sideshow.* Seattle: Brennan Dalsgard Publishers.

Gresham, William Lindsay. 1953. *Monster Midway.* New York: Rinehart & Company.

The Guinness Book of Records: 1999. 1998. New York: Guinness Publishing.

Hall, Ward. 1981. *Struggles and Triumphs of a Modern Day Showman: An Autobiography.* Sarasota, Fla.: Carnival Publishers.

———. 1991. *My Very Unusual Friends.* N.p.: n.p.

———. 2000. Interview by Joe Nickell and Benjamin Radford, York, Pa., September 9.

———. 2001. Interview by Joe Nickell and Benjamin Radford, Allentown, Pa., September 1.

———. 2004. Interview by Joe Nickell, Gibsonton, Fla., March 21.

Hammer, Carl, and Gideon Bosker. 1996. *Freak Show: Sideshow Banner Art.* San Francisco: Chronicle Books.

Harris, Neil. 1973. *Humbug: The Art of P. T. Barnum.* Chicago: University of Chicago Press.

Hartt, Rollin. 1909. *The People at Play.* Quoted in Nelson 1999, 81, 103–4.

Hay, Henry. 1949. *Cyclopedia of Magic.* Philadelphia: David McKay.

Hibben, Gil. 1998. *The Complete Gil Hibben Knife Throwing Guide.* 2nd ed. Sevierville, Tenn.: United Cutlery Corp.

Higley, Doug. 1998. "Truth or Fiction." *Circus Report* 44 (November 2).

———. 1999. Letter to author, January 13, accompanied by "The Last Museum" and other printed materials.

———. 2000. Letter to author, [January 25].

Hilton, Daisy, and Violet Hilton. [1942]. "The Ultimate Hilton Sisters: Siamese Twins." Cited in Bogdan 1990, 306.

Hoffmann, Professor. N.d. *Modern Magic.* Philadelphia: David McKay.

Holbrook, Stewart H. 1959. *The Golden Age of Quackery.* New York: Macmillan.

Holtman, Jerry. 1968. *Freak Show Man: The Autobiography of Harry Lewiston.* Cited in Drimmer 1991, 320–21.

Hopkins, Albert A. 1898. *Magic: Stage Illusions, Special Effects and Trick Photography.* Reprint, New York: Dover Publications, 1976.

Houdini, Harry. 1920. *Miracle Mongers and Their Methods.* Reprint, Toronto: Coles Publishing Co., 1980.

Hugard, Jean, ed. 1980. *Encyclopedia of Card Tricks.* Toronto: Coles Publishing Co.

Hyman, Ray. 1977. "Cold Reading: How to Convince Strangers That You Know All About Them." *Skeptical Inquirer (The Zetetic)* 1 (Spring/Summer): 18–37.

Jamieson, Bill. 2001. Interview by Joe Nickell and Benjamin Radford. Web site: www .head-hunter.com.

Jay, Ricky. 1987. *Learned Pigs & Fireproof Women.* London: Robert Hale.

———. 2001. *Jay's Journal of Anomalies.* New York: Farrar, Straus & Giroux.

Johnson, Randy, et al. 1996. *Freaks, Geeks, & Strange Girls: Sideshow Banners of the Great American Midway.* Honolulu: Hardy Marks Publications.

Keyes, Ralph. 1992. *"Nice Guys Finish Seventh": False Phrases, Spurious Sayings, and Familiar Misquotations.* New York: HarperPerennial.

Keyser, Wayne N. 2001. "Carny Lingo." In *On the Midway: Behind the Scenes of the Circus, Carnival & Sideshow.* CD-ROM available from http://www.goodmagic.com/cd.

Kleber, John E., ed. 1992. "Martin Van Buren Bates." In *The Kentucky Encyclopedia.* Lexington: University Press of Kentucky.

Kunhardt, Philip B., Jr., et al. 1995. *P. T. Barnum: America's Greatest Showman.* New York: Alfred A. Knopf.

LaMar, Leona. N.d. [ca. 1920s]. "The Girl with 1,000 Eyes." Englewood, N.J.: privately printed.

Leikind, Bernard. 1995. "What Is the Proper Way to Eat a Light Bulb?" *Skeptic* 3, no. 3: 107–8.

Leland, Charles G. 1882. *The Gypsies.* Boston: Houghton, Mifflin. Cited in Gresham 1953, 113–14.

Lentini, Frank. N.d. "The Life History of Francesco A. Lentini." In Taylor and Kotcher 2002, 1–3.

Lewis, Clarence O. 1991. *The Seven Sutherland Sisters.* Lockport, N.Y.: Niagara County Historical Society.

The Lincoln Library of Essential Information. 1946. Vol. 2. Buffalo, N.Y.: Frontier Press.

Loxton, Howard. 1997. *The Golden Age of the Circus.* New York: Smithmark.

Mannix, Daniel P. 1996. *Memoirs of a Sword Swallower.* San Francisco: V/Search Publications. Illustrated edition of *Step Right Up!* 1951.

———. 1999. *Freaks: We Who Are Not as Others.* New York: Juno Books. (Originally published 1976.)

Mariani, John F. 1994. *The Dictionary of American Food and Drink.* New York: Hearst Books.

McCandlish, James. 2003. "The Human Pincushion: New World Record." *National Inquirer,* March 25, p. 40.

McKennon, Joe. 1972. *A Pictorial History of the American Carnival.* Vols. 1 and 2. Sarasota, Fla.: Carnival Publishers of Sarasota.

———. 1981. *A Pictorial History of the American Carnival.* Vol. 3. Sarasota, Fla.: Carnival Publishers of Sarasota.

McWhirter, Norris. 1981. *Guinness Book of World Records.* 1982 ed. New York: Sterling Publishing Co.

Meah, Johnny. 1996. "Cunning Crafters of Dreams," "Notes on Fat People," "Notes on Alligator Skinned People," "Notes on Geeks." In Johnson et al. 1996, 47–50, 90, 120, 138.

———. 1998. "The Frog Prince." In Taylor 1998, 54–61.

Mencken, H. L. 1919. *The American Language.* Reprint, New York: Alfred A. Knopf, 1965.

"Midway Torture Feats." N.d. [Shawahnee, Calif.]: Harmur Productions.

Miller, Pete. 2003. "Dying for Fame: Elmer McCurdy's Death. . . ." www.newsobserver.com/bookreview/story.

Minor, Jason Temujin. 1996. "Makin' 'em Bigger 'n' Smaller." In Wilson et al. 1996, 180–82.

Mooney, Julie, et al. 2002. *Ripley's Believe It or Not! Encyclopedia of the Bizarre, Amazing, Strange, Inexplicable, Weird, and All True!* New York: Black Dog & Leventhal Publishers.

Mortado. N.d. "Mortado the Human Fountain." Reproduced in Taylor and Kotcher 2002, 48–51.

Munsey, Cecil. 1970. *The Illustrated Guide to Collecting Bottles.* New York: Hawthorn.

Nelson, Derek. 1999. *The American State Fair.* Osceola, Wisc.: MBI Publishing Co.

Newton, Michael. 2002. *The Encyclopedia of Robberies, Heists, and Capers.* New York: Checkmark Books.

Nickell, Joe. 1970. "Magic in the Carnival." *Performing Arts in Canada* 7, no. 2 (May): 41–42.

———. 1972. Personal journal, August 17.

———. 1974. Personal journal, August 3.

———. 1991a. "Historical Sketches: The Alligator Boys." *Licking Valley Courier,* April 4.

———. 1991b. *Wonder-Workers! How They Perform the Impossible.* Buffalo, N.Y.: Prometheus Books.

———. 1993. "Outlaw Impostors." In *Encyclopedia of Hoaxes,* ed. Gordon Stein. Detroit: Gale Research.

———. 1995. *Entities: Angels, Spirits, Demons, and Other Alien Beings.* Amherst, N.Y.: Prometheus Books.

———. 1999. "Sideshow! Carnival Oddities and Illusions Provide Lessons for Skeptics." *Skeptical Briefs* 9, no. 4 (December): 5–9.

———. 2001. *Real-Life X-Files: Investigating the Paranormal.* Lexington: University Press of Kentucky.

———. 2002. "Psychic Pets and Pet Psychics." *Skeptical Inquirer* 26, no. 6 (November/December): 12–15, 18.

The Oxford English Dictionary. 1971. Compact ed. New York: Oxford University Press.

Packard, Mary, et al. 2001. *Ripley's Believe It or Not!* Special ed. New York: Scholastic.

Parker, Mike. 1994. *The World's Most Fantastic Freaks.* London: Hamlyn.

Pele the Fire Goddess. 2003. E-mail to Benjamin Radford, November 5.

Polacsek, John. 1996. "Alive and on the Inside: Historian Notes on Sideshow Paintings & Banners." In Johnson et al. 1996, 31–36.

Premanand, B. 1994. *Science Versus Miracles.* Delhi, India: Indian CSICOP.

Randi, James. 1987. *The Faith-Healers.* Buffalo, N.Y.: Prometheus Books.

———. 1992. *Conjuring.* Buffalo, N.Y.: St. Martin's Press.

———. 1995. *The Supernatural A–Z.* London: Brockhampton.

Ray, Fred Olen. 1993. *Grind Show: Weirdness as Entertainment.* Hollywood, Calif.: American-Independent Press.

Reese, Ralph. 1996. "The Art of Gaffing Freaks." In Wilson et al. 1996, 189–91.

Reynolds, Bobby. 2001. Interviews by Joe Nickell and Benjamin Radford, Erie County Fair, Hamburg, N.Y., August 12; and New York State Fair, Syracuse, N.Y., August 31.

Rinaldo, Tom. 1991. *Robbery on the Midway.* N.p.: privately printed.

Ripley, Robert L. 1929. *Believe It or Not!* New York: Simon & Schuster.

Schiffman, Nathaniel. 1997. *Abracadabra! Secret Methods Magicians and Others Use to Deceive Their Audience.* Amherst, N.Y.: Prometheus Books.

Schneider, Hanspeter. 2004. *The Last Sideshow.* London: Dazed Books.

Scot, Reginald. 1584. *The Discoverie of Witchcraft*. Reprint, New York: Dover Publications, 1972.

Secreto, Jim. 1996. "Larger than Life: Positively Fat." In Johnson et al. 1996, 87–91.

Shepp, James W., and Daniel B. Shepp. 1893. *Shepp's World Fair Photographed*. Chicago: Globe Bible Publishing Co.

Sideshow. 2000. Documentary on the Learning Channel, aired December 30.

Sideshow Central. 2004. Hall & Christ World of Wonders for Sale. http://www .knddesign.com/sc/wowpr.html. Accessed January 14.

"Side Show Tricks Explained." N.d. Peoria, Ill.: A. B. Enterprises.

Siegel, Lee. 1991. *Net of Magic: Wonders and Deceptions in India*. Chicago: University of Chicago Press.

Sonntag, Ned. 1996. "Baby Ruth." In Wilson et al. 1996, 140–42.

Spindler, Konrad. 1994. *The Man in Ice*. New York: Crown Trade Paperbacks.

Stein, Gordon. 1993. *Encyclopedia of Hoaxes*. Detroit: Gale Research.

Stein, Harvey. 1998. *Coney Island*. New York: W. W. Norton.

Stencell, A. W. 1999. *Girl Show: Into the Canvas World of Bump and Grind*. Toronto: ECW Press.

———. 2002. *Seeing Is Believing: America's Sideshows*. Toronto: ECW Press.

Stone, Lisa, and Randy Johnson. 1996. "Depicting the Demons Inside and Out." Introduction to Johnson et al. 1996, 11–15.

Taber's Cyclopedic Medical Dictionary. 2001. Philadelphia: F. A. Davis.

Taggart, S. M. 1996. "The Lobster Boy Murder Caper." In Wilson et al. 1996, 169–74.

"Tallest Man in Iceland." 2003. http://www.islandia.is/~juljul/johann/johannuk.htm.

Taylor, James. 1997. *Shocked and Amazed!—On and Off the Midway*. No. 4. Baltimore: Dolphin-Moon Press.

———. 1998. *Shocked and Amazed!—On and Off the Midway*. No. 5. Baltimore: Dolphin-Moon Press.

———. 2001. *Shocked and Amazed!—On and Off the Midway*. No. 6. Baltimore: Dolphin-Moon Press.

Taylor, James, and Kathleen Kotcher. 2002. *James Taylor's Shocked and Amazed!—On and Off the Midway*. Guilford, Conn.: Lyons Press.

Teller. 1997. "Gorilla Girl." In Taylor 1997, 24–26.

Thompson, C. J. S. 1968. *Giants, Dwarfs, and Other Oddities*. New York: Citadel Press.

Treves, Frederick. 1923. *The Elephant Man and Other Reminiscences*. Excerpt reprinted in Drimmer 1991, 322–45.

Weiss, Alan. 1996. "Omi the Great." In Wilson et al. 1996, 132–38.

Wels, Byron G. 1977. *The Great Illusions of Magic.* Brooklyn, N.Y.: D. Robbins.

Whisnant Galleries. 2000. Information sheet on Fred G. Johnson's banner, "Major John, Frog Boy," citing Hammer and Bosker 1996.

Whitehead, Ruth Holmes. 2002. *Tracking Doctor Lonecloud.* Fredericton, New Brunswick: Goose Lane Editions; Halifax, Nova Scotia: Nova Scotia Museum.

Willey, David. 1999. "The Physics behind Four Amazing Demonstrations." *Skeptical Inquirer* 23, no. 6 (November/December): 44–46.

Wilson, Gahan, et al. 1996. *The Big Book of Freaks.* New York: Paradox Press.

Wiseman, Richard. 2002. "The History and Performance of the Flea Circus." Manuscript.

Tricks and Illusions of the World's Greatest Magicians (Becker), 298
"Amazing Mister Lifto." *See* Hermann, Joe
"Amazon Snake Charmer" banner, 58
Amburgh, Isaac Van, 300–301
Ament, W. D. "Mexican Billy," 264, 289
American Museum. *See* Barnum's American Museum
American State Fair (Nelson), 30–31, 64
Amos and Andy dolls, 38
"Anatomical Wonder." *See* Burkhart, Melvin
anatomical wonders, 73, 165–77; Burkhart, Melvin, 148, 161, 162, 175–77, 201, 240, 352; Carson, Rex "Americo," 176; contortionists, 2, 11, 53, 72, 95, 126, 165–68; India-rubber people, 168–71; special-effects performers, 171–75
Anderson, Bud, 26
androgen, 150
animal acts: acrobatics with bulls, 2; animal showmen, 21, 302–3; bears, xx, 4, 303, 304, 305; birds, 8, 304; Clever Hans (horse), 304; Consul (chimp), 305; dancing rooster, 305–6; dogs, trained, 4, 58, 303, 304; exhibits vs. acts, 306; Fatima the Hoochie-Coochie Bear, 305; flea circuses, 172, 314–21; heads, restoring severed, 1–2; in history, 303–4; horse-riding, trick, 6–7, 8–9; Josephine (chimp), 154; kangaroo, boxing, 303, 305; Lady Wonder (horse), 304; "Learned Pig," 304; "Learned Seal," 302; lion taming, 1, 31, 49, 64, 301; monkeys, 9, 300, 304; Munito the celebrated dog, 304; pigs, 17, 304; "scientific" Spanish pony, 304; Serrano the Psychic Horse, 305; singing mice, 305; snake charmers, xx, 57, 58, 65, 66, 67, 70, 72, 109, 193, 205, 250–54, 263, 306, 352; snake

pits, 18, 207; snake wrestling, 176; talking horse, 304; Toby the Sapient Pig, 304; "Two Curious Birds," 304; wild-animal training, 1, 2, 49, 301; "Wonderful Intelligent Goose," 304
animal exhibits: armadillos, 78, 309; bears, 53, 302, 306; bison, 53; camels, 17, 53, 301, 306; coatimundi, 309; elephants, 17, 300, 302, 303, 306–7; elephants (stuffed), 17, 330, 341; Giant Flesh-Eating Frogs, 308; "Giant Rat" show, 307–8, 311; "Giant Snake eating Frog," 75; "Great Living Whale," 302, 306; Jungle Mother, 78; killed in fires, 14, 303; lions, 49, 302, 303, 306; monkeys, 2, 78–79, 299; snakes, 14, 18, 52, 75; stuffed, 11, 17, 75, 330, 341; turkey buzzards, 309; whales, 14, 302, 333; Zeno the Ape Man (baboon), 52
animal freaks, 74, 309–14; alleged hybrids, 311, 312; bull with "elephant feet," 310; "Calf with 5 Legs & 6 Feet," 311; "Cow with 5 Legs," 311; "Daisy Mae the 2 Headed Cow," 311; "double-bodied cows," 309; "enormous pigs," 309; fetuses, 74, 311, 313, 328; five-legged cow, xx, 74, 311, 313; five-legged horse, 65; five-legged sheep, 311; "4 Wing Goose," 311; "Four Horn Sheep," 311; "Freaks of Nature and Pet Zoo" sideshow, 311; "Giant Alligator," 314; "Giant Chicken," 311; "Giant Rat" show, xxi, 307–8, 311; "Goat without Ears," 312; "Hairless Dog," 312; "'Hercules' the Giant Horse," 314; in history, 309; horse, with long mane and tail, 309–10; Jumbo the elephant, 17, 309; "Living Three-Horned Bull," 309; "Midget Bull," 311; "Nature's Living Tripod" (three-legged sheep), 311; "Nature's Mistakes" animal freak show, 310;

299, 309; *banner lines* at, 53; concessions at, 28–29, 33; contortionist at, 53, 165–66; dwarf at, 6; Fawkes, Isaac at, 6, 53, 165, 261; rides and amusements at, 40, 44–45; Siamese twins at, 122
Bates, Finis, 329
Bates, Martin Van Buren, 86–89
Battalia, Francois, 225–26
Battersby, Hannah, 55, 160
Battersby, John, 55, 101, 160
"Bearded Girl." *See* Jones, Annie
bearded ladies, 12, 72; Barnell, Jane, 152–53; "Brenda Beatty the Bearded Lady" (Bernie Rogers), 198–99; Clofullia, Josephine, 150–51; Delait, Clementine, 151; Devere, Jane, 153; female impersonators as, 198–99; Furella, Jean, 182; gaffed, 198; Gilbert, Grace, 153, 154; Jones, Annie, 80, 151–52, 252; Macgregor, Betty, 198–99; Madame Fortune, 198; Meyers, Mrs., 153; Murphy, Frances, 198; Percilla the Monkey Girl, 143, 150, 154–55, 199
"Bearded Lady of Thaon, The." *See* Delait, Clementine
bears, xx, 4, 53, 302, 303, 304, 305, 306
Beatty, Clyde, 58
Becker, Herbert L., 298
Beckman, Fred, 64
beds of nails, xxi, 69, 204, 232, 237, 242, 246, 247
Bejano, Emmitt, 143, 154–55
Bejano, Johnny, 143
Bejano, Percilla. *See* Percilla the Monkey Girl
Belgian Giant (aka the French Giant). *See* Bihin, E.
"Believe It or Not!" *See* "Ripley's Believe It or Not!"
Bellis, George, 242, 267, 294
benders. See contortionists

Bentley, Claude, 143
Berent, Stanley, 148
Bernadin ("fish boy"), 141
Bertolotto, L., 315–16
Best, Dick, 74, 190
Bibrowsky, Stephan. *See* Lionel the Lion-Faced Man
Biddenden Maids. *See* Chulkhurst, Mary and Eliza
"Big Cleo, World's Tallest Girl" mummy, 330
Big Eli Wheel, 41
Bigelow, "Texas Charlie," 18–19
Bigfoot, 81, 338
"Big Sea Horse" mummy, 338
Bihin, E., 84
Biped Armadillo, 150
bird call imitations, 5
"black-art" principle, 297
Black Prince and his Fairy Queen (midgets), 113
Blackwelder, Emmitt, 150
blade box. *See* "Coffin Blade Box" illusion
Blaine, David, 2
blind opening, 77, 78
blowdown, 26
blowing the route, 26
blowoff, xxi, 52, 76–79, 191, 195; as *after-catch* for next show, 77; for children, 78; "Egress, The," 76–77, 345–52; fat ladies on, 101; human pincushions, 77, 235, 236; for men, 78; shows as, 77; snake wrestling, 176; two-headed pickled punk, 323; and *walk-throughs*, 79
"Blue Man." *See* Walters, Fred
Bobby Reynolds's International Circus Sideshow Museum & Gallery, 75, 77, 185, 330–31, 349; *banner lines* at, 241, 249, 272, 273; and Cardiff giant hoax, 344; *illusion shows* at, 273, 280. *See also* Reynolds, Bobby

Frederick I, King, of Prussia, 82–83
"French Giant," 9, 55
Frierson, Mark, 338
Fritz, Delmo, 222–23
"frog boys," 145–48; Davis, Earl, 148; El
  Hoppo the Living Frog Boy, xix, 146–
  47; Flip the Frog Boy, 146; "frog girl
  show," 74, 148; Jordan, Otis ("Otis
  the Frog Boy"), 146, 349; Major
  John the Frog Boy, 58–59, 61, 146;
  Norwood, Carl, 146; Parks, Samuel D.
  ("Hopp the Frog Boy"), 145–46
front end of midway, 28
Fulkerson, Lorett, 186
Fulton, Scott, 334
Furella, Jean, 182

Gabriel, Mademoiselle, 135
gaffed acts, 201–8; flea circuses, 318–21;
  with glass eating, 231–32; human
  pincushion, 238; iron tongue act, 186;
  knife throwing, 256–58; vs. magic,
  294; strongmen, 201–2; swallowing
  objects, 232–33; swords, climbing a
  ladder of, 242; "wild man" or "wild
  woman" act, 202–8
gaffed oddities, xxi, 178, 194–202; "alligator" people, 197–98; bearded ladies,
  198; "Brenda Beatty the Bearded
  Lady" (Bernie Rogers), 198–99;
  Clark, Marguerete (or Margaret),
  196; "devil baby" exhibits, 336–38;
  extraterrestrial corpses, 75, 333,
  338–41; fetuses, 326; giants, 66, 67;
  "Gorilla Girl," 199–200; half and
  halfs, 73, 196–97; hybrid animals,
  312; Josephine-Joseph, 196–97; Koo-
  Koo the Bird Girl, 200–201; Lionella
  the Lion-Faced Girl, 200; mummies, 66, 67, 338; Murphy, Frances,
  198; Sasquatch/Bigfoot, xx, 81, 338;
  shrunken heads, 331–32; Siamese
  twins/"one-and-a-halfs," 124, 195–96;

"Three-Eyed Man"/"Man with
  Three Eyes," 161, 162, 194–95; "Two-
  Headed Mexican" (Pasquel Pinon),
  195. See also mermaids
gaffs: with games, 36, 39. See also bogus
  creatures; gaffed acts; gaffed oddities;
  hoaxes
Galyon, Wesley, 126–27
Galyon, Ronnie and Donnie, xx, 126–28
games: Bottle Roll, 39; "buyer beware,"
  34–35; cat rack, 38–39; Dime Pitch,
  39; prizes, 36–38; shell game, 35;
  Sunday school show, 36; three-card-
  monte, 35; types, 36; wheel of fortune,
  xx, 39. See also rides and amusements
games of chance, 36
games of skill, 36
Ganthony, Robert, 318
Gardner, Dick, 89, 171, 182, 191, 209,
  238, 252; and fire-eaters, 219–20, 222;
  and phenomenal ingesters, 226, 227,
  229, 230, 231, 232; and sword swal-
  lowers, 220, 222, 225
Garey, Malcolm, 308
Garneau, Mimi, 317–18
Garrett, "Speed," 280
Garth, Benjamin, 215, 218, 219
Gaskill, Frank W., 22–23, 49
geek. See "wild man" or "wild woman"
  acts
"General Tom Thumb," 12, 14, 113–18,
  302. See also Stratton, Charles
  Sherwood
"General Tom Thumb Company," 118
"Genuine Monster-Mouthed Ubangi
  Savages," 189–90, 204
George, David E., 329
"Georgia Magnet." See Hurst, Lulu
Gertsacov, "Prof." A. G., 314, 315, 316,
  320–21
Ghost Mansion, 47
Ghost Ride, 44
"Giant Alligator," 314

Malone, Jerry and Charlotte, 333
"Maltese Fountain." *See* Manfrede, Blaise
Manfrede, Blaise, 227
Mangels, W. E., 42
"Man-Monkey." *See* Johnson, William
  Henry
Mannix, Daniel P., 101, 146, 162, 238; and
  anatomical wonders, 167, 169, 170;
  and created oddities, 184, 189, 201;
  and fire-eating, 210, 214; and human
  pincushions, 234–35; and molten lead,
  244; and phenomenal ingesters, 228,
  229, 231, 232; and special-effects per-
  formers, 171, 172; and sword swallow-
  ing, 220, 224; and sword walking, 242;
  the *ten-in-one*, 57, 64–66, 70, 77; and
  whip snapping, 259
"Man of Iron." *See* breaking stone on
  chest
"Man of the Woods, The" banner, 53. *See
  also* bears
"Man Who Grows." *See* Willard, Clarence
  E.
"Man Without a Stomach." *See* Burkhart,
  Melvin
"Man with Three Eyes." *See* Durks,
  William (Bill)
"Man with Two Faces." *See* Milwin,
  Robert
Maori tattoos, 180
Marchand, Floram, 227, 228
Mariani, John F., 30
Mariedl (giantess), 84
mark, 35
Marquesas Islands, 178, 180
Martin sisters, 160
"Master Magician" banner, 263
"Master of Magic" banner, 263
"Maxine the Half Lady" banner, 73
Mayfield, Dr., 214
Mbuti tribespeople, 106
McCandlish, James, 238
McClory, Bill, 263

McCrary, Billy and Benny, 94
McCurdy, Elmer, mummy of, 328–29
McDaniels, Grace, 150, 162–63
McGreggor, Harry, 187
McGrow, Steve, 263
McGuire brothers. *See* McCrary, Billy
  and Benny
McKennon, Joe, 6, 35, 108; and carnivals,
  history of, 18, 20, 21, 22, 23, 24, 49,
  252, 260, 264, 283, 302; and concessions, 30, 34; and *geeks*, 205, 207; and
  illusion shows, 281, 284; and menageries, 302, 303, 304; and the midway,
  setting up, 25, 26, 28; and rides and
  amusements, 40, 41, 42, 46; the *ten-
  in-one*, 50, 52, 53, 62, 63, 73–74, 77
McLane, Fred. *See* Cliquot, Chevalier
McWhirter, Norris, 83, 84, 93, 94, 102,
  104, 106, 112
Meadowlands Fair (New Jersey), 291
Meah, Johnny, "The Great," 57, 146, 171,
  172, 205; and "alligator" people, 142,
  143; and "alligator" people, gaffed,
  197; banners by, 60–61, 67, 352; and
  fat people, 94–95, 96; "Suzy/Nature's
  Enigma" banner, 144
medicine shows, 5, 18–19, 261
Meleke, Zoe, 192, 193. *See also* Circassian
  beauties
menageries, 9, 48, 299–303; in ancient
  times, 299; circuses and tricks
  vs. educational, 300, 301; fire at
  Baltimore, 303; fire at Barnum's
  Museum, 14; in history, 299–300,
  302–3, 305; as sideshow, 302; snakes
  at, 252; stuffed animals, as part of,
  330–31; traveling, 300, 301–2, 309;
  wild-animal training at, 300–301,
  303. *See also* animal acts; animal
  exhibits; animal freaks; animal shows
Mencken, H. L., 62
Mendell the Mentalist, xix
mentalists, 264–66; "Lady Yava,

tors, 66, 67, 252, 253, 254; Serpentina, 72, 254; "Snake Trainer," 254; Terhurne, Pete, 254
"Snake Girl" banner, 254
"snake girl" illusion, 254, 281, 282
Snake Man. *See* Randian, Prince
snake-oil peddlers, 18–19
snakes, 65; biting heads off, 205; wrestling with, 176. *See also* snake charmers
"Snake Trainer" banner, 254
snake-wrestling, 176
Snowden, Bruce, 96, 99–101, 349
Sober Sue, 170–71
Sonney, Louis, 329
Sonntag, Ned, 98
Sparks' Show, 252
special-effects performers: Bradley, Oscar, 174; "eye-poppers," 172–74; eye tricks, 174; Holt, F. G., 174; Langevin, Alfred, 174; Laurello, Martin Joe, 171–72; Leather, John, 174; "Man Without a Stomach," 176; miscellaneous uses of anatomy, 174–75; Mundial, Feria, 174; Noggins, Oscar "Popeye," 172; Perry, "Popeye," 172–74; revolving head, 171–72; "rubber neck" effect, 177; Russell, Marguerite, 174; Saylors, J. T., 174; "two-faced man" feat, 177; Willard, Clarence E., 174–75
Spencer, Dave, 290–91
Sphinx, The. *See* living heads illusion
"spider girl" illusion. *See* Spidora illusion
Spidora illusion, xxi, 73, 170, 278, 280–82; techniques, 281
spielers. See grinders
Spindler, Konrad, 178
Sprague, Isaac W., 103–4
Stall, George, 203
Stebbings, "Couteau Gene," 255
Stein, Gordon, 15, 336

Stein, Harvey, 176
"Stella the Bearded Lady." *See* Macgregor, Betty
Stencell, Al W., 48, 293, 325, 326, 329, 330, 338, 342; and animals, 299, 301, 305, 309; and gorilla girl illusion, 288, 289, 290; and *illusion shows*, 260, 272, 278, 280, 283, 284, 291; and psychic marvels, 264
Stepping Stones (Broadway show), 257
Step Right Up! (Mannix), 64–66
Steve McGrow Carnival, 263
sticks (shills), 66
Stiles, Cathy, 148, 149, 150
Stiles, Donna, 148
Stiles, Grady, III, 149
Stiles, Grady, Jr., 148–50
Stiles, Grady, Sr., 148
Stiles, Mary Teresa, 148–50
stock, 36–37
Stone, Lisa, 119
stone eating, 225–26
"Stone Man." *See* Shouse, John
straitjacket, escaping from, 232, 260, 262
"Strange as It Seems" show, New York World's Fair (1939), 174, 177, 188, 198; human blockhead at, 238; human pincushions at, 235
Strange Eeka, 205
"Strange Girls" banner, 148, 190
Strates, James E., 25, 143
Strates Shows, 25, 45, 161; buzz-saw illusion, 272; Claude Bentley's Freak Circus, 143
Stratton, Charles Sherwood, 12, 14, 113–18, 302; and Lavinia, courtship and marriage to, 115–18; pretense of baby of, 116–18; touring, 114–15; visit to England, 114. *See also* "General Tom Thumb"
"Stretch." *See* Turner, Gary
Stretch, Jack, 170
string show, 50; *ten-in-one* as type of, 53

INDEX

Zahara (gorilla girl), 291

"Zalumma Agra, 'Star of the East'," 192

Zambora the Gorilla Girl, 290

Zamora the Torture King. *See* Cridland, Tim

Zancig, Julius, 265

Zanobia, Zana, 192

Zeleke, Zula, 192

Zeno the Ape Man, 52

Zercon, 107

Zerm, Patricia, 223

Zimmerman (giant), 82–83

"Zip." *See* Johnson, William Henry

Zobedia, Zoe, 192

"Zoe Meleke: Biographical Sketch of the Circassian Girl," 193

Zoledod, 192

Zoma, 205

"Zoma Depraved" banner, 205

"Zoma the Sadist" banner, 205

"zonkey" (half zebra-half donkey), 312

Zoological Institute (New York), 301

Zribeda, 192

Zulu, Millie, 192

Zwinge, Randall James Hamilton. *See* Randi, James "The Amazing"